Fully worked-out programmes for Quiet Days

A Quiet Word

Nick Fawcett

Kevin
Mayhew

First published in 2001 by
KEVIN MAYHEW LTD
Buxhall, Stowmarket, Suffolk IP14 3BW
Email: info@kevinmayhewltd.com

9 8 7 6 5 4 3 2 1 0

ISBN 1 84003 774 1
Catalogue No 1500446

Cover design by Jonathan Stroulger
Typesetting by Richard Weaver

Printed in Great Britain

CONTENTS

FOREWORD

During my time as a minister in Cheltenham, a local church asked me to lead a Quiet Day. It was an unremarkable request, except that I had no experience of either leading or sharing in such an event, so I was neither sure what to do or expect. As it turned out, I found the day a revelation, not because of the material I produced for it but simply due to the whole ambience of the occasion. Paradoxically, it wasn't really a Quiet Day at all – the one thing I failed to include in the programme being a time for silence! – yet, using a mixture of slides, music, readings and meditations, I glimpsed as never before the importance and potential of something that is all too often lacking in our churches; namely, an opportunity for prolonged reflection. Typically, we fill our worship with words and songs, with scarcely a pause for breath. Both of these have their place of course – where would I be as an author and hymn-writer without them! – but I found myself increasingly convinced that we need to use other mediums in worship, such as music and pictures, to engage the senses and the imagination. The result of such deliberations was my first book, *No Ordinary Man*, from which much of the material in this compilation derives; this followed several books later by a 'sequel', *No Ordinary Man (Book 2)*, which accounts for the rest of this collection.

My purpose in both volumes of *No Ordinary Man* was very simple – to encourage people, through a series of meditations, to reflect on the person of Jesus. I did not set out to provide answers so much as to provoke questions; to get people asking: 'Who was this man?' 'What did he do?' 'Why did he do it?' Above all, 'What does he mean for me today?' Each meditation explores such questions from the perspective of particular biblical characters who met with Jesus, either in person or through his Spirit – people like Mary and Joseph, Simon Peter and Mary Magdalene, John the Baptist and Paul. The first part of both books comprised one hundred such meditations; the second gave outlines for services and Quiet Days. This compilation brings together in a single unified book the Quiet Days and appropriate meditations from the two volumes of *No Ordinary Man*. Some of the material from the first volume has been slightly adapted to allow more time for silence but, apart from that, the sessions are unchanged. The aim of this collection is to provide a resource in an accessible format and designed for ease of use, specifically intended to promote quiet reflection. In an age where life is lived at an ever more frenetic pace, we need time to pause and reflect. It is my hope that the material in this book may prove helpful in affording such an opportunity.

Nick Fawcett

PRACTICAL MATTERS

When using slides and music, there are obviously certain basic requirements. A good hi-fi system, slide projector and screen are essential, as is an effective amplification system so that readers can be heard over any background music. You will also find the services of an assistant invaluable when it comes to presenting the material – ideally somebody to control the slide projector, and possibly someone to fade the music in and out as appropriate. Remember, too, to ensure that those reading the meditations are given proper time to prepare beforehand, and that they are instructed to read slowly and clearly, beginning by announcing the title of the meditation.

You can probably borrow much of the recommended music from your local library or a friend. Should you prefer to buy it, much is available on budget CD sets. I made particular use of *The Voices of Angels (100 Heavenly Classics)*, *100 Romantic Classics*, *100 Relaxing Classics* and *100 Popular Classics* (Castle Communications); *Discovering the Classics* (three volume double CD set), *Renaissance Choral Treasures* and *Classical Favourites for Relaxing and Dreaming* (Naxos); the *Classic Experience* discs 1 and 3 (EMI); and Classic FM's *All Time Christmas Greats*. Other works extensively used are Handel's *Messiah*, Mozart's *Requiem, Mass in C minor* and *Coronation Mass*, and a recent composition called *Fountain of Life*, written by Margaret Rizza and available from Kevin Mayhew Publishers Ltd.

Slide collections are not easy to find nowadays. You may be able to buy some from 'The Slide Centre' in Chatham (see Appendix), but many, sadly, are out of print. Your best bet may be to borrow them from your local Diocesan Resource Centre if you have one. Failing that, you might once more try your local library. When using slides always run through them beforehand making sure they are the right way up and in the correct order. Make sure also that you have a spare bulb in case one should blow, and arrange all electrical leads so that no one can inadvertently fall over them. The less you leave to chance, the less possibility there will be of anything going wrong.

One final point: these Quiet Days make extensive use of music, meditations, readings and visual images, but equally important is the place of silence. Do not neglect this. Participants need time to reflect on what they have heard and seen if God is to speak through it. I have indicated opportunities for silent reflection at numerous points throughout the sessions. Encourage people to make the most of these times, and to respect the space and quiet of other participants.

Quiet Days

The Life of Christ

Suggested visual material   Jesus of Nazareth 1-6
Bread and Wine
The Life of Christ IV

Introduction   Jesus of Nazareth – a man we are told who changed history, and a man with the power to change our lives. So who was he? What did he do? Why did he do it? And what does he have to say to us today? It is questions such as these we shall be asking today, not directly, but through reflecting on the experiences of those who witnessed the life of Jesus firsthand. We shall follow that life from beginning to end – from birth to death – and then on beyond to the resurrection. Through the words of Scripture, through music, pictures, silence and meditations, we consider not only what those events meant to those involved at the time, but what they mean for us, here and now.

SESSION ONE – *Beginnings*

Music   *Saviour's Day* Cliff Richard

Prayer

Lord Jesus Christ,
    time and again throughout your ministry
    you made time to be still,
    to draw away from the crowds
    so that in the quietness
    you could reflect on your calling.
You needed those moments,
    just as we need them in our turn.
So now we have made a space in our lives,
    away from the daily demands,
    away from the usual routine.
We are here, Lord, with time for you,
    in stillness and in quietness to seek your will.

Lord Jesus Christ,
   use these moments
   to refresh us, to feed us,
   to challenge us, to inspire us.
Fill them with your love
   and so may we be filled to overflowing.
Amen.

Slides   Annunciation and birth
Music   *The Angel Gabriel* Basque Carol
        during which Luke 2:1-7 is read

Meditation of the innkeeper

I felt sorry for that couple, I really did.
They were at their wits' end, the pair of them,
   just about all in.
But it was the lady who concerned me most;
   fit to drop she was,
   and hardly a surprise given her condition –
   not that I'm an expert in these matters
   but I felt sure her pains had already started;
   and so it was to prove, poor lass.
As for him, he was beside himself,
   frantic with worry,
   almost abusive in his frustration;
   and I can't say I blamed him –
   I'd have been the same in the circumstances.
Yet what could I do?
There wasn't a room to spare, that was the fact of the matter.
We were packed already,
   bulging at the seams,
   and I could hardly turf someone else out
   just to fit them in,
   could I?
I mean – be reasonable –
   that would have caused a right-old to-do,
   no use to anybody.
So I offered them the stable, if they could make use of it.
Not much of a prospect I agree,
   especially on such a night as that turned out,
   but it was a roof over their heads,
   a shelter from the worst of the wind if nothing else.

All right, so I still feel bad about it,
  wish now I'd taken the wife's advice
  and given up our room for them.
But to be honest we were both whacked,
  what with all the extra custom to see to.
We had an inn to run, remember,
  and we were rushed off our feet,
  longing only for a good night's sleep ourselves.
So we gave them the stable and that's the end of it –
  no point brooding over what might have been.
And to be fair, they were grateful,
  glad of anywhere to put their heads down.
But when I heard the baby crying,
  that's when it got to me –
  out there in those conditions!
I felt ashamed,
  disgusted with myself.
So we hurried out, the wife and I,
  anxious to help,
  not sure what we might find
  though fearing the worst.
But what a surprise!
There was no panic,
  no sign of confusion.
Quite the contrary –
  they seemed so peaceful,
  so full of joy,
  utterly content.
And the way they looked at that child –
  I mean, I've heard of worshipping your kids
  but this was something else –
  they were over the moon,
  absolutely ecstatic!
And that wasn't the half of it,
  for suddenly there in the shadows
  I spotted a bunch of shepherds –
  God knows where they came from.
Thought for a moment they were up to no good,
  but they weren't.
They just stood there gawping into the manger,
  wide-eyed with wonder,
  almost as though they'd never seen a baby before!

And then they walked away,
  joy in their faces,
  delight in their steps.
It's all quiet now, the inn and the stable,
  as if that night had never happened.
And so far as I know both mother and child are well.
You could say that's down to me in part,
  for at least I did something to help if no one else did.
Yet I can't help feeling I should have done more,
  that I let everyone down somehow –
  that it wasn't finally them I left out in the cold –
  it was me.

Silent reflection

Meditation of Mary

What a day it's been!
I'm shattered, exhausted,
  and yet I'm over the moon!
Does that sound strange?
Well, let me tell you what happened, then you'll understand.
It could hardly have started worse,
  arriving in Bethlehem like that to find the place packed.
My heart sank.
I knew we wouldn't find anywhere, not a chance,
  but Joseph wouldn't have it.
'Next time,' he kept saying, 'you'll see.'
Next time indeed!
A stable, that's what we ended up with –
  hardly the accommodation I had in mind!
It wouldn't have mattered, mind you,
  not in the usual run of things,
  but I was nine months pregnant
  and my pains had started that morning,
  getting stronger by the minute.
I was in agony by the end, you can imagine,
  just about desperate by then,
  not bothered where we stopped
  just so long as I could rest.
That's why we accepted the innkeeper's offer,
  makeshift though it was.
I lay there with cattle breathing down my neck,
  straw prickling my back,

and what felt like a gale whistling beneath the door –
   but I didn't care;
   I didn't care about anything by then,
   just wanted the baby to be born.
Poor Joseph, he was beside himself.
No idea how to cope or what to do next,
   but thankfully one of the women from the inn took pity on us.
You'll never know how good it was
   to see her kindly reassuring face,
   her confident smile beaming down at me
   through the haze of pain.
It seemed like an eternity for all that,
   but it wasn't long really.
And then that sound,
   that wonderful exhilarating sound,
   my son, Jesus, crying!
I didn't want to let go of him,
   but I had to, of course, eventually.
I was exhausted,
   just about all in.
So I wrapped him in strips of cloth
   and laid him in a manger.
Sleep came easy after that,
   blissful peace at last,
   but a moment ago I woke with a start,
   remembering those words in that vision I had –
   'And they shall name him Emmanuel,
   God with us'.
My child, Emmanuel?
Can it really be true?
God come to his people?
He's everything to me, I admit that,
   I could gladly worship him.
But others? I wonder.
Time alone will tell, I suppose.
Anyway, no more time for talking, I need my sleep.
But wait, who's this knocking on the door?
Shepherds!
What on earth can they want at this time of night?
I don't know.
What a day it's been!
What a day!

Slides   Shepherds
Music   *Pastoral Symphony (Messiah)* Handel
                during which Luke 2:8-20 is read

Meditation of the shepherds

It was just an ordinary day, that's what I can't get over;
   nothing special about it,
   nothing different,
   just another ordinary day.
And we were all just ordinary people,
   that's what made it even more puzzling;
   not important,
   not influential,
   just plain ordinary shepherds out working in the fields.
Yet we apparently were the first,
   singled out for special favour!
The first to know,
   the first to see,
   the first to celebrate,
   the first to tell!
I'm still not sure what happened –
   one moment night drawing in,
   and the next bright as day;
   one moment laughing and joking together,
   and the next rooted to the spot in amazement;
   one moment looking forward to getting home,
   and the next hurrying down to Bethlehem.
There just aren't words to express what we felt,
   but we knew we had to respond,
   had to go and see for ourselves.
Not that we expected to find anything mind you,
   not if we were honest.
Well, you don't, do you?
I mean, it's not every day the Messiah arrives, is it?
And we'd always imagined when he finally did
   it would be in a blaze of glory,
   to a fanfare of trumpets,
   with the maximum of publicity.
Yet do you know what?
When we got there
   it was to find everything just as we had been told,
   wonderfully special,

yet surprisingly ordinary.
Not Jerusalem but Bethlehem,
   not a palace but a stable,
   not a prince enthroned in splendour
   but a baby lying in a manger.
We still find it hard to believe even now,
   to think God chose to come
   through that tiny vulnerable child.
But as the years have passed –
   and we've seen not just his birth but his life,
   and not just his life but his death,
   and not just his death but his empty tomb,
   his graveclothes, his joyful followers –
   we've slowly came to realise it really was true.
God had chosen to come to us,
   and more than that, to you –
   to ordinary, everyday people,
   in the most ordinary, everyday of ways.
How extraordinary!

Slides   Magi
Music   *Arrival of the Queen of Sheba* Handel
          during which Matthew 2:1-12 is read

Meditation of the magi

We knew it would be worth it the moment we saw the star,
   worth the hassle,
   worth the effort,
   worth the sacrifice.
But there were times when we wondered, I can tell you!
As we laboured over those dusty barren tracks,
   as we watched fearfully for bandits in the mountains,
   as the sun beat down without a break,
   and still no sign of an end to it,
   we wondered, all too often.
We asked ourselves whether we'd got it wrong,
   misread the signs.
We argued over whether we'd taken the wrong turning
   somewhere along the way.
We questioned the wisdom of carrying on as the days dragged by.
And when finally we got to Jerusalem
   only to find his own people had no idea what was going on,
   then we really became worried.

Quite astonishing – the biggest event in their history,
　　and they didn't even realise it was happening!
Thankfully they looked it up, eventually,
　　somewhere in one of their old prophets,
　　and we knew where to go then.
It was all there in writing if only they'd taken the trouble to look –
　　God knows why they couldn't see it!
Anyway, we made it at last,
　　tired, sore and hungry,
　　but we made it.
And it was worth it, more than we had ever imagined,
　　for in that child was a different sort of king,
　　a different sort of kingdom,
　　from any we'd ever encountered before.
As much our ruler as theirs,
　　as much our kingdom as anyone's.
So we didn't just present our gifts to him,
　　we didn't just make the customary gestures of acknowledgement.
We fell down and worshipped him.
Can you imagine that?
Grown men,
　　respected,
　　wealthy,
　　important,
　　kneeling before a toddler.
Yet it seemed so natural,
　　the most natural response we could make,
　　the only response that would do!

Silent reflection

Slide　　　Herod
Reading　　Matthew 2:16-18

Meditation of Herod
Could they have been right,
　　those visitors from the East?
Were they not so misguided after all?
I laughed when they first arrived,
　　rambling on about a star like that –
　　a bunch of cranks I thought,
　　but we humoured them just in case.

They were wealthy after all,
    the sort who might well show appreciation worth having.
So I called together the chief priests,
    summoned the scribes,
    and set them to work –
    about time they did something useful.
But what did they come up with?
Bethlehem, that's what!
Foretold apparently by the prophet Micah.
Bethlehem! I ask you!
That provincial backwater!
It's in the middle of nowhere,
    hardly the place for a king to be born.
No, it would have to be Jerusalem,
    any fool could have told them that,
    but it was all academic anyway,
    no king had been born;
    well, I'd have been the first to know, wouldn't I?
Stands to reason.
Unless some usurper, some would-be Messiah,
    had designs on my throne;
    there's always enough of those,
    blasted troublemakers!
But I couldn't see it,
    not after what we did to the last impostor.
No, I didn't pay much attention,
    but just in case I told them to come back,
    let me know when they found him
    so that I could pay my respects in turn.
They never did, of course –
    never expected them to either.
No doubt slunk off home with their tails between their legs.
Yet I've not been able to sleep these last few days,
    not since I heard this rumour doing the rounds –
    three strangers apparently,
    who turned up recently in Bethlehem and offered gifts,
    costly gifts,
    gold, frankincense and myrrh,
    and all for some child not yet out of his cradle.
There may be nothing in it, of course,
    but it sounds like them, doesn't it?
And if it was, then who was the child?

What did they know about him?
Why didn't they come back?
Could there be something going on,
    some plot I don't know about,
    a rival to my throne?
Could it be that prophet knew what he was talking about,
    all those years ago?
It's unlikely, I grant you, but I'm making certain,
    deadly certain –
    just in case they were right.

Slide   Temple
Music   *For unto us a child is born (Messiah)* Handel
                during which Luke 2:36-38 is read

Meditation of Anna

I really felt I'd missed it,
    truthfully.
I mean, I wasn't just old,
    I was ancient!
And still there was no sign of the Messiah,
    no hint of his coming.
I began to wonder whether all those years of praying and fasting
    had been worth it,
    or simply one almighty waste of time.
I doubted everything,
    questioned everything,
    despite my outward piety.
Why hadn't God answered my prayers?
Why hadn't he rewarded my faithfulness?
Why believe when it didn't seem to make a scrap of difference?
I still kept up the facade mind you –
    spoke excitedly of the future,
    of all that God would do –
    but I didn't have much faith in it,
    not after so many disappointments.
Until that day when,
    hobbling back through the temple after yet more prayers,
    suddenly I saw him,
    God's promised Messiah.
Don't ask me how I knew,
    I just did,
    without any shadow of a doubt,

and it was the most wonderful moment of my life,
a privilege beyond words.
It taught me something, that experience.
It taught me never to give up,
never to let go,
never to lose heart.
It taught me there is always reason to hope
no matter how futile it seems.
It taught me to go on expecting
despite all the blows life may dish out.
It taught me God has never finished
however much it may feel like it.
I nearly lost sight of all that.
I was right on the edge,
teetering on the brink,
fearing God had passed me by.
But he'd saved the best till last,
and I know now, even though the waiting is over,
that there's more to come,
more to expect,
more to celebrate.
For though my life is nearly at an end,
it has only just begun!

Silent reflection

Meditation of a resident of Bethleham

Have you heard the news?
They're saying the Messiah's been born
right here in Bethlehem.
Honestly, that's what I was told,
the Christ,
God's promised deliverer,
come at last to set us free.
Do I believe it?
Well, I'm not sure.
It's hard to credit, I admit,
but this friend I spoke to seemed pretty certain.
Heard it from a shepherd apparently,
some chap who claimed to have seen the child for themselves,
and by all accounts he was delirious with excitement,
absolutely full of it.

He may have been mistaken, of course,
  or simply spinning some old yarn –
  you never can be sure, can you?
And, believe me, I don't go round believing everything I hear.
But this friend of mine,
  the one who heard it from the shepherd,
  he was full of it too.
You would have thought he'd been there,
  in the stable,
  beside the manger,
  the way he spoke.
He was utterly convinced, there's no question about that,
  and as I listened to him chattering on,
  I felt the urge welling up inside me,
  just as he had done,
  to tell someone else,
  to share the good news with those around me.
If he was right then this wasn't something to keep to myself,
  not for the privileged few,
  but a message for everybody,
  one they all needed to hear.
But before I say anything more,
  risk making a complete fool of myself,
  there's something I have to do –
  something my friend should have done
  and which the shepherds presumably did –
  and that is go and see for myself.
Call me a cynic if you like but I believe it's important –
  no, more than that, vital –
  for if you're going to accept something,
  let alone expect others to do the same,
  you have to be sure of your ground,
  as certain as you can be that it's not just all some grand delusion.
So I'm going now,
  off to find out the truth for myself,
  off to see this child,
  if he really exists, with my own eyes.
And if I find everything just as I've been told,
  the baby lying there in a manger,
  wrapped in strips of cloth,
  then I shall go and tell others what I have seen –
  for let's be honest, what else would there be to do?
What else could anybody do in my place?

Prayer

Loving God,
    you have given us and all the world Good News in Christ.
Help us to hear that news afresh each day,
    recognising it is as Good News for *us*.
Help us to receive it with both our minds and our hearts,
    always looking to understand more of what it continues to say.
And help us to share what Christ has done for us
    so that others in turn may celebrate what he has done for them.
Amen.

Music   *Rejoice, rejoice greatly (Messiah)* Handel

SESSION TWO – *Ministry*

Music   *Comfort ye (Messiah)* Handel

Prayer

Lord, we have thought of your birth;
    we reflect now on your life and ministry.
Speak through all you did
    of all you can do now
    for we ask it in your name.
Amen.

Slides   John the Baptist
Music   *O thou that tellest (Messiah)* Handel
            during which Matthew 3:13-17 is read

Meditation of John the Baptist

It still doesn't seem right,
    after all this time;
    me baptising Jesus!
I tried to stop him,
    couldn't believe my eyes when he came down into the water.
Actually thought for a moment he was going to baptise me.
But then I looked in those quiet eyes of his,
    and I knew he meant it,
    he wanted me to do the honours.
Even then I tried to change his mind.
'You can't be serious,' I told him.

But he was.
Amazing!
Well, what could I do?
I could hardly refuse, even though it seemed so out of place.
I wasn't worthy even to tie up his shoelaces,
    that's the way I saw it.
I'd spent my whole ministry looking forward to his coming,
    never pointing to myself but always to him.
To help prepare his way,
    that was all I asked,
    all I expected,
    all I wanted.
And I'd have been happy just to have seen him,
    to have been assured I'd done my bit.
But he thought different,
    so I did as he asked,
    trembling with anxiety,
    overcome with emotion,
    stunned at the privilege:
    I, John, baptised him!
It meant a lot to Jesus, that was obvious –
    his face was glowing,
    radiant with delight,
    almost as if he could hear God speaking.
But what people seem to forget is that it was memorable for me too:
    a day I shall always treasure,
    a day I shall never forget,
    the most special day in my life!

Slides   Temptation
Music   *Confutatis (Requiem)* Mozart
             during which Matthew 4:1-13 is read

Meditation of Mary, mother of Jesus

He looked awful,
    absolutely drained.
And it's hardly surprising, is it?
Forty days out in the wilderness –
    that's hell enough for anyone,
    but without food – I ask you?
He was lucky to be alive!
Barely was, mind you, when he came staggering back into Nazareth.

A complete wreck he was,
    just about done in!
'Why did you do it?' I asked him.
'What got into you?'
And all he could say was that he had to,
    that everything depended on it.
He was never the same afterwards.
I used to joke the sun had got to him.
But it wasn't the sun, of course,
It was much more than that.
He wrestled out there,
    with himself,
    with the world,
    with all the forces of evil,
    and in some way I don't quite understand,
    he won.
It was a costly time, there's no doubt about that,
    a disturbing, frightening time –
    I could see the pain in his eyes afterwards.
He'd had to struggle,
    make painful choices,
    confront life at its darkest.
And though I never told him, I admired him for that.
It takes courage to face reality,
    to ask youself what it's really all about.
Mind you, I always knew he had it in him.
He'd always been such a good boy,
    right from the start;
    too good some said.
Well, perhaps he was in a way –
    look where it got him after all.
Yet it wasn't as easy as many thought.
He was still tempted, all too often,
    and there were times
    when it would have been so easy for him to give in,
    so easy to compromise,
    to bend just the once.
I know that's what he faced out there in the wilderness
    though he never told me what exactly happened.
But he came back stronger, I have to admit it,
    more certain,
    more determined.

Not that he didn't have his moments afterwards –
    don't make that mistake.
It wasn't all plain sailing from then on.
He had to battle like you and I,
    harder if anything,
    for the path he took was so much more demanding.
Oh no, he endured temptation all right,
    as real as any we might face.
The difference is he overcame it,
    right to the end.
That's what made him so special.
That's why people follow him, even now!

Slides   Synagogue
Music   Adagio cantabile from *Pathetique Sonata* Beethoven
         during which Luke 4:14-30 is read

Meditation of a member of the synagogue in Nazareth

He had a wonderful voice,
    a real joy to listen to:
    so clear,
    so deep,
    so nicely-spoken.
I felt I could have sat there all day,
    letting the words wash over me:
    good news for the poor,
    release for the captives,
    recovery of sight for the blind –
    familiar,
    comfortable,
    reassuring words.
Or so I'd always thought.
Only this time they didn't sound quite as reassuring as they used to.
I don't know what it was
    but somehow as he spoke they came to life,
    possessed of a power they had never held before,
    as if I were hearing them for the very first time;
    only the prophet was speaking not to people long ago,
    but to me,
    here,
    now.

And suddenly I didn't want to hear,
   didn't want to listen any more,
   for the words were no longer what I'd thought they were,
   but unexpected,
   discomforting,
   troubling words.
They leapt at me and pinned me down.
They lunged at me piercing my very soul.
They left me anxious,
   guilty,
   fearful,
   asking what they meant to someone like me
   who was neither poor or blind,
   but rich and free.
I closed my ears
   but still he spoke,
   and listening again, despite myself, I heard him say,
   'A prophet is without honour in his own country.'
That was the end,
   too much.
The voice no longer seeming beautiful but strident,
   no longer bringing joy but rousing rage.
For I realised this man came not to soothe but to challenge,
   not to praise but to question;
   not only to us but to others.
I rose in rage,
   cursing him for his blasphemy,
   calling for his death!
Yet somehow, though all around me did the same,
   he walked straight by,
   unharmed,
   untouched.
Don't ask me how, for I just don't know.
But what I do know, deep down –
   much though I try to deny it,
   much though I try to ignore it –
   is that Jesus had been right to say,
   'These words have been fulfilled today.'

Slides   Matthew
Music   *Pathetique Sonata* (continued)
         during which Matthew 9:9-13 is read

Silent reflection

Meditation of Matthew

He had time for me,
   incredible, I know, but true.
He saw beneath the surface,
   beneath the greed, the selfishness and the corruption,
   and uncovered a person I didn't even know existed.
I groaned when I saw him coming, I won't pretend otherwise;
   another self-righteous prig coming to tell me my business,
   that's what I imagined.
And I'd had my fair share of those –
   well, nobody likes a tax collector, do they?
But I'd always given as good as I got.
I mean, it's not easy when you've a wife and kids at home to feed –
   we all have to earn a living somehow –
   and since the only people ready to give me a chance were the Romans
what could I do?
Or did any of them really imagine I enjoyed working for them?
Anyway, someone had to do it, didn't they, so why not me?
I suppose Jesus understood that, for he didn't criticise or condemn –
   none of the two-faced hypocrisy of the Pharisees,
   none of the usual accusing glances or obscene gestures –
   just those two lovely words:
   'Follow me.'
You could have knocked me over.
It was the last thing I expected,
   took the wind right out of my sails.
But more than that I was excited,
   moved,
   fascinated,
   because he had time for me.
He hadn't written me off,
   he hadn't seen only the outside –
   he accepted me as I was,
   with all my sin sticking to me.
And the funny thing was, once he did that
   it was me who pointed to my faults,
   not him.
I felt ashamed,
   painfully aware of all that was wrong,

longing to be different;
yet at the same time set free,
forgiven,
offered a new beginning.
I followed, of course,
What else could I do?
Would you refuse a man like that?
Well, perhaps you would, but I'm glad I didn't,
    because despite everything since –
    the times I've let him down,
    the occasions I've misunderstood,
    the mistakes I've made,
    the faults I still have –
    he goes on accepting me day after day,
Not for what I might become.
But for what I am!

Slides   Feeding of the five thousand
Music   *Pathetique Sonata* (continued)
               during which Luke 9:10-17 is read

Meditation of one of the 5000

We were starving,
    fit to drop,
    our stomachs rumbling something rotten.
And it's hardly surprising, is it?
We'd been up there on the mountain for ages and not a bite to eat.
It was our own fault, of course –
    we should have come prepared –
    but it just never occurred to us it would be necessary.
We thought we'd only be gone a while,
    a few hours at the most.
Only he kept on talking,
    and we kept on listening,
    rooted to the spot in wonder.
That's not like me, I can tell you –
    usually twenty minutes is my limit, no matter how good the speaker –
    but I could have listened to that man for ever
    because his words touched my heart,
    stirred my spirit,
    answered my deepest needs.

We were sorry when he stopped,
    each of us urging him to continue,
    but he knew I think, before we did,
    that we needed physical as well as spiritual nourishment.
And suddenly it hit us just how hungry we were,
    and how far from home.
We began to feel quite faint, what with the heat as well,
    and I honestly believe
    some of us wouldn't have had the strength to get back.
But suddenly he turned to his disciples, and told them to feed us.
You should have seen their faces –
    they didn't know whether to laugh or cry!
Neither did we, come to that.
As one of them finally put it,
    once he realised Jesus wasn't having him on:
    'Where are we to get bread out here?'
It was the back of beyond,
    the middle of nowhere;
    you couldn't just pop round the corner for a few thousand loaves!
But Jesus just looked amused,
    and then asked quietly if anyone had any food left.
Well, there weren't many who were going to answer that, were there?
Not if they had any sense.
Even supposing they had a morsel tucked away somewhere
    they were hardly going to admit it,
    not with five thousand starving wretches breathing down their necks!
But then a young lad stepped forward,
    all innocence,
    and produced five loaves and two fishes,
    handing them over with the sweetest and most trusting of smiles.
I didn't think Jesus would have the heart to take them,
    but he did,
    solemnly giving thanks to God before breaking them
    and getting his disciples to hand round the pieces.
Don't ask me what happened next –
    I still can't make sense of it –
    but somehow we all had a feast.
It wasn't just a few token crumbs or a desperate mouthful for the strongest,
    but more than we could eat
    and enough left afterwards to fill twelve baskets.
A miracle some say it was, and yes, I suppose they're right,
    but you know, what's always lived with me,

and what counts most looking back,
is not the way he fed our bodies but the way he fed our souls as well;
for I've been hungry physically many times since then,
but my spirit has found contentment, full to overflowing.

Slides   Blind man
Music   *'Moonlight' Sonata* Beethoven
        during which Mark 10:46-52 is read

Meditation of Bartimaeus

He made me see!
For the first time in my life,
   after all those years of darkness,
   all those years listening and wondering what the world must be like,
   I was able to look and see for myself!
I saw clouds scudding through the sky,
   grass waving in the breeze,
   flowers blooming in the meadow,
   waves breaking on the seashore.
I saw birds nesting in the trees,
   and animals wandering in the mountains,
   the moon and stars glowing in the night sky,
   the beauty of sunrise and sunset, bathing the earth in its golden glow.
I saw children playing,
   the faces of loved ones,
   the bustle of towns and city,
   the pomp of priest and temple.
I saw fields of corn and ripening fruit,
   bubbling streams and tranquil pools,
   a world of colour, form and contrast,
   more lovely than in my wildest dreams.
All this, thanks to Jesus, I can see!
Yet there is more,
   much more, that I owe him,
   for it is not just my eyes he has opened,
   but my mind,
   my heart,
   my soul.
I looked at him
   and I did not see just a man:
   I glimpsed the face of God,
   smiling through his welcome;

I glimpsed the hand of God,
   reaching out through his touch;
I glimpsed the love of God,
   accepting me through his call.
He made me see, Jesus,
   not just with my eyes, though I can't thank him enough for that,
   but with my soul –
   the things that really matter,
   that really count,
   that meet my deepest needs.
And now I know that even when it is dark,
   even when life is at its blackest,
   even when I cannot see the way ahead,
   I am walking in the light.

Silent reflection

Slides   Lazarus
Music   *Lacrimosa (Requiem)* Mozart
           during which John 11:32-44 is read

Meditation of Lazarus

It was so weird,
   so unreal.
At least that's how it felt.
And yet it happened!
I'd breathed my last, no question about that.
After those long dark days of sickness,
   the pain growing
   the strength failing;
   after those final terrible hours,
   sweat pouring down my face,
   lungs gasping for air;
   at last came peace,
   darkness closing about me,
   suddenly welcome though it had long been feared.
An end to the struggle,
   the battle nearly over.
For a moment I was a child again, comforted by my mother's embrace,
   a youth running wild as the wind,
   a man setting out afresh on life's great adventure,
   a father, taking my child into my arms.

And then rest.
The light went out,
   the flame extinguished,
   the game completed.
Only it wasn't,
   for suddenly a voice summoned me back to the fray,
   sunshine burst into the tomb,
   and consciousness returned.
No wonder they gasped,
   no wonder they swooned,
   no wonder they wept for joy,
   for I who had been taken from them,
   I who had been dead,
   was alive!
And yes, I thanked him, of course I did,
   once the confusion had cleared anyway,
   but it took a while, I can tell you.
And even now just once in a while
   I wonder if he really did me any favours
   for I know that one day I must face it all over again.
Yet it will be different then,
   very different,
   not just because I've been there before and know there's nothing to fear,
   but because Jesus has shown me
   that death is not so much the end as the beginning.
That's why he raised me from the tomb.
Not just to restore life,
   not simply to defer death,
   but to point to a new birth,
   a resurrection which only he can bring.
He came back too, you know,
   back from beyond the grave.
Three days in his tomb,
   long enough for decay to take hold,
   but he appeared to Mary,
   to Peter,
   to the Apostles,
   to us all.
And we know that even though we die
   one day we shall live
   even as he lives now!

Slides   Entry into Jerusalem
Music   *Gloria (Gloria)* Vivaldi
          during which Luke 19:29-41 is read

Meditation of Simon the Zealot

What a day it was,
    a day I shall never forget –
    the voices raised in jubilation,
    the arms outstretched in welcome,
    the crowds lining the streets,
    waving their palm branches,
    hurling down their cloaks,
    welcoming their king,
    the Son of David,
    the one who came in the name of the Lord.
They believed that at long last the waiting was over,
    the Messiah finally come to set them free.
We believed it too, come to that.
After all his talk of suffering and death we dared to hope he'd got it wrong,
    and for a moment as I watched him I wondered if he felt the same –
    the way he responded to the cheers,
    laughter playing on his lips,
    a smile on his face,
    a twinkle in his eyes.
He was enjoying himself, I'm sure of that,
    determined to savour the moment.
But then I noticed it,
    as we drew near to Jerusalem,
    a tear in the corner of his eye –
    so unexpected.
Not a tear of joy but of sorrow,
    trickling slowly down his face,
    silent testimony to his pain.
He wasn't fooled by it all,
    not like the rest of us.
He knew what they wanted,
    how they would change.
He knew they would offer the cross if he rejected their crown,
    but still he continued, resolute to the end;
    that's the extraordinary thing.
It was a day to remember,
    a day on which they welcomed their king.

But none imagined, least of all I,
   that the crown would be made of thorns,
   and the throne reached via a cross.

Slides   Cleansing of Temple
Music   *Montagues and Capulets* Prokofiev
           during which Luke 19:45-48 is read

Meditation of James

Why did he have to spoil it all?
That's what I want to know.
It was all going so well,
   way beyond our expectations,
   until he went and ruined it.
All right, so maybe he had to do something,
   maybe they were abusing the temple,
   making a mockery of what it was meant to be,
   but couldn't he have been more careful,
   more conciliatory,
   more diplomatic?
A quiet word in the right ears, surely that was the best way?
Perhaps a gesture of disapproval to get the point home,
   even a scathing condemnation, though preferably out of earshot.
But this –
   overturning their tables in a fit of rage,
   smashing their stalls,
   driving out their livestock,
   lashing out in fury;
   it was asking for it,
   guaranteed to make enemies,
   and let's face it, hardly good for his image.
A troublemaker they called him after that,
   and can you blame them?
Why couldn't he have left things as they were?
They were right behind him,
   ready to do whatever he asked,
   dancing for joy in the streets,
   tearing down branches to greet him.
Oh, I know a few might still have turned against him,
   once they realised what he was saying,
   and what he wasn't –
   there would still have been some determined to do him in, I realise that.

But why did he make it easy for them?
Why invite hostility?
Why refuse to compromise?
I'm trying to understand, I really am, but it's hard.
If it had been me I'd have taken the easy way, despite my convictions –
    toned things down,
    avoided confrontation,
    kept in with those who mattered.
That's why I'm still alive today and he's not.
Yet, deep down, I realise he had no other choice,
    not if he was going to be true to himself.
And he always was, I have to give him that.
That's what made him so special,
    that's why I followed him.
    that's why I still do, even now.

Prayer

Lord Jesus Christ,
    we want to be true to our convictions,
    to stand up for what is right,
    but it's hard when the pressure is on.
It's hard not to bend when all around us disagree,
    it's hard not to compromise for the sake of peace,
    it's hard not to tone things down
    when we find ourselves in the firing line.
Yet there are times when we need to stick our necks out
    for what we believe in,
    even when doing so may make us unpopular with others.
Give us wisdom to know when those times are,
    and give us courage then to hold fast through them all.
Amen.

Music   *Clair de lune* Debussy

SESSION THREE – *Death*

Music *Miserere* Allegri

Prayer
Lord Jesus Christ,
   you came to us, you died for us.
Help us to understand all that means.
Amen.

Music Final movement of *Pathetique Symphony* Tchaikovsky
during which the following are used, the music fading
for meditations

Slides Gethsemane
Reading Matthew 26:36-46, after which music fades

Meditation of Matthew

He was scared, that much is certain.
I've never seen him like it before.
He'd always seemed so sure,
   so confident,
   so at ease with himself,
   even when he talked about death
   and he'd done that often enough.
I really thought it didn't worry him, the way he'd spoken,
   but this time it was different,
   so different.
We'd just finished supper,
   and he'd seemed strangely preoccupied throughout,
   so we weren't surprised when he suggested going out for a little air –
   a stroll to clear our heads, that's what we expected.
But then he asked us to pray for him,
   and off he went alone into the darkness.
Gone for ages it seemed,
   and when he came back you should have seen him.
Shaking like a leaf he was,
   eyes wide with fear,
   sweating buckets,
   a right old state.

We were shocked, I can tell you.
It made us nervous just to look at him.
And the tone of voice he used with us,
   just because we'd dozed off for a few minutes.
I know he was hurt, but I ask you, it was past midnight!
Three times he went off,
   and each time he came back the same –
   terrified.
He was scared, make no mistake.
It wasn't as easy as we all thought.
Not easy at all.

Silent reflection

Meditation of Peter

He was broken-hearted, if you ask me,
   and I can't say I blame him.
I think I'd have felt the same.
You see, he'd expected it from the others –
   the Scribes and Pharisees –
   he knew they had it in for him from the start.
And the crowds who'd followed him, welcomed him into Jerusalem –
   he wasn't taken in by them,
   not for a moment.
Even Judas,
   he saw the truth about him before anyone else had an inkling.
But the rest of us, I think he'd hoped for something better.
Not that he asked much.
He knew I'd deny him, despite all my protestations of loyalty,
   and he knew we'd all run for it when it was our skins on the line.
He'd accepted that, and still loved us, God knows why!
But there in the garden, that's when he needed us most,
   that's when he'd hoped for that little bit more.
Just to know we cared,
   that we were behind him,
   that we were there.
It would have meant so much.
And we failed him, even in that one simple thing.
I still don't know how it happened.
I tried,
   I really tried,
   but somehow I just couldn't keep my eyes open.

I can forgive myself the rest;
   it was my life at stake after all.
But to stay awake just one hour.
It wasn't much to ask, was it?
And I couldn't do even that.
He was broken-hearted,
   the stuffing knocked right out of him,
   and I know in large part it was all down to me.

Silent reflection

Slide   Judas hangs himself
Reading Matthew 27:1-5a, after which music fades

Meditation of Judas
Oh God, what have I done? What have I done?
The man I called my friend,
   taken before Caiaphas,
   tried by the Council,
   condemned to the most dreadful of deaths,
   and all down to me.
I've tried telling myself that it's not my fault,
   that it's the priests,
   Herod,
   Pilate to blame,
   anyone but myself.
They're the ones who want him dead after all.
They're the ones who pronounce the sentence,
   so why accuse me?
I've tried telling myself that my part was irrelevant,
   that if I hadn't betrayed him someone else would,
   that it was only a matter of time,
   that all I did was bring things to a head –
   so why condemn me?
I've tried telling myself I had no choice,
   that I had to bring him down to earth,
   make him see reason,
   stop the crowds getting carried away.
All for the best possible motives –
   so why judge me?
I've tried telling myself it's what he wanted,
   even that I've been used,

an innocent pawn in God's cosmic plan,
a helpless puppet dancing to his tune,
made in such a way that I had no choice –
so why blame me?
But I do, that's the trouble;
  I do blame myself.
It's not others I'm worried about;
  it's me.
For I know, despite all my excuses,
  that there's no escaping my responsibility.
It's there before me, every second, every moment,
  deep in my heart –
  the doubt,
  the fear,
  the greed,
  the selfishness,
  which sent him to his death with a kiss.
Oh God, what have I done? What have I done?
God forgive me, forgive me.
For I can't forgive myself.

Slides   Trial
Reading   Luke 23:6-12, after which music fades

Meditation of Herod

He was innocent, you could tell that immediately,
  innocent of any crime.
I should have known it when Pilate sent him to me, the wily old fox –
  wanting me to do his dirty work as usual.
Well, no thank you, not this time.
But I was glad at first,
  I'd wanted to see this Jesus for some time;
  heard so much about him, you'll understand.
The greatest attraction in Judea,
  pulling in the crowds like nobody's business.
We'd all been looking forward to judging for ourselves.
But what a disappointment!
What a let-down!
Would he perform for us, give us some proof of his talents?
Would he hell!
A trickster, that's what we called him,
  and made him suffer for it too.

Yet he wasn't;
   I knew it,
   we all knew it.
He wasn't a fraud, or any of the things they accused him of.
You only needed to look at him to see that.
Those eyes, they went straight through you,
   not a hint of deceit,
   not a trace of malice,
   not a sign of evil.
A good man, the best I've come across.
We couldn't let him go, of course, not given the mood the crowd were in,
   but I was damned if I was going to be the one to have him killed.
I've had enough regrets about that Baptist fellow,
   whatever his name was.
No, let Pilate sort it out, that's what I decided.
And funnily enough he understood.
He didn't thank me for it, but he understood.
Knew what Jesus was like, I suppose.
He was innocent,
   innocent of any crime,
   we both knew that;
   we only wish we could feel the same about ourselves.

Silent reflection

Meditation of Pilate

He was different,
   I have to admit it.
Not a bit like I'd expected.
I'd heard the stories, of course.
Who hadn't?
Teacher, miracle worker, Messiah.
But I just thought he'd be like all the others:
   a charlatan out for what he could get,
   or some crazy fanatic who dared imagine
   he could take on the might of Rome.
Give me five minutes and I'll usually break them down.
A good flogging will see to that if all else fails.
Not this one though –
   I tried that,
   I tried everything;
   we gave him the full works.

And still he just stood there looking at me,
   as if I was the one on trial,
   as if he was the one in charge.
He was quite innocent, of course; any fool could see that.
But he wouldn't help himself,
   almost like he wanted to die.
Maybe he knew it was useless,
   that the crowds would never let me get away with it,
   though why they wanted him killed beats me.
I had no choice, that's what I keep telling myself.
It was my duty.
And anyway, it was them, not me, who had the last word.
Yet I can't help thinking I should have done more,
   feeling guilty.
The wife doesn't help, nagging me about him all the time.
Does she think that I can sleep any better than her?
What would she have done in my place?
I washed my hands of him in the end, literally.
But I still feel dirty, as though it's finally down to me.
He was different all right,
   but what sort of man was he?
That's the mystery.

Slides   The Cross
Reading   Matthew 27:27-31, 45-46, after which music fades

Meditation of a Roman soldier at the cross

He was in agony,
   believe me, I know.
I've seen it often enough, crucifixion.
All in a day's work for me.
And I've heard a few howl for mercy over the years.
There's few things to touch it so they tell me for sheer pain,
   slow, lingering, dreadful.
But he was different, that was the curious thing.
I could see he was suffering all right;
   it was there in his eyes,
   in the gritted teeth,
   in the writhing body,
   in the sweat pouring from him,
   and most of all in that last awful groan.

But he never complained,
  never screamed,
  never swore.
Funny that.
To be honest, I've never seen anyone quite like him.
That look he had, even in death,
  as though we were the ones suffering,
  as though we were the criminals deserving punishment,
  as though he felt sorry for us.
Ridiculous, of course.
But you know, I could swear as he drew his last breath
  there was a smile on his face,
  almost like he felt he'd achieved something.
An odd business,
  very odd.

Slide   Jesus dies
Reading   Luke 23:44-47, after which music ends

Meditation of the centurion at the foot of the cross

He was special, that's all I can say,
  and it's not like me to hand out compliments, ask anyone.
I've seen all kinds,
  the real dregs of society,
  murderers, rapists, bandits, muggers, you name it.
And I've watched them all suffering without a shred of conscience.
Good riddance to them, that's the way I look at it.
Felt the same with this one too, at first.
Blasted troublemaker.
Should have thought more carefully, shouldn't he,
  before he started raising expectations, stirring up the crowd?
But as I watched him that all changed;
  you couldn't help but be impressed.
There was something about him –
  the quiet dignity,
  the complete composure,
  the sheer courage of the man.
Nothing could shake him –
  not the mocking or the spitting,
  not the lying or the jeering,
  not the flogging or the interrogation,
  not even the thorns twisted so cruelly into his head.

And when it came to the end,
   as he staggered under that cross, just about all in,
   as the blood spurted from those hands and feet,
   as the life seeped from his broken body,
   still the same.
He actually had time for others,
   more than for himself!
Time for one of the two wretches hanging there alongside him,
   time for his mother, for his friends,
   time for his people who'd stood to gloat,
   time even for us.
Amazing!
The Son of God some of them called him.
And you know what, I think they might have been right.
He was special, there's no doubt about that.

Silent reflection

Meditation of James

He was dead, and I still can't believe it.
I kept on hoping it was all a bad dream,
   that any moment I'd wake up and find we were back together again;
   there on the mountainside as he preached to the crowd,
   there in the boat as he stilled the storm,
   there on the road as he healed the sick,
   there in the upstairs room as we shared supper.
But I didn't wake up and I knew then it was no dream – it was real.
Yet still I couldn't accept it;
   I was waiting for another miracle,
   waiting for him to come down off the cross
   and wipe the smile off their faces,
   waiting for God to do something, anything to put a stop to this madness.
I still can't understand it.
Why did he have to die?
Why the waste of such a beautiful life?
It doesn't make any sense to me.
But it did to him, that's the extraordinary thing.
He warned us of it often enough,
   told us it had to happen,
   even said we should welcome it.
Well, it's happened now,

It's over.
I witnessed his last gasp,
   I heard his last cry,
   I watched them drive the spear into his side,
   I was there when they cut him down, limp and lifeless,
   and I saw the stone rolled against the tomb.
I still can't believe it,
   but I've seen it with my own eyes.
He was dead.

Silent reflection

Slide   Women at Cross
Music   *Rhapsody on a theme of Paganini* Rachmaninov

Meditation of Mary, mother of Jesus

Why me?
That's what I kept on asking myself.
Why me?
I mean, it was obvious what people were going to say, wasn't it?
The sly looks,
   the knowing grins,
   the wagging tongues.
And Joseph?
Well, he really hit the roof.
Furious he was, and who can blame him?
If we'd been married it would have been different,
   but engaged – it was bound to cause a scandal.
And it hurt, more than anyone will know;
   I never realised people could be so cruel.
I didn't even want a baby, that's what made it worse;
   it was the last thing on my mind.
I was still young,
   not ready for that kind of responsibility,
   wanting to enjoy life a little.
I could have done without those sleepless nights,
   the endless washing,
   the countless extra demands.
And believe me, it didn't get any easier.
Well, it never does, does it?

I'll never forget how he disappeared like that
   on the way back from Jerusalem –
   a right old panic he had us in.
But was he sorry?
Well, if he was he had a funny way of showing it.
'You should have known where to find me,' he said –
   'My Father's house, where else?'
Cheeky monkey!
And then, just when life was plodding along nicely,
   back on an even keel,
   he went swanning off into the wilderness to be baptised.
Oh, I know he had to make his own way, don't get me wrong,
   but I couldn't help feeling
   he was getting mixed up in something dangerous.
And so it proved.
We could all see it coming,
   all except him apparently.
He said the wrong things
   to the wrong people
   in the wrong places,
   and there could only be one result.
It nearly broke my heart to watch it –
   my beautiful boy, broken and bleeding,
   struggling with that cross,
   hanging in agony.
But then he looked down,
   not at the rest of them
   but at me.
And in his eyes was such love,
   such care,
   such tenderness!
I saw suddenly the eyes of God looking at me
   through the eyes of my child,
   and I asked myself then,
   as I'd asked so many times before,
   yet differently this time,
   so very differently:
      Why me?
      Why me?

Music   *Meditation* Massenet
Reading   Luke 2:33-35

Meditation of Mary, mother of Jesus

What was that Simeon said –
'A sword will pierce your soul'?
I spent so long wondering what that meant,
tossing and turning on my bed,
brooding and fretting when I'd a moment to myself.
It seemed such a strange thing to say,
especially at what was meant to be a time of joy.
We'd only had Jesus a few days,
and my heart was still bursting with happiness.
We were both over the moon,
Simeon too, that's the odd thing –
he was almost dancing with delight.
But then his expression clouded,
and he gave that awful warning which has haunted me ever since.
I just haven't been able to forget it, try as I might.
Always the question has been there,
nagging away in the back of my mind,
even in the brightest moments:
what did he mean?
And if you'd asked me as little as a week ago
I still wouldn't have been sure.
Oh, I'd a fair idea by then, of course –
the fears were mounting up –
but I'd still kept on hoping,
praying that I might be wrong.
Now I know though,
all too well.
My heart is not just pierced –
it's broken!
For I've stood here today and seen my son die.
I watched him cursed and ridiculed, scourged and beaten.
I watched as they hammered nails through his hands
and lifted him on to a cross.
I watched as he twisted in agony and cried out in despair.
And a moment ago I watched as they plunged a spear into his side.
At least he didn't feel that –
thank God he was dead by then –
but I did.
It thrust deep inside,
running me through without mercy.

I've never known such pain,
   such agony,
   such horror.
And now life has gone for me too;
   I feel it has nothing left to offer.
Yet he's given me joy,
   no one can take that away.
He was with me for thirty wonderful years,
   everything a son could be –
   not many mothers can say that.
I've had joy,
   and now I have pain.
Maybe that's the way it had to be,
   the way it has to be,
   if there's to be any joy at all.

Silent reflection

Prayer

After joy comes sorrow;
   after laughter, tears;
   after pleasure, pain.
Deep down we know
   that we cannot have one without the other.
But sometimes when life is dark
   we find that hard to accept,
   even wishing we experienced no joy at all
   if it would save us pain afterwards.
Yet you were there equally, O God,
   in the joy of Jesus' birth
   and the sorrow of his death.
Teach us, we pray,
   to live with both the good and the bad,
   the times of celebration
   and the times of despair,
   realising, though we may not see it,
   that you are present in both.
Amen.

Music   *Miserere* Allegri

SESSION FOUR – *Life*

Music   *Kyrie ('Coronation' Mass)* Mozart

Prayer
Lord Jesus Christ,
   you died and you rose again.
Live in us now
   and help us to live for you.
Amen.

Slide   Mary
Music   *I know that my redeemer liveth (Messiah)* Handel
               during which Mark 16:9-11 is read

Meditation of Mary Magdalene

They're not going to listen, I can tell you that now.
They've always been suspicious of me, right from the start,
   wondering what Jesus was thinking of,
   getting mixed up with someone like me.
I know what they'll say, you mark my words –
   'Making it all up.'
   'Wanting to be the centre of attention as usual.'
   'A lovesick fool.'
Not that I can blame them;
   it didn't do his cause any good, after all, when I came along.
A few tax-collectors those Pharisees could stomach,
   but me, I really put the cat among the pigeons.
I know how the tongues wagged,
   how easy it became to criticise.
Maybe I should have stayed away,
   kept my distance,
   but I loved him.
No, not in the sense they meant with their sly, dark innuendo,
   but deeper,
   with everything I am,
   everything I've got,
   in a way that I've never loved before.
Yet not even the disciples really trusted me, I know that.
They found it hard to accept,
   hard to forgive what I'd been.

And I can understand that –
   let's face it, I'm finding it hard to forgive them for running away,
   failing him when he needed them most.
But what I hold on to is those words from the cross:
   'Father, forgive them, for they do not know what they do.'
He understood we all fail him,
   that we're all unworthy,
   none of us perfect,
   yet he forgave us and loved us despite that.
I thought I'd lost him,
   the only one who ever truly accepted me,
   and I was reconciled to struggling on alone,
   no one to understand,
   no one to offer their support.
But I was wrong, for he came to me.
There in the garden, overwhelmed by my grief,
   he came to me, and hope was born again.
Not that I could believe it at first.
The voice was familiar,
   the face,
   the eyes,
   but I told myself it couldn't be,
   that it had to be the gardener,
   anyone but Jesus.
And they'll do the same, I'm sure of it,
   tell me I got it wrong,
   that I'm overwrought,
   ready to believe anything.
They won't listen, I can tell you that now,
   but then I'm used to that, aren't I?
And it doesn't matter any more,
   for he's accepted me
   as he's accepted them,
   as he accepts everyone who's ready to respond to his love
   and receive his forgiveness.

Silent reflection

Meditation of Peter
They said he was alive! Can you believe that?
All right, I know they were upset, cut up about what had happened,
   but then we all were, each one of us.

We'd all loved him,
   all believed he was someone special,
   all hoped he was the one we were waiting for.
And we were crushed by what had happened, utterly devastated.
We understood how they felt.
But you have to face facts, don't you?
It's no good burying your head in the sand
   and pretending the worst hasn't happened.
There's no point trying to fool yourself when you know the truth full well.
And we knew, believe me, all too well.
We'd seen him crying out in agony,
   we'd heard him draw his last breath,
   and we'd been there when they laid him in the tomb.
At a distance, true – keeping well out of sight, just in case,
   but he was dead, there's no question about that.
So what were they playing at, those women, claiming he's alive?
They didn't seriously expect any of us to swallow it, surely?
I guess they'd finally gone over the edge, lost their marbles?
Women! We might have guessed they'd go under in a crisis.
No wonder Jesus stuck to men for his disciples –
   clear-headed, realistic, down to earth, sensible.
Jesus alive! We'd like to believe it, of course we would.
But it's nonsense, any fool can see that.

Version for three voices

Peter   They said he was alive! Can you believe that?

John   All right, I know they were upset, cut up about what had happened.

James   But then, we all were, each one of us.

Peter   We'd all loved him.

John   We'd all believed he was someone special.

James   We'd all hoped he was the one we were waiting for.

Peter   And we were crushed by what had happened, utterly devastated.

John   We understood how they felt.

Peter   But you have to face facts, don't you?

John   It's no good burying your head in the sand and pretending the worst hasn't happened.

James   There's no point trying to fool yourself when you know the truth full well.

Peter   And we knew, believe me.

John   We'd seen him crying out in agony.

James   We'd heard him draw his last breath.
Peter   And we'd been there when they laid him in the tomb.
James   At a distance, true – keeping well out of sight, just in case.
John   But he was dead, there's no question about that.
Peter   So what were they playing at, those women, claiming he's alive?
John   They didn't seriously expect any of us to swallow it, surely?
Peter   I guess they'd finally gone over the edge, lost their marbles?
James   Women! We might have guessed they'd go under in a crisis.
John   No wonder Jesus stuck to men for his disciples – clear-headed,
        realistic, down to earth, sensible.
Peter   Jesus alive! We'd like to believe it, of course we would.
John   But it's nonsense, any fool can see that.

Slide   Mary
Music   *How beautiful are the feet (Messiah)* Handel
        during which John 20:11-18 is read

Meditation of Mary Magdalene

I was shattered at the time,
   inconsolable.
It was as though the bottom had fallen out of my world
   and there was nothing left to live for.
How could they do that to him, I asked myself?
How could they destroy someone so loving and gentle,
   so caring,
   so good?
Yet they had.
I'd seen it myself,
   I'd watched as he drew his last agonised breath;
   and it was dreadful,
   more terrible than I can ever describe.
It wasn't just the pain he went through, though that was awful enough;
   it was the isolation of it all –
   standing there before Pilate, alone,
   forsaken by his friends,
   one man against the might of an empire;
   groaning under the lash of the whip, alone,
   no one to offer him comfort,
   no one to bathe his wounds;
   hanging upon that cross, alone,
   crying out in such heart-breaking anguish,
   as though he were separated not just from us but from God himself.

I felt at the time I would never forget it,
  that the memory would haunt me for the rest of my days.
And so it would have,
  unquestionably,
  were it not for what came after.
It was all so unexpected –
  suddenly, in the nightmare of my grief, a ray of sunshine,
  and then joy, immersing me in its light.
One moment despair,
  then the stone rolled away,
  the tomb empty,
  the mysterious stranger appearing from nowhere,
  and that familiar voice speaking my name.
One moment tears,
  the next laughter.
One moment death,
  the next life.
And now my heart dances with delight.
I still can scarcely take it in though;
  sometimes I have to pinch myself to be sure it's not all a dream.
But no, it's true.
He died yet rose again!
He was killed yet conquered death!
He lived and lives again!
I really thought that life was over,
  not just for him but for me.
But I was wrong, wasn't I?
For it wasn't over;
  it was only just beginning.

Slide   Risen Jesus
Music   *Morning (Peer Gynt)* Grieg
             during which Luke 24:13-20, 25-31 is read

Meditation of Cleopas

So that's who it was!
I see it now, staring me in the face.
But how could we have not realised it before?
That's what I don't understand.
You see, we'd been to Jerusalem,
  watched with our own eyes what they did to him,
  even stood at the foot of the cross,
  yet we didn't recognise him when he walked beside us.

Why?
Was it sorrow that blinded us,
   our hearts too full of grief to glimpse the truth?
It's possible, for we were devastated, there's no denying that;
   we'd thought he was the one we longed for,
   coming to redeem our people,
   and it had been a terrible blow after arriving full of hope,
   anticipating his kingdom,
   to see him nailed to that cross,
   bruised and broken,
   the life seeping from his bleeding body.
We'd been so certain,
   so sure he was the Messiah,
   but we'd seen his death
   and were making our way back home,
   our dreams in tatters,
   our lives in ruins.
That could have clouded our eyes, unquestionably,
   for we had little time for anything or anyone.
He was the last person we expected to meet, I can tell you that.
Oh, I know he'd talked of rising again,
   returning from the grave –
   we were talking of it even as we walked –
   but we'd taken it all with a pinch of salt,
   and in our hearts we'd given him up,
   reluctantly making our way back to reality.
We never imagined for a moment we might see him;
   the thought simply never entered our heads.
So yes, perhaps that explains it,
   why for all that time the penny failed to drop.
Yet it was more than that,
   for it wasn't finally the face we recognised at all.
It went far deeper –
   the way he spoke,
   the way he acted,
   the way our hearts burned within us as we walked.
And above all the meal that we shared.
He took the bread,
   and broke it,
   and suddenly we realised, with a certainty nothing could shake,
   that this was Jesus,
   risen,

alive,
   victorious.
Yet even as we saw it he disappeared,
   vanishing before our eyes,
   and we've never seen him since.
It's funny that, isn't it,
   how we saw him most clearly when we couldn't see him at all,
   how our eyes were opened when we weren't even looking –
   and how we know he's with us now, even though he's departed from us!

Slide   Empty Tomb
Music   *Hallelujah Chorus (Messiah)* Handel
          during which John 20:19-20 is read

Meditation of Andrew

We've seen Jesus!
No, don't laugh,
   we've seen him, I tell you!
We made the mistake of dismissing it ourselves,
   scoffing when the women came racing back wild-eyed with excitement.
'Pull yourselves together!' we told them,
   'For God's sake calm down!'
We couldn't believe he was alive,
   refused to accept it could possibly be true.
And when they admitted they couldn't be certain,
   that they'd only seen the empty tomb rather than Jesus himself,
   then we looked for some simpler explanation,
   an answer more in line with common sense.
Even when Mary returned, tears of joy in her eyes,
   even when the two from Emmaus spoke of having seen him,
   we wouldn't accept it, certain that we knew best.
It's understandable, I suppose;
   I mean, you'd think twice, wouldn't you,
   if you'd seen your best friend murdered,
   sealed in the tomb,
   only to be told he'd been spotted down the street?
And anyway, we didn't want to build our hopes up.
We were still reeling from the shock, the horror, the sorrow of it all.
Yet if I'm honest there's more to it than that,
   for most of all our pride was hurt.
If he was alive, we reasoned, then why hadn't we seen him?

Why should Mary,
    or those two disciples,
    or anyone else come to that,
    have seen him before we did?
We were his chosen disciples,
    we the ones who'd given up everything to follow him,
    we those who had taken all the risks –
    so if he had risen surely we'd have known?
It's awful, I know, but that's the way we saw it
    until he finally appeared to us.
We should have remembered, of course, what he'd said so often,
    how the first will be last,
    the least greatest;
    but we still had much to learn
    and were too full of ourselves by half.
Anyway, there we were,
    huddled together in that upstairs room,
    arguing about what it all meant,
    when there he was,
    standing among us,
    arms outstretched in welcome.
Where he came from or where he went after I've no idea.
I only know that it was him –
    Jesus –
    and that he was alive,
    wonderfully,
    amazingly,
    gloriously,
    alive!

Slides   Thomas
Music   *Kyrie ('Coronation' Mass)* Mozart
                during which John 20:24-25 is read

Meditation of Thomas

Would you believe it!
They're all at it now, the whole daft lot of them!
I never thought I'd see the day.
Not Peter, anyway – I thought he had more sense.
And James and John, hot-headed at times perhaps,
    but they had their heads screwed on, or so I thought.
OK, maybe the others were a little suspect.

Simon for one.
To be honest, I felt like he'd believe anything sometimes.
And the rest, they had their moments too, to put it kindly.
But this? Jesus alive and kicking, dropping in on them for a quiet chat . . .
    who are they trying to kid?
It really is beyond me.
I mean, they were the first to mock when the women came back
    trembling and laughing like a bunch of mixed-up children.
We all agreed it was nothing more than hysteria, poor things.
So what's changed? What's got into them?
If you ask me it's this cursed waiting:
    waiting for the sound of footsteps,
    waiting for the knock on the door,
    waiting for the moment when we know it's all up for us
    just as it was for him.
That's enough to make anyone go off their trolley.
But even so you won't catch me rabbiting on about Jesus being alive –
    I'll want more than a few fanciful visions before I start doing that.
Let me touch him perhaps,
    see the scars,
    put my hand in that spear-wound,
    feel where they smashed those nails home,
    and then, who knows, it might be different.
But be honest, what chance is there of that?
Do you believe it could happen?
I don't.

Silent reflection

Slides   Peter
Music   *In trutina (Carmina Burana)* Orff

Meditation of Peter
He called me to follow,
    to lay down my nets and follow him.
No time to think,
    no time to weigh up the pros and cons;
    then and there the need to decide.
So I did,
    on the spot –
    left everything to become one of his disciples.
And I'm glad.

No, honestly, despite everything I'm glad,
    for I know it was the right decision,
    the only decision I could have made.
Yet if I'd known then what I know now
    it might all have been very different.
I'd have thought twice, that's for certain –
    made sure I understood the small print –
    and very likely I'd have got cold feet.
You see, I'd no real idea what I was taking on, even though I thought I had.
I imagined he wanted me for a few days,
    a few weeks at most,
    and then, having done my bit, I could return home,
    back to friends and family,
    back to the security of my fishing nets,
    back to the way things had always been.
But he soon put me right on that, didn't he?
Made it quite clear that discipleship is a lifelong commitment,
    not an option you can walk away from as the mood takes you.
Well, to be honest, a few of us soon considered chucking it in,
    cutting our losses before we got in too deep.
Only we couldn't do that,
    not when it came to it,
    for we knew, though he was asking much, he was offering more.
He had the answers we were looking for,
    the words of eternal life,
    and to have walked away then
    would have been to turn our backs on our one true chance of happiness.
So we carried on,
    day after day,
    week after week,
    month after month,
    following in his footsteps,
    sharing in his work.
And it was tough going, I can tell you,
    really tough –
    and believe me, as a fisherman I know what I'm talking about.
Yet somehow we always found the strength we needed,
    just as he said we would;
    or at least we did until that awful last week
    when suddenly it all went wrong –
    the week Judas betrayed him, the soldiers arrested him,
    Pilate condemned him;

the week when we all ran for our lives,
  our love and loyalty forgotten.
It was terrible,
  more dreadful than my worst nightmares –
  I've never known fear like I felt then,
  or sorrow either;
  and I asked myself as never before,
  'Why did I ever get mixed up with Jesus?'
I still ask that sometimes, more often than you might imagine,
  for it's not got any easier following him.
There've been sacrifices to make, suffering to endure, rejection to face;
  and I know that one day, unless I'm much mistaken,
  I shall pay the ultimate price.
So yes, if I'd known then what I know now I might have decided differently.
It's possible – I really don't know – but I'm glad I didn't,
  for though it's been difficult and invariably demanding,
  it's been wonderful also;
  and I know that not only was it the right decision,
  it was the best I could ever have made.

Prayer

Lord Jesus Christ,
  it is not easy to follow you –
  not if we are serious about discipleship.
You call us to a new way of thinking, a new way of loving,
  a new way of living that is more costly and demanding
  than we can ever imagine.
Yet though the cost is high the reward is greater,
  for in you we find life in all its fullness.
Lord Jesus Christ,
  help us to follow.
Amen.

Hymn   *At the name of Jesus*

Blessing

Music   *Gloria (Gloria)* Vivaldi

The Ministry of Christ

Suggested visual material Jesus of Nazareth 3 and 4
The Life of Christ II
The Gospel: Life of Jesus

MORNING SESSION

Music Slow movement from *Concerto for two violins* J. S. Bach

Silent reflection

Introduction Christ crucified and risen – for most of us a summary of what the Gospel is all about. And yet, of course, all that finally derives its meaning from what went before – the words and actions of Jesus throughout his earthly ministry. It was these that inspired the Apostles to leave all and follow him, these that drew the crowds in such numbers to see for themselves, and these which first led people to believe here was God, come to the world through his promised Messiah. So today we focus not on the birth of Jesus, nor on his death and resurrection, but upon his life, and we ask ourselves what some of those touched by his ministry might have said to us could we have been there to hear first-hand of their experiences. Imagine yourself beside them, imagine yourself in their shoes – for the Christ who touched their lives has power still to touch yours today.

Prayer
Lord Jesus Christ,
   we hear much about your life,
   your death and your resurrection;
   and so, of course, we should
   for these are central to our faith.
But there is a danger,
   through emphasising these too much,
   that we forget what is just as important,

if not more so –
the three wonderful years of your ministry,
in which you taught the multitude,
healed the sick,
responded to the needy,
cared for the poor.
Lord Jesus Christ,
it is easy to lose sight of those things,
to let the message you proclaimed
be obscured rather than enlightened
by our concern
to preach the Cross and resurrection.
Yet we cannot fully make sense of one
without the other.
So help us today,
as we reflect on the period of your ministry,
to hear again what you said
and see again what you did during that time,
so that we may hear your voice
and better know your will.
Amen.

Slides and Music

Nimrod (Enigma Variations) Elgar, during which Luke 4:14-30 is read

Meditation of a member of the synagogue in Nazareth

He had a wonderful voice,
a real joy to listen to:
so clear,
so deep,
so nicely-spoken.
I felt I could have sat there all day,
letting the words wash over me:
good news for the poor,
release for the captives,
recovery of sight for the blind –
familiar,
comfortable,
reassuring words.
Or so I'd always thought.
Only this time they didn't sound quite as reassuring as they used to.

I don't know what it was
   but somehow as he spoke they came to life,
   possessed of a power they had never held before,
   as if I were hearing them for the very first time;
   only the prophet was speaking not to people long ago,
   but to me,
   here,
   now.
And suddenly I didn't want to hear,
   didn't want to listen any more,
   for the words were no longer what I'd thought they were,
   but unexpected,
   discomforting,
   troubling words.
They leapt at me and pinned me down.
They lunged at me piercing my very soul.
They left me anxious,
   guilty,
   fearful,
   asking what they meant to someone like me
   who was neither poor or blind,
   but rich and free.
I closed my ears
   but still he spoke,
   and listening again, despite myself, I heard him say,
   'A prophet is without honour in his own country.'
That was the end,
   too much.
The voice no longer seeming beautiful but strident,
   no longer bringing joy but rousing rage.
For I realised this man came not to soothe but to challenge,
   not to praise but to question;
   not only to us but to others.
I rose in rage,
   cursing him for his blasphemy,
   calling for his death!
Yet somehow, though all around me did the same,
   he walked straight by,
   unharmed,
   untouched.
Don't ask me how, for I just don't know.

But what I do know, deep down –
  much though I try to deny it,
  much though I try to ignore it –
  is that Jesus had been right to say,
  'These words have been fulfilled today.'

Slides and music

Domine Deus (Gloria) Vivaldi, during which Matthew 10:1-4 is read

Meditation of Peter

I had no doubts at the beginning,
  not when he first called me.
There was something about the man –
  the authority in his voice,
  the honesty in his eyes –
  which made it almost impossible to say no.
He was unique,
  I was certain of that immediately;
  the sort of man you could trust,
  stake your life on if necessary.
And I believed if anyone was worth following,
  anyone quite clear what they were all about,
  it was Jesus.
But I'm not sure now,
  not sure at all,
  for he's just come back with a new bunch of recruits,
  And, honestly, you ought to see them –
  a motley crew if ever there was one!
There's this chap Matthew for a start –
  a tax-collector of all people! –
  he's really going to win us some friends, isn't he?
Then there's Simon, the so-called Zealot –
  well, we've all heard about him,
  a real rabble-rouser by all accounts;
  you can bet your last shekel when there's trouble brewing,
  rebellion in the air,
  he'll be there in the thick of it.
To be fair I can't say yet about the others, but I have my doubts.
  especially Judas –
  a bit of a snob if you ask me,
  too full of himself by half.

And Thaddeus? Well, he's just the opposite,
a nobody really,
quiet as a mouse;
I can't see him making much of an impression.
Nor Bartholomew for that matter.
So what's Jesus thinking of?
I just don't know.
It's shaken me, all of this, I don't mind telling you.
Don't misunderstand me, I'm still more than happy to follow Jesus,
no question about that,
but not if it means getting mixed up with this lot.
Why couldn't he have stuck to fishermen,
decent, honest, sensible folk like us?
Why complicate everything,
involve people from different backgrounds
with a different way of looking at life?
We knew where we stood at the beginning,
just James, John and me, together with Jesus.
If he needed others there were plenty more we could have recommended,
friends and colleagues we could guarantee would never rock the boat.
But now who's to say what might happen?
I suppose Jesus knows what he's playing at, even if I can't see it yet.
Maybe he knows something about these fellows that I don't,
maybe he has some purpose in mind which I haven't quite understood.
So fair enough, I'll go along with him,
for the moment anyway,
despite my misgivings.
He obviously wants us to work together,
obviously thinks we can too.
Well, we'll see.
Time will tell, won't it?
But if it's going to work it will need a miracle, that's all I can say.
An absolute miracle.

Slides and music

Pathetique Sonata Beethoven, during which Matthew 9:9-13 is read

Meditation of Matthew

He had time for me,
incredible, I know, but true.
He saw beneath the surface,
beneath the greed, the selfishness and the corruption,

and uncovered a person I didn't even know existed.
I groaned when I saw him coming, I won't pretend otherwise;
   another self-righteous prig coming to tell me my business,
   that's what I imagined.
And I'd had my fair share of those –
   well, nobody likes a tax collector, do they?
But I'd always given as good as I got.
I mean, it's not easy when you've a wife and kids at home to feed –
   we all have to earn a living somehow –
   and since the only people ready to give me a chance were the Romans
what could I do?
Or did any of them really imagine I enjoyed working for them?
Anyway, someone had to do it, didn't they, so why not me?
I suppose Jesus understood that, for he didn't criticise or condemn –
   none of the two-faced hypocrisy of the Pharisees,
   none of the usual accusing glances or obscene gestures –
   just those two lovely words:
   'Follow me.'
You could have knocked me over.
It was the last thing I expected,
   took the wind right out of my sails.
But more than that I was excited,
   moved,
   fascinated,
   because he had time for me.
He hadn't written me off,
   he hadn't seen only the outside –
   he accepted me as I was,
   with all my sin sticking to me.
And the funny thing was, once he did that
   it was me who pointed to my faults,
   not him.
I felt ashamed,
   painfully aware of all that was wrong,
   longing to be different;
   yet at the same time set free,
   forgiven,
   offered a new beginning.
I followed, of course,
What else could I do?
Would you refuse a man like that?

Well, perhaps you would, but I'm glad I didn't,
   because despite everything since –
   the times I've let him down,
   the occasions I've misunderstood,
   the mistakes I've made,
   the faults I still have –
   he goes on accepting me day after day,
Not for what I might become.
But for what I am!

Slides and music

Pié Jesu (Requiem) Andrew Lloyd Webber
during which Mark 1:40-45 is read

Meditation of a leper

He touched me!
That was all.
No magic spells,
   no wonder potions,
   no hype,
   just that one little action.
So simple,
   so special;
   the first time I'd been touched in as long as I can remember,
   the first time someone has looked at me with love
   rather than revulsion in their eyes.
And the moment I felt his hand upon me I felt clean.
It was as though a weight had been lifted from me,
   a burden of disease,
   isolation,
   despair.
As though God himself had reached out into my darkness
   and told me that he cared after all,
   that even I had a place in his heart.
I looked down and my hands could move again,
   I reached out and they could feel again,
   and suddenly I was dancing,
   skipping,
   laughing,
   running,
   like a little child,
   celebrating the joy of life!

I'm one of the crowd again now,
   back amongst my own,
   able to share with my family as in the old days,
   to walk in the market place,
   worship in the synagogue,
   as much a part of society as the next man.
But I don't blame anyone for the way they treated me,
   for I know I'd have done the same in their place.
We live in fear of leprosy, all of us.
We've seen its power,
   the way it can slowly destroy a person;
   we've stood by helpless as lives have been turned inside out,
   those who were once so beautiful hideously disfigured –
   and we all shy away,
   all keep our distance,
   all push the problem out of sight.
It's cruel, I know,
   hard for those who suffer,
   separated from everything and everyone they've ever loved.
I know, for I've been there.
But what choice is there?
We know the score,
   and I can tell you this:
   there isn't one of us who would wish that curse on our worst enemy.
No, I can't blame anyone for what they did,
   yet I'll never forget Jesus,
   the man who saw me as I was,
   the man who touched me as I was,
   the man who made me what I am.

Slides and music

And he shall feed his flock (Messiah) Handel
during which Luke 9:10-17 is read

Meditation of one of the 5000

We were starving,
   fit to drop,
   our stomachs rumbling something rotten.
And it's hardly surprising, is it?
We'd been up there on the mountain for ages and not a bite to eat.
It was our own fault, of course –
   we should have come prepared –

but it just never occurred to us it would be necessary.
We thought we'd only be gone a while,
   a few hours at the most.
Only he kept on talking,
   and we kept on listening,
   rooted to the spot in wonder.
That's not like me, I can tell you –
   usually twenty minutes is my limit, no matter how good the speaker –
   but I could have listened to that man for ever
   because his words touched my heart,
   stirred my spirit,
   answered my deepest needs.
We were sorry when he stopped,
   each of us urging him to continue,
   but he knew I think, before we did,
   that we needed physical as well as spiritual nourishment.
And suddenly it hit us just how hungry we were,
   and how far from home.
We began to feel quite faint, what with the heat as well,
   and I honestly believe
   some of us wouldn't have had the strength to get back.
But suddenly he turned to his disciples, and told them to feed us.
You should have seen their faces –
   they didn't know whether to laugh or cry!
Neither did we, come to that.
As one of them finally put it,
   once he realised Jesus wasn't having him on:
   'Where are we to get bread out here?'
It was the back of beyond,
   the middle of nowhere;
   you couldn't just pop round the corner for a few thousand loaves!
But Jesus just looked amused,
   and then asked quietly if anyone had any food left.
Well, there weren't many who were going to answer that, were there?
Not if they had any sense.
Even supposing they had a morsel tucked away somewhere
   they were hardly going to admit it,
   not with five thousand starving wretches breathing down their necks!
But then a young lad stepped forward,
   all innocence,
   and produced five loaves and two fishes,
   handing them over with the sweetest and most trusting of smiles.

I didn't think Jesus would have the heart to take them,
  but he did,
  solemnly giving thanks to God before breaking them
  and getting his disciples to hand round the pieces.
Don't ask me what happened next –
  I still can't make sense of it –
  but somehow we all had a feast.
It wasn't just a few token crumbs or a desperate mouthful for the strongest,
  but more than we could eat
  and enough left afterwards to fill twelve baskets.
A miracle some say it was, and yes, I suppose they're right,
  but you know, what's always lived with me,
  and what counts most looking back,
  is not the way he fed our bodies but the way he fed our souls as well;
  for I've been hungry physically many times since then,
  but my spirit has found contentment, full to overflowing.

Slides and music

Wonderful world Louis Armstrong, during which Mark 10:46-52 is read

Meditation of Bartimaeus

He made me see!
For the first time in my life,
  after all those years of darkness,
  all those years listening and wondering what the world must be like,
  I was able to look and see for myself!
I saw clouds scudding through the sky,
  grass waving in the breeze,
  flowers blooming in the meadow,
  waves breaking on the seashore.
I saw birds nesting in the trees,
  and animals wandering in the mountains,
  the moon and stars glowing in the night sky,
  the beauty of sunrise and sunset, bathing the earth in its golden glow.
I saw children playing,
  the faces of loved ones,
  the bustle of towns and city,
  the pomp of priest and temple.
I saw fields of corn and ripening fruit,
  bubbling streams and tranquil pools,
  a world of colour, form and contrast,
  more lovely than in my wildest dreams.

All this, thanks to Jesus, I can see!
Yet there is more,
    much more, that I owe him,
    for it is not just my eyes he has opened,
    but my mind,
    my heart,
    my soul.
I looked at him
    and I did not see just a man:
    I glimpsed the face of God,
    smiling through his welcome;
    I glimpsed the hand of God,
    reaching out through his touch;
    I glimpsed the love of God,
    accepting me through his call.
He made me see, Jesus,
    not just with my eyes, though I can't thank him enough for that,
    but with my soul –
    the things that really matter,
    that really count,
    that meet my deepest needs.
And now I know that even when it is dark,
    even when life is at its blackest,
    even when I cannot see the way ahead,
    I am walking in the light.

Silent reflection

Blessing

AFTERNOON SESSION

Music   *Chanson de Matin* Elgar

Silent reflection

Slides and music
And the glory of the Lord (Messiah) Handel, during which Mark 9:2-3 is read

Meditation of John
It was fantastic,
   extraordinary,
   mind-blowing;
   a once-in-a-lifetime experience,
   and I was lucky enough to be there –
   me, and Peter and James up on the mountain with Jesus.
We knew something was going to happen;
   we could see it from his manner when he asked us to join him,
   but we never dreamt of anything like that.
He seemed to change before our eyes,
   his clothes to glow,
   his face to shine.
And then – would you believe it –
   who did we see with him but Moses and Elijah!
Clear as day they were,
   chatting together like old friends.
We were struck dumb for a moment,
   lost for words,
   and then dear old Peter got stuck in as usual.
'Can I do something?' he blurted out,
   'You will stay, won't you?'
And why not?
I mean, we were all enjoying ourselves,
   didn't want the moment to end,
   almost too good to be true!
But strangely, as soon as Peter finished speaking,
   the spell seemed to break.
The sky darkened as clouds came over
   and then, as a peal of thunder broke the silence,
   Moses and Elijah disappeared,
   leaving Jesus standing there alone,
   looking just as he always had,
   as ordinary as you or me.

Did we imagine it?
We've often asked ourselves that.
Or was it a vision,
   brought on perhaps by the heat
   or the altitude,
   or simply having one too many before we set off?
It must have been something like that, surely?
There's no other logical explanation.
Yet it's funny how we all saw the same thing,
   all down to the last detail.
I don't know what to make of it,
   but I wouldn't have missed it for the world.
It helped me understand what Peter had already begun to grasp,
   that Jesus was the Messiah,
   the answer to all our prayers,
   the fulfilment of the Law and the Prophets.
It was just a glimpse,
   a moment's wonderful insight
   which I thought at the time could never be repeated.
And that was true in a sense,
   for no one will ever witness quite what we saw in the way we saw it.
But we have all seen his glory now,
   not just the three of us,
   but Thomas, Andrew, Mary, Matthew, and so many others –
   the glory of the Father revealed in him.
We see it day after day after day,
   full of grace and truth,
And, believe me, that too is fantastic,
   extraordinary,
   unforgettable!

Slides and music

Chi Mai Ennio Morricone, during which Mark 10:13-16 is read

Meditation of Andrew

I could have brained those children,
   rushing around like that with their yelling and shrieking,
   shattering our peace and quiet.
We'd had him alone at last,
   just us and Jesus;
   a rare opportunity to sit and listen undisturbed,
   drinking in his every word.

And it was wonderful,
  a truly magical moment,
  until, that is, they turned up –
  those wretched kids ushered forward by their doting parents,
  just so that he could touch them.
Really, how ridiculous!
Superstition, that's all it was –
  no real faith behind any of it –
  just sentimental rubbish,
  nauseating!
So we tried to stop them; you can understand that, surely?
We wanted to get back to the business in hand,
  before we were so rudely interrupted;
  back to more serious matters.
OK, so maybe we were a bit over the top,
  a touch more heavy than the situation demanded,
  but we were angry,
  disappointed.
I mean, could *you* have concentrated with that row going on?
I couldn't.
Yet did they care?
Not likely!
We fully expected Jesus to back us up,
  send the lot of them packing.
But can you believe this? He didn't!
He actually turned on us,
  and there was anger in his eyes,
  anger touched almost with pity.
'Leave them alone,' he said. 'Let them come to me. What's your problem?'
Well, we didn't know what to say, did we?
It caught us right on the hop.
So we just fidgeted uncomfortably, trying to cover our embarrassment.
It was so unfair.
We'd meant no harm, after all,
  certainly hadn't meant to upset anybody;
  yet there they were now,
  the kids bawling their eyes out,
  the mums looking daggers at us,
  the dads having a go at everyone –
  what a mess!
I honestly didn't know what to do next.
But thankfully Jesus came to the rescue as always.

He reached out and took the children in his arms, one by one,
  a great loving hug.
And then he lifted them up for all to see.
'These are special,' he told us,
  'More precious than you will ever know –
  each one treasured by God.'
And you could tell from the way he smiled at them,
  and the way they smiled back at him,
  that he meant every word he was saying,
  and they knew he meant it.
I still feel a bit aggrieved by it all –
  well, you can tell that, can't you?
But I realise now we made ourselves look rather silly that day,
  even childish, you might say;
  and I'm beginning to understand Jesus has no room for the childish,
  only the childlike.

Slides and music

Chanson de Matin Elgar, during which John 4:1-7 is read

Meditation of the woman at the well

He was full of surprises, that man,
  from the moment I first met him.
I thought he'd just push me aside like all the rest;
  either that or walk away with his head in the air.
He was a Jew, remember, and I a Samaritan;
  and worse than that,
  a woman,
  alone.
Yet he stayed where he was, a smile on his face,
  quite happy, apparently, to be associated with me.
Well, call me suspicious if you like, but I wasn't sure what he was up to,
  so I asked him straight out, 'What's your game?'
He laughed at that, and then offered me a drink of water –
  at least I thought that's what he was doing though I wasn't sure.
You see, he had no bucket,
  and he could hardly shin down the well, could he?
So where was this water he was on about meant to come from?
To be frank I suspected he was pulling my leg,
  but I was beginning to like him despite the nonsense he talked.
He had a nice way with him,
  kind,

gentle,
  a bit of all right in an unconventional sort of way.
So I played along, wondering where it would all lead.
If only I'd known –
  what an embarrassment I might have saved myself.
I'll never know how he guessed,
  but suddenly he looked straight at me
  and for the first time I noticed his eyes.
They didn't undress you like so many men's seem to do,
  but looked much deeper,
  almost as if into my very soul.
And then he started talking about my lovers,
  my husbands,
  my past,
  every detail correct.
It was uncanny,
  frightening,
  far too near the knuckle,
So I tried to fob him off with some old chestnut about worship.
But even then he threw me;
  none of the usual pat answers
  but a response that reached right to the heart of the matter,
  cutting through all the trivia.
And it was after that he produced the biggest surprise of all –
  told me he was the Messiah!
I didn't know what to say,
  just stood there gawping, flabbergasted.
I mean, I realised he was a prophet,
  but the Messiah?
It couldn't be, I told myself,
  no way.
I went back down to the village, seeking reassurance,
  wanting someone to tell me he was just another religious nutcase.
But they didn't.
They were curious,
  wanted to see for themselves.
And when they heard him,
  listened to his teaching,
  they believed he was the Messiah.
Me? I still don't know, but I wouldn't be surprised,
  not if I'm honest;
  nothing would surprise me about him.

Slides and music

Andante Religioso (Holberg Suite) Grieg
during which Mark 10:35-45 is read

Meditation of James, son of Zebedee

I honestly don't know what came over us.
What on earth we could have been thinking of.
Believe me, we don't usually go around acting like that,
    thrusting ourselves forward, seeking special favours.
Yet this time we just couldn't help ourselves.
It was all that talk of death, I suppose,
    his warnings of disaster lurking round the corner –
    those were enough to unsettle anybody.
So when he suddenly spoke of resurrection,
    light at the end of the tunnel,
    we just reached out for it,
    without a second thought.
After all, let's face it, we'd given up a lot to follow Jesus,
    waved goodbye to any hope of a normal life getting mixed up with him;
    and if he seriously expected us to stand by him
    while the sparks were flying,
    well, we simply felt we deserved some kind of reward;
    wasn't that reasonable enough?
But when the others got to hear of it, what a rumpus!
It was as though all hell had broken loose.
Don't ask me who started it, but all at once there we were,
    arguing among ourselves like a bunch of washer-women,
    each claiming to be his number one,
    the greatest in the kingdom of heaven.
We were acting like spoilt children, of course –
    making a right spectacle of ourselves into the bargain –
    but it didn't matter at the time;
    nothing mattered then but our wounded pride,
    our punctured self-importance,
    our frustrated self-interest.
Pathetic!
We realised that later, once we'd had time to stop and think.
But it was too late by then,
    the damage was done.

No, not to ourselves, I don't mean that,
   though we had let ourselves down undeniably;
   but to him,
   the one we claimed to stand for,
   who we'd talked so much about,
   who we were meant to be representing.
'Do not let the sun go down on your anger' – that's what he had told us,
   and we'd been snarling at each other like spitting camels.
'Love your enemies' – that's what he'd commanded,
   and we couldn't even love each other.
'Turn the other cheek' –
   and we'd traded insult for insult.
'Judge not, lest you be judged' –
   and we'd condemned each other without a flicker of compunction.
We let Jesus down; that's what hurts now.
It doesn't matter about us, not when it comes down to it –
   we had only ourselves to blame.
But Jesus?
He'd put his faith in us,
   called us to a position of trust, responsibility,
   and we'd thrown it all back in his face.
I ask you, who's going to listen to us now?
We can talk all we like about changed lives,
   about becoming new people,
   but they've seen for themselves, all too clearly,
   that we're no different from the rest of them.
He forgave us, of course –
   well, he always does, doesn't he?
Told us to put the whole business behind us.
So we're trying,
   we really are;
   trying to be the people he called us to be,
   trying to be more like him.
I only hope we've learned our lesson,
   seen the error of our ways,
   for I'm telling you straight, unless we're together in this,
   seen to practise what we preach,
   you can hardly expect anyone to take us seriously, can you?
Well, can you?

Slides and music

'Moonlight' Sonata Beethoven, during which Luke 19:1-4 is read

Meditation of Zacchaeus

I only wanted to see him, that's all,
 find out what all the fuss was about.
I'd no intention of getting involved, absolutely none.
It was the last thing I wanted, the last thing I expected.
I was simply curious, you'll understand that, surely?
I'd heard so much about him –
 the man who could perform miracles, forgive sins, change lives.
He was the talk of the town;
 we all wanted to see him, everyone.
But that was the trouble,
 the streets were packed,
 crowds ten, fifteen deep,
 and I knew straightaway I'd no chance of getting close,
 not even, given my size, so much as a look in.
It was the same old story: poor old Zacchaeus,
 the butt of so many jokes over the years,
 once again missing out when the competition started.
I'd grown used to it, even immune,
 but strangely this time it hurt as never before;
 to be denied the opportunity of a little colour in the drabness of my life –
 all because God had been sparing with the inches.
It seemed so unfair,
 the final nail in the coffin,
 and I felt like lifting a fist to heaven and cursing my creator.
But then a brainwave.
Why not climb a tree, I thought?
And brilliant – a grandstand view!
There he was, just below me, as clear as day!
Well, you can imagine, I was well pleased.
It was to be my claim to fame;
 the proud boast that at last would make men look up to me –
 I'd seen Jesus.
Only then he spotted me.
I hadn't bargained on that.
I'd expected him simply to walk on by.
Maybe a smile, even a wave, but no more,
 but he stopped and smiled and spoke to me.
I was dumbfounded,
 unable to take in for a moment what he was saying,
And when it finally registered I could barely believe it.
He wanted to visit my home,
 share a meal with me, Zacchaeus!

A bit of a cheek really, inviting himself like that,
 yet I could hardly say no, could I, not with all the crowd watching?
They weren't best pleased, I can tell you,
 always considered me a mean old so and so,
 a tight-fisted, two-faced swindler,
 and let's face it, I was.
But this was my chance to show them
 I could push the boat out once in a while,
 so I hurried down to welcome him.
The trouble was, one thing led to another,
 and before I knew it I was letting my heart rule my head,
 paying back all those I'd defrauded, four times over,
 giving away half my possessions to the poor.
A moment's madness?
Well perhaps, but that was the effect Jesus had on you.
He made you want to be different, to be like him.
I've regretted my impulsiveness once or twice since then,
 I won't pretend otherwise,
 yet I wouldn't change anything given my time again,
 for though I'm poorer materially now,
 I feel richer than I ever dreamt I could be.

Slides and music

The trumpet shall sound (Messiah) Handel
during which John 11:32-44 is read

Meditation of Lazarus

It was so weird,
 so unreal.
At least that's how it felt.
And yet it happened!
I'd breathed my last, no question about that.
After those long dark days of sickness,
 the pain growing
 the strength failing;
 after those final terrible hours,
 sweat pouring down my face,
 lungs gasping for air;
 at last came peace,
 darkness closing about me,
 suddenly welcome though it had long been feared.

An end to the struggle,
   the battle nearly over.
For a moment I was a child again, comforted by my mother's embrace,
   a youth running wild as the wind,
   a man setting out afresh on life's great adventure,
   a father, taking my child into my arms.
And then rest.
The light went out,
   the flame extinguished,
   the game completed.
Only it wasn't,
   for suddenly a voice summoned me back to the fray,
   sunshine burst into the tomb,
   and consciousness returned.
No wonder they gasped,
   no wonder they swooned,
   no wonder they wept for joy,
   for I who had been taken from them,
   I who had been dead,
      was alive!
And yes, I thanked him, of course I did,
   once the confusion had cleared anyway,
   but it took a while, I can tell you.
And even now just once in a while
   I wonder if he really did me any favours
   for I know that one day I must face it all over again.
Yet it will be different then,
   very different,
   not just because I've been there before and know there's nothing to fear,
   but because Jesus has shown me
   that death is not so much the end as the beginning.
That's why he raised me from the tomb.
Not just to restore life,
   not simply to defer death,
   but to point to a new birth,
   a resurrection which only he can bring.
He came back too, you know,
   back from beyond the grave.
Three days in his tomb,
   long enough for decay to take hold,
   but he appeared to Mary,
   to Peter,

to the Apostles,
to us all.
And we know that even though we die
one day we shall live
even as he lives now!

Prayer

Lord Jesus Christ,
you became flesh,
walking our earth, sharing our humanity,
identifying yourself with each one of us:
we praise you for that great truth.
But save us, we pray,
from allowing it to make us over-familiar,
believing we know all about you there is to know.
Help us always
to keep a sense of awe and wonder in worship,
recognising that through you we are privileged
to glimpse a little of the majesty
and greatness of God.
Amen.

Music   *Chanson de Matin* Elgar

Peter – In the Footsteps of Jesus

Suggested visual material   Jesus of Nazareth 2-6
The Life of Christ IV

MORNING SESSION

Music   *Sheep may safely graze* J. S. Bach

Introduction   Of all the Apostles there are perhaps none we ident-ify with more readily than Simon Peter – the man whom Jesus called 'The Rock' and on whom he built his Church; yet a man who exhibited just about all the human failings we know ourselves to be guilty of. At one moment he could show deep spiritual insight, at the next an almost complete lack of under-standing. In one breath he could profess loyalty to Christ, in the next deny him three times. Impulsive, impetuous, stubborn, idealistic, Peter is a man we can relate to. His story gives us the confidence that for all our faults we can be used by Jesus to fulfil his purpose and bring nearer his kingdom.

Prayer

Lord Jesus Christ,
   you call us to follow you
   just as you called the Apostles
   during your ministry.
It's easy for us to feel inadequate
   compared with them,
   to wonder what contribution we,
   ordinary everyday people
   with all manner of failings and precious few gifts,
   can make to your kingdom.
But today we come to reflect
   on one of the greatest of those Apostles,
   and yet perhaps the most human.

A man capable of great insights –
  and total misunderstanding;
  of enormous faith – and pathetic faithlessness,
  of great courage – and feeble cowardice.
Lord Jesus Christ,
  as we reflect on the experiences of Peter,
  help us to reflect on our own experiences too,
  and to recognise that just as you used him,
  so you can use us!
Amen.

Slides and music

Domine Deus (Gloria) Vivaldi, during which Matthew 10:1-4 is read

Meditation

I had no doubts at the beginning,
  not when he first called me.
There was something about the man –
  the authority in his voice,
  the honesty in his eyes –
  which made it almost impossible to say no.
He was unique,
  I was certain of that immediately;
  the sort of man you could trust,
  stake your life on if necessary.
And I believed if anyone was worth following,
  anyone quite clear what they were all about,
  it was Jesus.
But I'm not sure now,
  not sure at all,
  for he's just come back with a new bunch of recruits,
  And, honestly, you ought to see them –
  a motley crew if ever there was one!
There's this chap Matthew for a start –
  a tax-collector of all people! –
  he's really going to win us some friends, isn't he?
Then there's Simon, the so-called Zealot –
  well, we've all heard about him,
  a real rabble-rouser by all accounts;
  you can bet your last shekel when there's trouble brewing,
  rebellion in the air,
  he'll be there in the thick of it.

To be fair I can't say yet about the others, but I have my doubts.
    especially Judas –
    a bit of a snob if you ask me,
    too full of himself by half.
And Thaddeus? Well, he's just the opposite,
    a nobody really,
    quiet as a mouse;
    I can't see him making much of an impression.
Nor Bartholomew for that matter.
So what's Jesus thinking of?
I just don't know.
It's shaken me, all of this, I don't mind telling you.
Don't misunderstand me, I'm still more than happy to follow Jesus,
    no question about that,
    but not if it means getting mixed up with this lot.
Why couldn't he have stuck to fishermen,
    decent, honest, sensible folk like us?
Why complicate everything,
    involve people from different backgrounds
    with a different way of looking at life?
We knew where we stood at the beginning,
    just James, John and me, together with Jesus.
If he needed others there were plenty more we could have recommended,
    friends and colleagues we could guarantee would never rock the boat.
But now who's to say what might happen?
I suppose Jesus knows what he's playing at, even if I can't see it yet.
Maybe he knows something about these fellows that I don't,
    maybe he has some purpose in mind which I haven't quite understood.
So fair enough, I'll go along with him,
    for the moment anyway,
    despite my misgivings.
He obviously wants us to work together,
    obviously thinks we can too.
Well, we'll see.
Time will tell, won't it?
But if it's going to work it will need a miracle, that's all I can say.
An absolute miracle.

Slides and music

Domine Fili unigenite (Gloria) Vivaldi, during which Mark 8:27-33 is read

Meditation

It was a wonderful moment,
    I really thought I'd cracked it.
After all the uncertainty,
    all the questions,
    all the confusion,
    I finally believed I understood who he was.
'You're the Messiah!' I told him,
    and he beamed at me with such delight that I felt my heart would burst.
No one else had grasped it you see,
    not properly.
They wondered, of course,
    but like so many others they were still guessing,
    groping in the dark.
He might as well have been Elijah or John for all they knew.
I was different, and Jesus knew it.
'Blessed are you,' he said, 'for God has revealed this to you and not man.'
What an accolade!
But then it all went wrong,
    just when I felt I'd arrived the bubble burst,
    and with a vengeance!
I suppose I got carried away,
    never stopped to think.
Typical of me, really.
It's just that it came as such a shock,
    him going on like that about the future,
    everything he had to suffer,
    all doom and gloom,
    even talking of death itself.
I wasn't having any of it.
'Not likely!' I shouted. 'No way!'
I meant no harm,
    I just didn't think such things could happen to the Messiah,
But you should have seen his face,
    the anger, the disappointment.
Satan, he called me!
Can you believe that?
Me, his right-hand man,
    the one who'd just hit the nail on the head,
    the pick of the bunch, so I thought –
    Satan!

I was hurt at the time,
    cut to the heart if I'm honest,
    but I can see now, all too clearly, that he was right and I was wrong.
I still had so much to learn,
    so much to understand,
    and I needed a reprimand, a stern hand, if I was to progress any further.
I'd only just begun to glimpse the truth
    and if I'd have had my way
    it would have meant him denying everything he stood for.
He *was* the Messiah but not in the way *I* meant it;
    he *had* come to establish his kingdom,
    but in a very different way than *we* expected.
His was the way of service, of sacrifice, or self-denial,
    offering his life for the life of the world.
I see that now and I marvel at his love,
    but what I marvel at even more is that
    even when I understood him so little
    he understood me so much.

Silent reflection

Slides and music
And the glory of the Lord (Messiah) Handel
during which Luke 9:28-36 is read

Meditation
I wanted to hold on to that moment for ever,
    to keep things just as they were for the rest of eternity,
    for I feared life would never be so special again.
It was just the four of us –
    well, six if you count Moses and Elijah, but I'm not sure you can do that –
    the four of us sharing a blessed moment of peace and quiet;
    no crowds pleading for a miracle,
    no lepers begging for healing,
    no Pharisees baying for his blood,
    no Sadducees spoiling for a fight.
Just us,
    together,
    as we'd all too rarely been.
And we knew it couldn't last;
    he'd made that perfectly clear when I dared suggest otherwise.

There was trouble round the corner,
  his enemies waiting to pounce,
  and he knew it was only a matter of time before they got him.
Not much of a prospect, was it –
  rejection, suffering, death?
I don't know how he stuck it, I really don't.
But we didn't want to think about such things,
  not then anyway,
  and up there on the mountain it all seemed a million miles away,
  out of sight, out of mind.
Can you blame me for wanting to stay,
  for wanting to hang on to the moment for as long as possible?
Only I couldn't, of course.
You can't stop the clock, can you, and make the world stand still?
You can't store those golden moments safely away,
  untarnished by the march of time.
Life goes on, as they say,
  and you have to go with it,
  like it or not.
It was hard to accept that,
  hard to go back to the daily round
  with its familiar demands and expectations.
Yet as I spoke to Jesus, coming down the mountain,
  I realised suddenly it had to be;
  that there was no other way –
  going back, I mean.
Without that there would have been no point,
  those sacred moments an empty illusion.
He knew that,
  and slowly, very slowly, I came to know it too.
It was a vital time, a special time,
  one that gave him new strength,
  new resolve,
  the inspiration he needed to face the future and fulfil his destiny.
But it was as much for us as for him
  a moment we could look back upon,
  so that afterwards we might keep on looking forward.

Slides and music

Thy rebuke has broken his heart (Messiah) Handel
during which Mark 14:32-42 is read

Meditation

He was broken-hearted, if you ask me,
   and I can't say I blame him.
I think I'd have felt the same.
You see, he'd expected it from the others –
   the Scribes and Pharisees –
   he knew they had it in for him from the start.
And the crowds who'd followed him, welcomed him into Jerusalem –
   he wasn't taken in by them,
   not for a moment.
Even Judas,
   he saw the truth about him before anyone else had an inkling.
But the rest of us, I think he'd hoped for something better.
Not that he asked much.
He knew I'd deny him, despite all my protestations of loyalty,
   and he knew we'd all run for it when it was our skins on the line.
He'd accepted that, and still loved us, God knows why!
But there in the garden, that's when he needed us most,
   that's when he'd hoped for that little bit more.
Just to know we cared,
   that we were behind him,
   that we were there.
It would have meant so much.
And we failed him, even in that one simple thing.
I still don't know how it happened.
I tried,
   I really tried,
   but somehow I just couldn't keep my eyes open.
I can forgive myself the rest;
   it was my life at stake after all.
But to stay awake just one hour.
It wasn't much to ask, was it?
And I couldn't do even that.
He was broken-hearted,
   the stuffing knocked right out of him,
   and I know in large part it was all down to me.

Silent reflection

Slides and music

God so loved the world (Crucifixion) Stainer
during which Luke 22:54-62 is read

Meditation

He warned me it would happen,
  told me exactly how it would be,
  but I just didn't believe him.
If he'd said anyone else I'd have thought otherwise –
  I mean you can't trust anyone finally can you, not even your friends?
And, to be honest, I expected a few of them to cave in
  when the pressure was on.
But me, I felt I was different.
It was me after all whom he called to be his first disciple,
  me who realised he was the Messiah
  when the rest were still groping in the dark,
  me he called 'The Rock'.
And I thought I was just that:
  unshakeable,
  firm,
  dependable.
I'm not saying I was better than anyone else,
  just that my faith always seemed stronger.
So I told him,
  confidently,
  proudly,
  'Though all else fail you I will not.
  Lord, I am ready to die for you.'
God, how those words haunt me now,
  how stupid they make me feel.
If only I'd kept my mouth shut,
  if only I hadn't been so full of myself,
  if only I'd had more courage.
We all failed him, all of us in our own way.
They look at me and say, 'He denied him.'
They talk of Judas and say, 'He betrayed him.'
They point at the others and say, 'They abandoned him.'
Well, let them judge if they want to.
Let them imagine they're a cut above the rest;
  I've learnt the hard way that I'm not.

Silent reflection

Prayer

Lord Jesus Christ,
   you could have chosen anyone
   as the foundation for your Church,
   but you didn't;
   you chose Peter –
   the man who misunderstood you,
   who denied you,
   who failed you time and time again.
A man *we* might have written off,
   but who *you* saw instead as a rock
   on which to build your kingdom.
Lord Jesus Christ,
   when we let you down in our turn,
   remind us of Peter
   and help us to believe you can still use us.
Amen.

Music   *Behold, and see if there be any sorrow (Messiah)* Handel

AFTERNOON SESSION

Music   *Surely (Messiah)* Handel

Prayer

Lord Jesus Christ,
   you were under no illusions
   about those you called to follow you.
You knew that Judas would betray you,
   Peter deny you,
   and the rest of the apostles forsake you,
   yet still you continued on your way to the Cross.
Lord Jesus Christ,
   we marvel at your amazing grace
   that goes beyond our understanding.
Help us as we recall the stories of Judas
   and Peter today
   to appreciate the wonder of your love for us
   who deserve it so little,
   and in return to love you who deserve it so much.
Amen.

Slides and music

Lacrimosa (Requiem) Mozart, during which Luke 23:32-38 is read

Meditation

He was bleeding,
　my friend Jesus,
　skewered to that cross,
　like a piece of meat,
　great drops of blood trickling slowly to the ground,
　from his head,
　from his hands,
　from his feet.
I watched, stricken with horror,
　numbed with grief,
　as the life seeped away.
And I asked myself tearfully,
　angrily,
　why?
Why had God let it happen?
Why didn't he step in and do something?
What was he thinking of?
It seemed criminal,
　a stupid, senseless waste to let such a wonderful man die –
　let alone to die like that!
And for a moment my faith was shattered,
　in myself,
　in God,
　in everything.
But then I remembered his words,
　just the night before when we had broken bread together:
　'This is my blood, shed for you and for many, for the forgiveness of sins.'
And even as I remembered, so that other time came back,
　there by the Sea of Galilee after he had fed the multitude,
　the crowd pressing round him asking for more:
　'Whoever comes to me will never be hungry,
　whoever believes in me will never be thirsty;
　my flesh is true food and my blood is true drink.'
They had been a mystery to me until then, those words,
　hard to stomach, if you'll pardon the pun.
But suddenly, there beneath that cross, I began to understand,
　just a little,
　only the merest fraction,

yet enough to help me realise it wasn't all in vain;
that somehow Jesus was hanging there for me,
for you,
for everyone.
I still ask why, mind you, and I think I always will,
for I'll never get that picture out of my mind;
that picture of Jesus broken on the cross.
Why that way, God, and not another?
Why not something less brutal,
less awful,
less messy?
Yet the strange thing is *he* never asked why,
not once in all the days I knew him.
Oh, he'd have liked there to be another way, of course;
he didn't want to die any more than the next man.
But he offered his life,
freely,
willingly,
lovingly,
in the conviction that, through his dying, we might truly live.

Slides and music

Vocalise in E minor Rachmaninov, during which Luke 24:1-11 is read

Meditation

They said he was alive! Can you believe that?
All right, I know they were upset, cut up about what had happened,
but then we all were, each one of us.
We'd all loved him,
all believed he was someone special,
all hoped he was the one we were waiting for.
And we were crushed by what had happened, utterly devastated.
We understood how they felt.
But you have to face facts, don't you?
It's no good burying your head in the sand
and pretending the worst hasn't happened.
There's no point trying to fool yourself when you know the truth full well.
And we knew, believe me, all too well.
We'd seen him crying out in agony,
we'd heard him draw his last breath,
and we'd been there when they laid him in the tomb.

At a distance, true – keeping well out of sight, just in case,
  but he was dead, there's no question about that.
So what were they playing at, those women, claiming he's alive?
They didn't seriously expect any of us to swallow it, surely?
I guess they'd finally gone over the edge, lost their marbles?
Women! We might have guessed they'd go under in a crisis.
No wonder Jesus stuck to men for his disciples –
  clear-headed, realistic, down to earth, sensible.
Jesus alive! We'd like to believe it, of course we would.
But it's nonsense, any fool can see that.

Version for three voices

Peter They said he was alive! Can you believe that?

John All right, I know they were upset, cut up about what had happened.

James But then, we all were, each one of us.

Peter We'd all loved him.

John We'd all believed he was someone special.

James We'd all hoped he was the one we were waiting for.

Peter And we were crushed by what had happened, utterly devastated.

John We understood how they felt.

Peter But you have to face facts, don't you?

John It's no good burying your head in the sand and pretending the worst hasn't happened.

James There's no point trying to fool yourself when you know the truth full well.

Peter And we knew, believe me.

John We'd seen him crying out in agony.

James We'd heard him draw his last breath.

Peter And we'd been there when they laid him in the tomb.

James At a distance, true – keeping well out of sight, just in case.

John But he was dead, there's no question about that.

Peter So what were they playing at, those women, claiming he's alive?

John They didn't seriously expect any of us to swallow it, surely?

Peter I guess they'd finally gone over the edge, lost their marbles?

James Women! We might have guessed they'd go under in a crisis.

John No wonder Jesus stuck to men for his disciples – clear-headed, realistic, down to earth, sensible.

Peter Jesus alive! We'd like to believe it, of course we would.

John But it's nonsense, any fool can see that.

Slides and music

Cum Sancto Spiritu (Gloria) Vivaldi, during which Acts 2:1-4 is read

Meditation

We shouldn't have been surprised,
   not if we'd had any sense;
   it was what we'd been told to expect,
   what he'd promised us.
But we never imagined anything quite so extraordinary.
We were waiting, it's true,
   gathered together as so often before,
   but we'd been doing that for days
   and our confidence had taken a hammering.
We were going through the motions, that's all,
   telling each other he hadn't forgotten us,
   talking of the future as though we still believed in it,
   yet wondering in our hearts if there was anything to look forward to.
I mean, what could we hope to achieve when all was said and done.
What reason to think that we, a motley bunch if ever there was one,
   should fare better than our master?
We wanted to carry on his work, don't get me wrong:
   we wanted to tell people what had happened,
   help them find faith for themselves,
   but how could we even hope to begin?
So we kept the doors locked
   and sang our hymns
   and said our prayers
   and hid our doubts.
Until suddenly it happened!
I can't properly describe it even now,
   but it changed our lives.
It was as though a mighty wind blew away the cobwebs,
   a refreshing breeze revived our flagging faith,
   a breath of air stirred our spirits.
As though a tiny spark rekindled our confidence,
   a tongue of fire set our hearts aflame,
   a raging inferno swept our fears away.
As though life had begun again,
   the world become a different place,
   and each of us been born anew.
I know that doesn't make sense,
   but it's the best I can do.

You'll have to experience it for yourself to understand.
And you can, just as we did.
Believe me, we never would have thought it possible,
   despite all Jesus said to us.
We were lost,
   lonely,
   frightened,
   hopelessly aware of our weaknesses,
   searching for any strengths.
We never thought we'd change a soul,
   let alone the world,
   but that's because we had no idea how God could change us!

Slides and music

In trutina (Carmina Burana) Orff, during which Matthew 4:18-20 is read

Meditation

He called me to follow,
   to lay down my nets and follow him.
No time to think,
   no time to weigh up the pros and cons;
   then and there the need to decide.
So I did,
   on the spot –
   left everything to become one of his disciples.
And I'm glad.
No, honestly, despite everything I'm glad,
   for I know it was the right decision,
   the only decision I could have made.
Yet if I'd known then what I know now
   it might all have been very different.
I'd have thought twice, that's for certain –
   made sure I understood the small print –
   and very likely I'd have got cold feet.
You see, I'd no real idea what I was taking on, even though I thought I had.
I imagined he wanted me for a few days,
   a few weeks at most,
   and then, having done my bit, I could return home,
   back to friends and family,
   back to the security of my fishing nets,
   back to the way things had always been.

But he soon put me right on that, didn't he?
Made it quite clear that discipleship is a lifelong commitment,
   not an option you can walk away from as the mood takes you.
Well, to be honest, a few of us soon considered chucking it in,
   cutting our losses before we got in too deep.
Only we couldn't do that,
   not when it came to it,
   for we knew, though he was asking much, he was offering more.
He had the answers we were looking for,
   the words of eternal life,
   and to have walked away then
   would have been to turn our backs on our one true chance of happiness.
So we carried on,
   day after day,
   week after week,
   month after month,
   following in his footsteps,
   sharing in his work.
And it was tough going, I can tell you,
   really tough –
   and believe me, as a fisherman I know what I'm talking about.
Yet somehow we always found the strength we needed,
   just as he said we would;
   or at least we did until that awful last week
   when suddenly it all went wrong –
   the week Judas betrayed him, the soldiers arrested him,
   Pilate condemned him;
   the week when we all ran for our lives,
   our love and loyalty forgotten.
It was terrible,
   more dreadful than my worst nightmares –
   I've never known fear like I felt then,
   or sorrow either;
   and I asked myself as never before,
   'Why did I ever get mixed up with Jesus?'
I still ask that sometimes, more often than you might imagine,
   for it's not got any easier following him.
There've been sacrifices to make, suffering to endure, rejection to face;
   and I know that one day, unless I'm much mistaken,
   I shall pay the ultimate price.
So yes, if I'd known then what I know now I might have decided differently.

It's possible – I really can't say – but I'm glad I didn't,
　　for though it's been difficult and invariably demanding,
　　it's been wonderful also;
　　and I know that not only was it the right decision,
　　it was the best I could ever have made.

Silent reflection

Slides and music

Agnus Dei ('Coronation' Mass) Mozart
during which 2 Peter 1:1-4, 12-15 is read

Meditation

This time I will not fail:
　　despite the terror,
　　despite the sorrow,
　　despite the pain,
　　I will not fail.
God knows I don't want to die –
　　I'm not the stuff of heroes,
　　but then I hardly need tell you that, do I?
You'll all know well enough about the last time.
It's been written about,
　　talked about,
　　preached about so many times –
　　Peter, the man who was all talk,
　　the apostle who lost his nerve when the pressure was on.
The memory has lived with me ever since,
　　searing into my conscience like a hot iron.
Not that Jesus didn't forgive me;
　　he soon put me right on that.
Three times he affirmed his call,
　　three times offered me the opportunity to declare my love,
　　one for each of my denials.
No, he never blamed me for my failure,
　　never condemned,
　　not even once the slightest hint of censure,
　　let alone telling me, 'I told you so.'
And to be fair neither has anyone else.
They all understood I meant well,
　　knew equally how easily they'd have done the same;

and if anyone felt it served me right for shooting my mouth off
    they never said.
Yet I've had to live with the knowledge of my own empty promises,
    my extravagant worthless claims;
    and sometimes, I can tell you, my skin still crawls with shame.
It's as though, deep down, I don't believe I can trust myself,
    and because of that I ask myself why anyone else should trust me either.
Well, now's the time to put the record straight,
    here as I rot in jail waiting for the final moment
    when the executioner comes,
    when death finally arrives.
It won't be easy, I know that.
They'll push me to recant,
    threaten me, torture me,
    maybe even promise life if I'm ready to deny my faith,
    willing to turn my back on Jesus as I did all those years ago.
But not this time:
    this time I will not fail.
I was given another chance to live,
    forgiven,
    restored,
    accepted;
    and I seized it with both hands,
    living life to the full in a way I never lived it before.
Now I have another chance to die,
    another chance to offer my life for the sake of Christ who died for me,
    and this time I will stay true to the end,
    for I know that in death, as in life, he will stay true to me.

Slides and music

O Come, O come, Emmanuel Traditional hymn
during which 2 Peter 3:1-4, 8-15a is read

Meditation

'How much longer?' they keep asking.
    'When will the waiting be over and the kingdom arrive?'
Well, how should I know?
In all honesty why should I have any more idea than the rest of them?
But they just don't get it.
They think because I was with Jesus,
    close to him for those three years,
    that I must have some special knowledge,

inside information,
  a hotline to heaven.
If only I had!
At least then I could shut them up and get a bit of peace.
At least I could give some answers
  instead of telling them yet again to be patient.
Patient!
Why should they be?
I'm not!
I'm consumed with frustration,
  chafing at the bit,
  desperate for something to happen,
  for it's hard, I can tell you, being a Christian today.
There are informers everywhere, looking to make a quick penny.
There's the Pharisees spitting poison.
There's the rest of them, our own kin, intent on destroying us.
And there's Caesar, mad Caesar, delighting in cruelty,
  any way of using us for sport.
We've seen brothers and sisters in Christ tortured,
  flogged,
  stoned;
  we've heard their screams, their groans, their sobs,
  listened to their cries for mercy, their pleas for help;
  and they want to know, who can blame them, when it will all end.
It's made worse by what Jesus told us –
  all that stuff about not seeing death before he comes.
If he hadn't said that, not raised our hopes, it might have been easier –
  we'd certainly have felt different –
  so what was he thinking of making such a promise?
Yet maybe that's not fair,
  for he told us after all not to speculate about the future,
  not to imagine we can ever be certain,
  not even to concern ourselves with dates or times.
'Leave it to God,' that was his advice.
  'Trust in him and get on with living.
  It may be hard,
  It may be costly,
  but you've a job to do, here and now.'
I'm not saying that answers everything,
  but the more I think about it, the more it does help.
  for, of course, he *has* come, through his Spirit,
  and his kingdom is *here*, all around us, if only we have eyes to see it.

He will return in person too, I've no doubt about that;
   sometime he will finally reign supreme.
But what matters is not *when* that happens;
   it's living each moment in the confidence that it will.
And if I'm really truthful, most of the time,
   when we're not facing danger,
   when we're not running for our lives,
   I'm quite happy with that.
For I love this life in so many ways and am in no hurry for it to end.
Is that wrong? I don't know.
All I can say is, 'In your time, Lord.
   In your own time.'

Prayer
Lord Jesus Christ,
   you know that despite our faith
   we have failed you time and time again.
The spirit is willing but the flesh is weak.
Yet however often we let you down,
   you set us back on our feet,
   offering us the chance to start afresh
   and make amends.
Lord Jesus Christ,
   help us to learn from our mistakes
   and to walk more faithfully in your footsteps,
   whatever it may cost.
Amen.

Music   *Sheep may safely graze* J. S. Bach

Women of Faith

Suggested visual material	Jesus of Nazareth 1, 4, 5 and 6
	The Life of Christ I-III
	Jesus, the Child
	Come let us adore
	The Gospel: Life of Jesus
	Oberammergau 1990
	St Paul
	The Story of Saint Paul

MORNING SESSION

Music   *Love's Theme* from *Midnight Express*

Introduction   All too often, even today, we hear the comment 'It's a man's world', and, despite all the efforts of recent years to overcome discrimination, there is still some truth in that remark. Yet if that's so today, it was all the more so in the days of Jesus; women then in countless ways treated as second class citizens. For some the fact that Jesus chose only men to be his Apostles shows that even he was influenced by the attitudes of his day, but this is to overlook the important place he gave to women throughout his ministry, time and again making it clear through words and actions that women counted to him just as much as men.

Today we look at some of those women whose lives were touched by Jesus. We consider their faith, their personal experiences, their courage, their convictions. Listen to their testimony, for the Christ who accepted them is the same Christ who accepts us today – Christ who values all people equally and welcomes all into his kingdom.

Prayer

Gracious God,
   you have told us that in Christ
   there is neither Jew nor Greek
   slave nor free,
   male nor female.
You tell us that you value us for what we are,
   and in the Scriptures you show that to be true.
In a world of prejudice and discrimination,
   you called people from all walks of life,
   all strands of society;
   each having a place in your kingdom
   and a contribution to make towards it.
Gracious God,
   we come today to remember especially
   some of the women you called –
   women who,
   despite the odds stacked against them
   in a male-dominated society,
   demonstrated a faith in you
   and commitment to you
   that puts many of us to shame.
Teach us through their example
   to see beyond the artificial barriers we create,
   to be open to all,
   to respect all,
   and to work together for your kingdom
   in the unity of your Son, Jesus Christ our Lord.
Amen.

Slides and music

Sinfonia (Messiah) Handel, during which Luke 1:39-43 is read

Meditation of Elizabeth

My baby jumped for joy, I swear it!
Oh I know you often feel them kicking,
   and you may well say it was only shuffling about in the womb,
   but this was different, I'm positive.
It was the first time I'd ever felt it move for a start,
   a wild lurch as Mary approached,
   almost as if it knew even then
   she was carrying the child who would shape its life.

Yes, I know that sounds ridiculous,
    and I wouldn't have given it another thought myself –
    I'm not usually given to romanticising.
But you see, when I saw Mary coming,
    I knew something special had happened,
    something quite out of the ordinary.
I realised she was pregnant for one thing,
    but then we women do spot those things, don't we?
Not that it was showing yet, mind you,
    but it was there in her eyes,
    in her expression,
    in the spring in her step,
    just as it had been in mine a few months earlier.
I knew,
    and I ran to embrace her,
    sharing her joy.
Yet there was more to it than that,
    I could feel it in my bones even before she began to speak.
I could sense that her child would be different,
    not just from mine but from every child,
    born to set us free,
    the fulfilment of our hopes,
    the answer to our prayers.
You think that's over the top?
Well, I may have over-reacted, I accept that,
    let my imagination run away with me.
I'd been a bit on edge, it's true,
    ever since that queer business with Zechariah –
    that day before I conceived when he came back from the temple,
    eyes staring,
    shaking his head in disbelief,
    unable to say a word until after John was born.
It got me down, I don't mind admitting it,
    and yes, perhaps I was a little overwrought,
    perhaps just plain excited.
But I still say it,
    despite what anyone may think –
    my child leaped in my womb,
    positively jumped for joy!

Slides and music

For unto us a child is born (Messiah) Handel, during which Luke 2:1-7 is read

Meditation of Mary, mother of Jesus

What a day it's been!
I'm shattered, exhausted,
　　and yet I'm over the moon!
Does that sound strange?
Well, let me tell you what happened, then you'll understand.
It could hardly have started worse,
　　arriving in Bethlehem like that to find the place packed.
My heart sank.
I knew we wouldn't find anywhere, not a chance,
　　but Joseph wouldn't have it.
'Next time,' he kept saying, 'you'll see.'
Next time indeed!
A stable, that's what we ended up with –
　　hardly the accommodation I had in mind!
It wouldn't have mattered, mind you,
　　not in the usual run of things,
　　but I was nine months pregnant
　　and my pains had started that morning,
　　getting stronger by the minute.
I was in agony by the end, you can imagine,
　　just about desperate by then,
　　not bothered where we stopped
　　just so long as I could rest.
That's why we accepted the innkeeper's offer,
　　makeshift though it was.
I lay there with cattle breathing down my neck,
　　straw prickling my back,
　　and what felt like a gale whistling beneath the door –
　　but I didn't care;
　　I didn't care about anything by then,
　　just wanted the baby to be born.
Poor Joseph, he was beside himself.
No idea how to cope or what to do next,
　　but thankfully one of the women from the inn took pity on us.
You'll never know how good it was
　　to see her kindly reassuring face,
　　her confident smile beaming down at me
　　through the haze of pain.
It seemed like an eternity for all that,
　　but it wasn't long really.
And then that sound,
　　that wonderful exhilarating sound,
　　my son, Jesus, crying!

I didn't want to let go of him,
   but I had to, of course, eventually.
I was exhausted,
   just about all in.
So I wrapped him in strips of cloth
   and laid him in a manger.
Sleep came easy after that,
   blissful peace at last,
   but a moment ago I woke with a start,
   remembering those words in that vision I had –
   'And they shall name him Emmanuel,
   God with us'.
My child, Emmanuel?
Can it really be true?
God come to his people?
He's everything to me, I admit that,
   I could gladly worship him.
But others? I wonder.
Time alone will tell, I suppose.
Anyway, no more time for talking, I need my sleep.
But wait, who's this knocking on the door?
Shepherds!
What on earth can they want at this time of night?
I don't know.
What a day it's been!
What a day!

Silent reflection

Slides and music

Rejoice, rejoice greatly (Messiah) Handel, during which Luke 2:36-38 is read

Meditation of Anna

I really felt I'd missed it,
   truthfully.
I mean, I wasn't just old,
   I was ancient!
And still there was no sign of the Messiah,
   no hint of his coming.
I began to wonder whether all those years of praying and fasting
   had been worth it,
   or simply one almighty waste of time.

I doubted everything,
  questioned everything,
  despite my outward piety.
Why hadn't God answered my prayers?
Why hadn't he rewarded my faithfulness?
Why believe when it didn't seem to make a scrap of difference?
I still kept up the facade mind you –
  spoke excitedly of the future,
  of all that God would do –
  but I didn't have much faith in it,
  not after so many disappointments.
Until that day when,
  hobbling back through the temple after yet more prayers,
  suddenly I saw him,
  God's promised Messiah.
Don't ask me how I knew,
  I just did,
  without any shadow of a doubt,
  and it was the most wonderful moment of my life,
  a privilege beyond words.
It taught me something, that experience.
It taught me never to give up,
  never to let go,
  never to lose heart.
It taught me there is always reason to hope
  no matter how futile it seems.
It taught me to go on expecting
  despite all the blows life may dish out.
It taught me God has never finished
  however much it may feel like it.
I nearly lost sight of all that.
I was right on the edge,
  teetering on the brink,
  fearing God had passed me by.
But he'd saved the best till last,
  and I know now, even though the waiting is over,
  that there's more to come,
  more to expect,
  more to celebrate.
For though my life is nearly at an end,
  it has only just begun!

Slides and music

Confutatis (Requiem) Mozart, during which Luke 4:1-13 is read

Meditation of Mary, mother of Jesus

He looked awful,
    absolutely drained.
And it's hardly surprising, is it?
Forty days out in the wilderness –
    that's hell enough for anyone,
    but without food – I ask you?
He was lucky to be alive!
Barely was, mind you, when he came staggering back into Nazareth.
A complete wreck he was,
    just about done in!
'Why did you do it?' I asked him.
'What got into you?'
And all he could say was that he had to,
    that everything depended on it.
He was never the same afterwards.
I used to joke the sun had got to him.
But it wasn't the sun, of course,
It was much more than that.
He wrestled out there,
    with himself,
    with the world,
    with all the forces of evil,
    and in some way I don't quite understand,
    he won.
It was a costly time, there's no doubt about that,
    a disturbing, frightening time –
    I could see the pain in his eyes afterwards.
He'd had to struggle,
    make painful choices,
    confront life at its darkest.
And though I never told him, I admired him for that.
It takes courage to face reality,
    to ask youself what it's really all about.
Mind you, I always knew he had it in him.
He'd always been such a good boy,
    right from the start;
    too good some said.

Well, perhaps he was in a way –
  look where it got him after all.
Yet it wasn't as easy as many thought.
He was still tempted, all too often,
  and there were times
  when it would have been so easy for him to give in,
  so easy to compromise,
  to bend just the once.
I know that's what he faced out there in the wilderness
  though he never told me what exactly happened.
But he came back stronger, I have to admit it,
  more certain,
  more determined.
Not that he didn't have his moments afterwards –
  don't make that mistake.
It wasn't all plain sailing from then on.
He had to battle like you and I,
  harder if anything,
  for the path he took was so much more demanding.
Oh no, he endured temptation all right,
  as real as any we might face.
The difference is he overcame it,
  right to the end.
That's what made him so special.
That's why people follow him, even now!

Silent reflection

Slides and music

Chanson de Matin Elgar, during which John 4:1-7 is read

Meditation of the woman at the well

He was full of surprises, that man,
  from the moment I first met him.
I thought he'd just push me aside like all the rest;
  either that or walk away with his head in the air.
He was a Jew, remember, and I a Samaritan;
  and worse than that,
  a woman,
  alone.
Yet he stayed where he was, a smile on his face,
  quite happy, apparently, to be associated with me.

Well, call me suspicious if you like, but I wasn't sure what he was up to,
 so I asked him straight out, 'What's your game?'
He laughed at that, and then offered me a drink of water –
 at least I thought that's what he was doing though I wasn't sure.
You see, he had no bucket,
 and he could hardly shin down the well, could he?
So where was this water he was on about meant to come from?
To be frank I suspected he was pulling my leg,
 but I was beginning to like him despite the nonsense he talked.
He had a nice way with him,
 kind,
 gentle,
 a bit of all right in an unconventional sort of way.
So I played along, wondering where it would all lead.
If only I'd known –
 what an embarrassment I might have saved myself.
I'll never know how he guessed,
 but suddenly he looked straight at me
 and for the first time I noticed his eyes.
They didn't undress you like so many men's seem to do,
 but looked much deeper,
 almost as if into my very soul.
And then he started talking about my lovers,
 my husbands,
 my past,
 every detail correct.
It was uncanny,
 frightening,
 far too near the knuckle,
So I tried to fob him off with some old chestnut about worship.
But even then he threw me;
 none of the usual pat answers
 but a response that reached right to the heart of the matter,
 cutting through all the trivia.
And it was after that he produced the biggest surprise of all –
 told me he was the Messiah!
I didn't know what to say,
 just stood there gawping, flabbergasted.
I mean, I realised he was a prophet,
 but the Messiah?
It couldn't be, I told myself,
 no way.

I went back down to the village, seeking reassurance,
   wanting someone to tell me he was just another religious nutcase.
But they didn't.
They were curious,
   wanted to see for themselves.
And when they heard him,
   listened to his teaching,
   they believed he was the Messiah.
Me? I still don't know, but I wouldn't be surprised,
   not if I'm honest;
   nothing would surprise me about him.

Slides and music

Aria from *Bachianas Brasileiras* Villa-Lobos
during which Luke 10:38-42 is read

Meditation of Mary, sister of Martha

I felt sorry for Martha, I really did;
   she was doing her best after all.
Someone had to see to the hospitality,
   make sure the dinner was all right,
   wash up after us,
   and, to be honest, I felt I wasn't pulling my weight.
I could see she was getting harassed
   despite the smile she kept on her face.
She didn't say anything, but she didn't need to,
   I could tell by the way she looked that she was angry.
And with good reason.
It was selfish of me,
   unforgivable,
   but I couldn't help myself.
He was so fascinating,
   so easy to listen to,
   so genuine.
It was as though every word he spoke was for me,
   answering the questions I'd never dared to ask,
   meeting the needs I never even knew existed,
   giving me the sense of purpose I had so longed to find.
How could I get up to wash dishes?
Interrupt him to offer another drink?
It would have been sacrilege.

I knew I might never have another chance like that again,
    and so, shame on me, I sat back and let Martha get on with it.
I wasn't surprised when she finally complained,
    but I was by the answer Jesus gave her.
I expected him to back her up, give me a ticking off –
    after all, fair's fair.
But instead he praised me
    and rebuked her!
He spoke gently, of course,
    almost tenderly,
    yet it was a rebuke for all that.
I don't know how she felt but I could have died of embarrassment.
It was my fault, you see –
    me who effectively earned her that reprimand,
    and I expected her to be furious afterwards;
    I know I would have been.
Yet funnily enough she wasn't.
She was very quiet for a time,
    very thoughtful,
    and then she told me not to look so guilty,
    for Jesus had been right.
He'd made her face herself for the first time,
    and she realised now she couldn't go on running for ever,
    couldn't go on hoping being busy would disguise the emptiness inside.
She'd been made to stop and ask herself what life was all about,
    and in Jesus she had begun to find the answers.
She's still the efficient hostess, of course,
    always will be.
And me?
    I'm just as ready to find an excuse for laziness given half the chance!
But we've changed, both of us,
    grown closer,
    found inner contentment,
    become more at peace with ourselves,
    because through meeting Jesus we've each discovered what really counts,
    the one thing we really need.

Silent reflection

Prayer
Loving God,
   we think we are so busy, so pressurised,
   having so much to do.
We rush around day after day
   with never a moment to spare.
Yet so often we forget the one thing we really need –
   to make time and space in our lives
   to meet with you,
   to hear your voice,
   and to look at the world from your perspective.
Loving God, teach us to be still
   and know your presence.
Amen.

Music   *Pie Jesu (Requiem)* Andrew Lloyd Webber

AFTERNOON SESSION

Music   *Pie Jesu (Requiem)* Andrew Lloyd Webber

Prayer
Almighty God,
   you are greater than our minds can fathom,
   higher than our highest thoughts,
   sovereign over all,
   worthy of praise and honour.
Forgive us that all too often
   we have lost our sense of awe
   and wonder before you.
Speak to us, as you spoke to Mary,
   and help us to catch a new sense
   of who you are
   and all you have done through Jesus.
Help us to magnify your name,
   singing your praises
   and telling of your greatness.

Slides and music
Puer Natus Scheidt
during which Luke 2:33-35 and John 19:25-27 are read

Meditation of Mary, mother of Jesus

What was that Simeon said –
  'A sword will pierce your soul'?
I spent so long wondering what that meant,
  tossing and turning on my bed,
  brooding and fretting when I'd a moment to myself.
It seemed such a strange thing to say,
  especially at what was meant to be a time of joy.
We'd only had Jesus a few days,
  and my heart was still bursting with happiness.
We were both over the moon,
  Simeon too, that's the odd thing –
  he was almost dancing with delight.
But then his expression clouded,
  and he gave that awful warning which has haunted me ever since.
I just haven't been able to forget it, try as I might.
Always the question has been there,
  nagging away in the back of my mind,
  even in the brightest moments:
  what did he mean?
And if you'd asked me as little as a week ago
  I still wouldn't have been sure.
Oh, I'd a fair idea by then, of course –
  the fears were mounting up –
  but I'd still kept on hoping,
  praying that I might be wrong.
Now I know though,
  all too well.
My heart is not just pierced –
  it's broken!
For I've stood here today and seen my son die.
I watched him cursed and ridiculed, scourged and beaten.
I watched as they hammered nails through his hands
  and lifted him on to a cross.
I watched as he twisted in agony and cried out in despair.
And a moment ago I watched as they plunged a spear into his side.
At least he didn't feel that –
  thank God he was dead by then –
  but I did.
It thrust deep inside,
  running me through without mercy.
I've never known such pain,
  such agony,
  such horror.

And now life has gone for me too;
   I feel it has nothing left to offer.
Yet he's given me joy,
   no one can take that away.
He was with me for thirty wonderful years,
   everything a son could be –
   not many mothers can say that.
I've had joy,
   and now I have pain.
Maybe that's the way it had to be,
   the way it has to be,
   if there's to be any joy at all.

Slides and music

Behold, and see (Messiah) Handel, during which John 19:25, 28-30 is read

Meditation of Mary, wife of Clopas

He was silent,
   quite still,
   his body limp and lifeless,
   like a rag doll,
   like a broken puppet.
And I thanked God that at last it was over,
   his ordeal finally ended.
But it wasn't,
   not quite.
He moved again,
   just the faintest twitch,
   the last flickering ember of life,
   but enough to prolong our hopes,
   enough to prolong his pain.
He was still breathing,
   still suffering.
We watched wretchedly, torn by conflicting desires –
   the longing to see him come down and prove his enemies wrong;
   the longing to see him find peace in the cold embrace of death.
But suddenly his eyes were open,
   wide,
   bright,
   triumphant;
   the lips were moving,

eager,
excited,
exultant;
and his voice rang out:
'It is finished!'
An acknowledgement of defeat, some said afterwards,
  a last despairing cry of sorrow.
But it wasn't,
  not for those who heard it,
  not for those with ears to hear.
It was altogether different –
  like sunshine after storm,
  like rain after drought,
  like laughter after tears –
  gloriously unexpected,
  wonderfully surprising.
He had stooped and conquered,
  staked all and won.
Defeat was victory,
  darkness was light,
  death was life.
I didn't see it then, mind you,
  I can't pretend that.
It was just a glimpse at the time,
  a glimmer barely understood.
But what I did see, with sudden staggering clarity,
  was that until that moment,
  until that last victorious shout,
  he had lived with the awful burden of holding the world's fate in his own
  and wondering whether he could see it through.
At last it was done –
  he had honoured his calling,
  fulfilled his mission,
  walked the way of the cross.
It was finished,
  and with a song in his heart and joy in his eyes
  he bowed his head and surrendered his spirit.

Silent reflection

Slides and music
Lift up your heads (Messiah) Handel, during which Mark 16:1-4 is read

Meditation of Salome

The stone was rolled away.
I'd no idea how,
   let alone what it meant,
   but we saw it for ourselves,
   pushed to one side,
   the tomb gaping open,
   almost inviting us to go inside.
And I can't tell you the relief we felt.
We'd been asking each other as we walked, 'How will we possibly get in?'
   knowing we'd never move the stone ourselves,
   not after watching it being rolled into place –
   grown men sweating with the exertion.
But we'd gone anyway,
   desperate for something to do,
   some way to express our grief,
   some gesture to pay our last respects.
A last look at the man we'd loved so much, that's what we expected;
   a final anointing with the attention he deserved.
But what a shock we had.
It was Mary, I think, who went in first,
   and I could tell at once something was wrong,
   the way she stopped and gasped,
   but I still wasn't prepared for what I saw,
   or rather what I didn't.
For he was gone,
   disappeared,
   just the folded grave-clothes left to mark where they had laid him.
We were speechless,
   all of us,
   overcome with disbelief,
   not knowing what to think or what to do.
And then this man appeared –
   don't ask me who he was –
   asking what we were looking for,
   as if that wasn't obvious;
   telling us to go elsewhere,
   to seek the living,
   not the dead.
Well, we were stunned, you can imagine;
   it was all such a shock,
   so unexpected,

and we stood for ages,
   simply nodding,
   grinning,
   trying to hide our embarrassment,
   trying to stop our hands from shaking.
But we went eventually,
   on to Galilee as instructed;
   the apostles too, once they'd got over their disbelief.
And we met him,
   just as we had been told –
   Jesus!
Risen!
Alive!
Victorious!
The stone was rolled away, and I still don't know how,
   but I know now what it means –
   thank God, I know!

Slides and music

I know that my Redeemer liveth (Messiah) Handel
during which John 20:11-18 is read

Meditation of Mary Magdalene

I was shattered at the time,
   inconsolable.
It was as though the bottom had fallen out of my world
   and there was nothing left to live for.
How could they do that to him, I asked myself?
How could they destroy someone so loving and gentle,
   so caring,
   so good?
Yet they had.
I'd seen it myself,
   I'd watched as he drew his last agonised breath;
   and it was dreadful,
   more terrible than I can ever describe.
It wasn't just the pain he went through, though that was awful enough;
   it was the isolation of it all –
   standing there before Pilate, alone,
   forsaken by his friends,

one man against the might of an empire;
   groaning under the lash of the whip, alone,
   no one to offer him comfort,
   no one to bathe his wounds;
   hanging upon that cross, alone,
   crying out in such heart-breaking anguish,
   as though he were separated not just from us but from God himself.
I felt at the time I would never forget it,
   that the memory would haunt me for the rest of my days.
And so it would have,
   unquestionably,
   were it not for what came after.
It was all so unexpected –
   suddenly, in the nightmare of my grief, a ray of sunshine,
   and then joy, immersing me in its light.
One moment despair,
   then the stone rolled away,
   the tomb empty,
   the mysterious stranger appearing from nowhere,
   and that familiar voice speaking my name.
One moment tears,
   the next laughter.
One moment death,
   the next life.
And now my heart dances with delight.
I still can scarcely take it in though;
   sometimes I have to pinch myself to be sure it's not all a dream.
But no, it's true.
He died yet rose again!
He was killed yet conquered death!
He lived and lives again!
I really thought that life was over,
   not just for him but for me.
But I was wrong, wasn't I?
For it wasn't over;
   it was only just beginning.

Silent reflection

Slides and music

Laudamus te (Mass in C minor) Mozart, during which Acts 16:11-15 is read

Meditation of Lydia

They all think I'm mad, getting mixed up in this Jesus business –
    ought to have more sense than become involved –
    and I can understand their reasons well enough.
You see, I'd have thought the same once:
    why take any chances when you've worked so hard
    to make a success of your life?
Why risk everything for the sake of some new-fangled religion?
Yet let's be fair, I'd already put myself out on a limb,
    rejecting the idols of Rome as I did, and worshipping the God of Israel.
That was bordering on the eccentric,
    more than a trifle suspect in some people's eyes.
Yet while it may have made me different,
    even perhaps considered a little odd,
    it hadn't actually harmed my prospects.
A matter of choice, that was the way people saw it;
    they go their way and I mine.
So I did just that.
And though I say it myself, I made a good fist of it –
    my business thriving,
    my lifestyle more than comfortable,
    myself respected,
    a valued member of the community,
    successful pillar of the establishment.
But then I heard about Jesus, and I was fascinated immediately.
I suppose it was the way Paul spoke of him.
His faith was so real,
    so alive,
    almost radiating from him,
    and I listened entranced to everything he had to say,
    knowing this man Jesus was for me,
    the one thing missing in my life,
    the answer I'd long been looking for.
What else could I do but accept him?
How else respond than declare him as Lord?
Yet I knew the controversy surrounding him,
    the hatred of the Jews,
    the suspicions of the Romans,
    and I understood from the beginning it might be costly,
    possibly risking everything I'd worked for,
    maybe even more.
Once I opened my home like that,
    welcomed his followers,

offered hospitality,
  there could be no going back.
I'd shown my colours,
  made my stand,
  identified myself with Jesus beyond all question.
So yes, perhaps I am mad,
  perhaps I ought to think again,
  but it makes no difference.
Though they urge me to keep quiet,
  implore me not to make a show,
  I have no choice –
  I have to follow, serve him, play my part, come what may.
Oh, I know they mean well,
  that they want to save me from myself,
  and I'm touched by their concern, believe me.
But even if they're right and I do end up losing everything,
  it doesn't matter,
  for I've found far, far more than anything I may ever have to sacrifice.

Prayer

Lord Jesus Christ,
  you identified yourself totally with humankind,
  sharing not just our life but our death.
Forgive us that sometimes we are reluctant
  to be identified with you.
We are afraid of what people may think,
  embarrassed by the possibility
  of being misunderstood,
  worried that it may affect our prospects,
  nervous about what it might lead to.
Lord Jesus,
  help us to put you first in our lives,
  even when that might mean
  putting other things we value second.
Teach us to show in our lives
  what we claim to be true with our lips.
Amen.

Blessing

Music   *Gloria (Gloria)* Vivaldi

People of the Spirit

Suggested visual material   Material for this Quiet Day is hard to come by, but some slides from the following can be used:

Jesus of Nazareth 6
Bread and Wine
The Life of Christ IV
St Paul
The Story of Saint Paul

MORNING SESSION

Music   *Violin Romance No. 2 in F major* Beethoven

Introduction   'If only I could have been alive when Jesus was! If only I could have been there when he healed the sick, fed the multitude, preached to the crowds on the hillside!' How often have you heard that said? How often perhaps even said it yourself? It's easy to imagine that if we could have been there then faith would come so much easier to us. But to think like that is to ignore the promise Jesus gave of his Holy Spirit – a promise which those in the early days of the Christian Church so clearly saw fulfilled. For them, although Jesus was no longer physically with them, he was as much present as he had ever been during his earthly ministry. In fact more so, for his Spirit dwelt within each one of them. Listen today to some of their stories, for they remind us that the Holy Spirit is equally Christ's gift to us, here and now!

Prayer

Living God,
    when we hear about the gift of the Holy Spirit
    our thoughts tend automatically to turn
    to the day of Pentecost –
    that incredible day
    when you turned the lives of the Apostles
    upside down,
    that day which in many ways marked the birth
    of the Christian Church.
Yet wonderful as that day was,
    it is only part of the story,
    for although many since have received the Spirit
    just as dramatically,
    for others it has been different.
While the gifts of some have caught the eye,
    those of others have passed almost unnoticed.
Yet each have been different expressions
    of the same Spirit.
Living God,
    as we consider today some of those first people
    touched by your Spirit,
    help us to recognise the way you come to us,
    the gifts you give to us,
    and the way you are able to use us
    in a multitude of different ways.

Slides and music

Cum Sancto Spiritu (Gloria) Vivaldi, during which Acts 2:1-4 is read

Meditation of Peter

We shouldn't have been surprised,
    not if we'd had any sense;
    it was what we'd been told to expect,
    what he'd promised us.
But we never imagined anything quite so extraordinary.
We were waiting, it's true,
    gathered together as so often before,
    but we'd been doing that for days
    and our confidence had taken a hammering.
We were going through the motions, that's all,
    telling each other he hadn't forgotten us,

talking of the future as though we still believed in it,
    yet wondering in our hearts if there was anything to look forward to.
I mean, what could we hope to achieve when all was said and done.
What reason to think that we, a motley bunch if ever there was one,
    should fare better than our master?
We wanted to carry on his work, don't get me wrong:
    we wanted to tell people what had happened,
    help them find faith for themselves,
    but how could we even hope to begin?
So we kept the doors locked
    and sang our hymns
    and said our prayers
    and hid our doubts.
Until suddenly it happened!
I can't properly describe it even now,
    but it changed our lives.
It was as though a mighty wind blew away the cobwebs,
    a refreshing breeze revived our flagging faith,
    a breath of air stirred our spirits.
As though a tiny spark rekindled our confidence,
    a tongue of fire set our hearts aflame,
    a raging inferno swept our fears away.
As though life had begun again,
    the world become a different place,
    and each of us been born anew.
I know that doesn't make sense,
    but it's the best I can do.
You'll have to experience it for yourself to understand.
And you can, just as we did.
Believe me, we never would have thought it possible,
    despite all Jesus said to us.
We were lost,
    lonely,
    frightened,
    hopelessly aware of our weaknesses,
    searching for any strengths.
We never thought we'd change a soul,
    let alone the world,
    but that's because we had no idea how God could change us!

Slides and music

Gloria ('Credo' Mass) Mozart, during which Acts 4:32-37 is read

Meditation of Barnabas

It wasn't much of a gift;
    at least I didn't think so.
In fact, I didn't feel I had a gift at all,
    not like the rest of them with all their stunning signs and wonders.
I envied them sometimes,
    so often in the limelight,
    stealing all the headlines –
    prophets,
    teachers,
    workers of miracles,
    speakers of tongues.
They were the ones who drew the crowds,
    the ones who people noticed,
    and all I did was plod quietly along,
    living the faith in my own simple way,
    speaking and doing and caring and sharing
    as I believed Christ would have me do.
And then they gave me this name –
    Barnabas,
    'Son of Encouragement.'
It was all so unexpected,
    a complete surprise,
    for what had I done to deserve any such honour.
But then they told me,
    one by one,
    that of all the gifts they valued,
    mine was chief among them.
A generous gesture,
    a word of praise,
    an expression of trust,
    an act of love –
    not causing gasps,
    not making heads turn;
    yet these, they told me
    (though I'd never dreamt it nor even realised they'd been done),
    these had stirred their hearts and cheered their spirits
    as signs and wonders could never do.
It doesn't seem much, does it –
    encouraging people?
Not a gift you'll find in any of the textbooks,
    nor one people will ever fight over.

Yet don't let that fool you as it did me –
　　don't waste time thirsting for those showy gifts you do not have –
　　for it's often when you're least aware of it,
　　through things you count unimportant,
　　that Jesus chooses to use you.
So if you are wondering, as I did, why you've been left out,
　　if you're feeling down,
　　or doubting your experience,
　　or waiting for the spirit and perplexed he hasn't come,
　　let me offer you some simple words of encouragement:
　　follow Jesus,
　　faithfully,
　　simply,
　　and maybe,
　　just maybe,
　　you'll find his spirit's been there all along.

Slides and music

O death, where is thy sting (Messiah) Handel
during which Acts 6:8-10, 12-15 is read

Meditation of Stephen

I'm too young to die,
　　far, far too young!
There's still so much to live for,
　　so much I want to do,
　　so much I've barely started.
It's not that I'm afraid of death,
　　don't get me wrong.
It's just that I love life
　　and I don't want to let it go unless I have to.
I love the sound of birds singing in the trees,
　　the wind whispering through the grass,
　　children laughing in the street.
I love the sight of clouds scudding across the sky,
　　the sun setting across the ocean,
　　the trees laden with summer fruits.
I love the feel of water fresh upon my skin,
　　the smell of flowers dancing in the breeze,
　　the taste of food, steaming from the oven.

I love the joy of sharing with my family,
   the pleasure of being among friends,
   the warmth of Christian fellowship –
   so much that is good which I just don't want to lose.
So why throw it away, I hear you ask me?
Why take a path that surely leads to death?
I've asked that too, believe me, countless times,
   searching for another way,
   an easier way that doesn't cost so much.
And yet although I wish there was,
   I know deep down there isn't.
I could have steered a different course – no doubt that's true –
   denied my faith or kept it under wraps.
I could have toned my message down or run away,
   not trod on toes or taken risks.
Yet what if Christ had done the same, I ask you that –
   put safety first and not caused such a stir?
What future then would we have had?
What hope, what joy, what faith to share?
But no, he gave his all,
   despite the pain,
   despite the fear,
   despite the sorrow –
   pursuing the way of love even to the cross.
That's why I'm here now,
   jostled by the crowds,
   dragged through the streets,
   waiting for the stones to fly.
I don't want to die,
   but neither did Jesus.
I'm too young to die,
   but so was he.
I want to live
   for I love life,
   passionately,
   deeply –
   but the thing is I love Jesus even more,
   just as he loved me.

Slides and music

Gratias (Mass in C minor) Mozart
during which John 1:43-46 and Acts 8:4-8 are read

Meditation of Philip

I have to tell you!
Forgive me if I'm intruding,
   barging in where I'm not wanted,
   but I have to tell you what Christ has done for me.
I'm not bragging, God forbid!
There's been no merit on my part,
   nothing about me that's special or deserving of praise.
I'm just an ordinary, everyday person,
   no different from anyone else,
   but I've suddenly discovered what really matters in life,
   what really counts.
I thought I knew already;
   well, we all do, don't we?
A good job,
   loving partner,
   nice home,
   children –
   you know the sort of thing.
And don't think I'm knocking those,
   for they can all be precious,
   all offer their own fulfilment.
But when I heard about Jesus,
   met him for myself,
   suddenly I discovered there is something else,
   something more important than any of those,
   able to give a whole new perspective on them all,
   and to answer my deepest needs.
I was set free from myself,
   my guilt,
   my sin,
   my shame;
   not suddenly becoming perfect
   but finding forgiveness,
   a new beginning,
   a multitude of new beginnings.
I was set free from the endless quest for pleasure,
   from the gods of greed and lust,
   pride and envy;
   learning there is more to life than the thirst for gain
   or the pursuit of success.

I was set free from fear and worry,
   despair and sorrow;
   even in my darkest days certain joy will surely come.
And above all I've been freed from death,
   knowing though this life shall end that I shall rise again!
So now do you see why I have to tell,
   why I have to let you know?
I've found so much,
   such hope,
   such peace,
   such happiness;
   and I can't just sit on that as though it's mine and mine alone.
I have to pass it on,
   share it out,
   let you find it too;
   so forgive me if I'm intruding,
   but if you've got a moment,
   please, please,
   let me tell you!

Slides and music

Nocturne in B flat minor Chopin, during which Acts 15:22-32 is read

Meditation of Silas

Who'd have believed it?
Who'd have believed after all I said I would end up with Paul,
   treading the roads of Macedonia,
   sailing the high seas,
   risking my life alongside him,
   his right-hand man.
I was against him, you see,
   when I first started out on the way of Christ.
He had my respect, of course –
   his courage and determination deserved at least that –
   but I thought he'd gone too far,
   preaching as he did to the Gentiles.
It was all right to a point maybe –
   they've always been welcome to join us
   should they follow our customs, accept our law, embrace our ritual;
   but Paul saw things differently,
   accepted them as they were,
   one law for us and another for them,

the law of Moses,
   the law of Christ.
It was over the top,
   too much, too soon,
   and we told him so in no uncertain terms.
A Jew first,
   a Christian second,
   that's the way I saw it –
   the two belonging inseparably together,
   the one depending on the other,
   but strictly in that order.
Only then I heard him for myself,
   brought to Jerusalem to account for his actions,
   to sort things out once and for all,
   and I couldn't help but be impressed.
He was right –
   I could see it immediately,
   though I tried to hold out against him.
Those Gentiles, they had come to faith,
   had met with Christ,
   had received his spirit,
   and if God was willing to welcome them,
   who was I to shut the door?
I realised suddenly it was I and not them who had to change,
   I who had to think again,
   and by God's grace I've done just that.
We're partners now, Paul and me,
   working together to preach the Gospel,
   Christians first,
   Jews second.
Who'd have believed it?
Who'd have ever thought I could change so much?
Yet that's what faith is all about:
   through meeting Jesus to be made new,
   remade,
   restored;
   born and born again.
And now I know that no one, no matter how it may seem,
   how impossible it may appear,
   no one is outside the transforming and renewing power of his love.

Slides and music

Laudamus te (Mass in C minor) Mozart, during which Acts 16:11-15 is read

Meditation of Lydia

They all think I'm mad, getting mixed up in this Jesus business –
   ought to have more sense than become involved –
   and I can understand their reasons well enough.
You see, I'd have thought the same once:
   why take any chances when you've worked so hard
   to make a success of your life?
Why risk everything for the sake of some new-fangled religion?
Yet let's be fair, I'd already put myself out on a limb,
   rejecting the idols of Rome as I did, and worshipping the God of Israel.
That was bordering on the eccentric,
   more than a trifle suspect in some people's eyes.
Yet while it may have made me different,
   even perhaps considered a little odd,
   it hadn't actually harmed my prospects.
A matter of choice, that was the way people saw it;
   they go their way and I mine.
So I did just that.
And though I say it myself, I made a good fist of it –
   my business thriving,
   my lifestyle more than comfortable,
   myself respected,
   a valued member of the community,
   successful pillar of the establishment.
But then I heard about Jesus, and I was fascinated immediately.
I suppose it was the way Paul spoke of him.
His faith was so real,
   so alive,
   almost radiating from him,
   and I listened entranced to everything he had to say,
   knowing this man Jesus was for me,
   the one thing missing in my life,
   the answer I'd long been looking for.
What else could I do but accept him?
How else respond than declare him as Lord?
Yet I knew the controversy surrounding him,
   the hatred of the Jews,
   the suspicions of the Romans,
   and I understood from the beginning it might be costly,
   possibly risking everything I'd worked for,
   maybe even more.

Once I opened my home like that,
  welcomed his followers,
  offered hospitality,
  there could be no going back.
I'd shown my colours,
  made my stand,
  identified myself with Jesus beyond all question.
So yes, perhaps I am mad,
  perhaps I ought to think again,
  but it makes no difference.
Though they urge me to keep quiet,
  implore me not to make a show,
  I have no choice –
  I have to follow, serve him, play my part, come what may.
Oh, I know they mean well,
  that they want to save me from myself,
  and I'm touched by their concern, believe me.
But even if they're right and I do end up losing everything,
  it doesn't matter,
  for I've found far, far more than anything I may ever have to sacrifice.

Prayer

Loving God,
  when we read the pages of Scripture,
  when we hear dramatic stories of testimony,
  when we meet sparkling Christians,
  it's hard sometimes not to feel a little daunted.
We do not have stunning gifts,
  we don't make the headlines,
  we haven't exciting stories to tell.
Yet you remind us through people like Barnabas
  that those behind the scenes with the unsung gifts
  can make just as great a contribution
  to your kingdom
  as any other.
Amen.

Music   Slow Movement from *Concerto for two Violins* J. S. Bach

AFTERNOON SESSION

Music   Largo from *Spring (Four Seasons)* Vivaldi

Prayer

Loving God,
   we thank you for your call that comes to us –
   your call to discipleship, to service,
   to be your people,
   sharing in the work of your kingdom.
We thank you that you call us as we are,
   with all our faults, weaknesses and doubts,
   accepting us not through our own deserving,
   but through your grace, your love,
   and your mercy.
And we thank you above all
   for the assurance we have
   that through his Holy Spirit Christ is within us,
   working in our hearts and minds and souls
   to change our lives
   and draw us ever closer to you.
Loving God,
   receive our praise in his name.

Slides and music

Adagio from *Clarinet Concerto in A major* Mozart
during which 1 Timothy 1:1-7 and 1 Timothy 4:11-16 are read

Meditation of Timothy

I was only a boy,
   a mere slip of a lad compared to most of them,
   and I really wondered what use I could be.
My heart was willing,
   positively bursting to get involved.
My faith was strong,
   bubbling up like a mountain spring from deep within,
   but I wondered whether anyone would accept me
   and whether I had any right to expect them to.
They had more experience of life after all,
   a store of wisdom accumulated over the years;

so why should they listen to someone half their age
    just because he believed God had called him?
Yet though a few balked at the idea,
    most had no objections.
They treated me with kindness,
    friendship,
    genuine respect;
    and if occasionally I went too far,
    carried away by youthful exuberance,
    they responded patiently,
    more than willing to make allowances.
None more so than Paul,
    my dear friend Paul.
How much I owe that man!
How much he changed my life!
Guiding me and helping me along the way of Christ.
And yet, though I've often tried to thank him,
    he's always shrugged it off,
    saying it's not him but Jesus I ought to thank.
Jesus who valued young and old,
    Jesus who welcomed little children,
    Jesus who's chosen me.
I've held on to that,
    day by day,
    year by year,
    and now suddenly it is I who am old,
    receiving from those who are young,
    I who have to recognise that God can work through all.
It's hard to accept that sometimes,
    even for me,
    until I look back,
    and remember those days long ago.
For I realise then, once again, that if Christ could use me
    he can use anyone!

Slides and music

Love's Theme from *Midnight Express*
during which 1 Corinthians 13:1-13 is read

Meditation of Paul

He taught me the meaning of love,
    what it really means to say, 'I love you'.
Slowly,
    gently,
    he taught me.
Not through words,
    nor through gestures,
    but through showing me love in action.
I thought I'd understood,
    that I loved as much as the next man, maybe more.
Not perhaps as a husband loves his wife, or a father his children –
    there's not been time for that, sadly –
    but deeper,
    beyond such natural ties –
    my fellow apostles,
    my family in Christ,
    my fellow human beings.
And I did love in my own way, of course I did –
    my only goal,
    my single aim,
    to help them,
    serve them,
    reach them.
And yet, despite all that, I sometimes wondered if I'd ever loved at all,
    for deep down, in my heart of hearts, I knew it was all about me –
    my preaching, *my* striving, *my* loving;
    my efforts, *my* successes, *my* ambitions –
    all finally for my own satisfaction
    and even, I fear, my own glory as much as his.
It's human, I realise that, or so at least we tell ourselves,
    but is that true?
Or does it have to be?
For when I look at Jesus,
    all he did for me,
    I see a different truth,
    a different kind of love;
    patient, kind, humble;
    not serving self or seeking gain,
    but putting others first.
A love that knows me as I am,
    understands my faults,
    yet still believes in me.

A love which, though I turn away, accepts me,
    even dies for me!
That's what it means, this thing called love,
    seeing the worst, believing the best,
    asking nothing, and giving all.
I thought I'd understood, all those years ago,
    but I hadn't, hardly at all.
I'm still learning even now,
    still struggling to let go of self.
I can't do it alone,
    I've come to realise that at last;
    I need his help, his love flowing through me,
    and I'll carry on praying for that,
    striving for that,
    until my dying day,
    for I understand now that without love all else is nothing.

Slides and music

Agnus Dei ('Coronation' Mass) Mozart
during which 2 Peter 1:1-4, 12-15 is read

Meditation of Peter

This time I will not fail:
    despite the terror,
    despite the sorrow,
    despite the pain,
    I will not fail.
God knows I don't want to die –
    I'm not the stuff of heroes,
    but then I hardly need tell you that, do I?
You'll all know well enough about the last time.
It's been written about,
    talked about,
    preached about so many times –
    Peter, the man who was all talk,
    the apostle who lost his nerve when the pressure was on.
The memory has lived with me ever since,
    searing into my conscience like a hot iron.
Not that Jesus didn't forgive me;
    he soon put me right on that.

Three times he affirmed his call,
   three times offered me the opportunity to declare my love,
   one for each of my denials.
No, he never blamed me for my failure,
   never condemned,
   not even once the slightest hint of censure,
   let alone telling me, 'I told you so.'
And to be fair neither has anyone else.
They all understood I meant well,
   knew equally how easily they'd have done the same;
   and if anyone felt it served me right for shooting my mouth off
   they never said.
Yet I've had to live with the knowledge of my own empty promises,
   my extravagant worthless claims;
   and sometimes, I can tell you, my skin still crawls with shame.
It's as though, deep down, I don't believe I can trust myself,
   and because of that I ask myself why anyone else should trust me either.
Well, now's the time to put the record straight,
   here as I rot in jail waiting for the final moment
   when the executioner comes,
   when death finally arrives.
It won't be easy, I know that.
They'll push me to recant,
   threaten me, torture me,
   maybe even promise life if I'm ready to deny my faith,
   willing to turn my back on Jesus as I did all those years ago.
But not this time:
   this time I will not fail.
I was given another chance to live,
   forgiven,
   restored,
   accepted;
   and I seized it with both hands,
   living life to the full in a way I never lived it before.
Now I have another chance to die,
   another chance to offer my life for the sake of Christ who died for me,
   and this time I will stay true to the end,
   for I know that in death, as in life, he will stay true to me.

Slides and music

Rex Tremendae (Requiem) Mozart, during which Revelation 21:1-4 is read

Meditation of John

One day we'll see him again.
Don't ask me when,
   don't ask me how,
   but one day
   when all this struggle is over –
   all the pain,
   all the grief,
   all the fear,
   all the doubt –
   then he will return to establish his kingdom.
I know that's hard to believe sometimes.
When you keep on battling against the odds and nothing seems to change,
   when you stand up for what is good yet evil seems to triumph,
   when love is met with hatred,
   gentleness with violence,
   truth with falsehood –
   of course you start to wonder.
When you're faced with suffering,
   sickness,
   death;
   when greed and corruption are rewarded with plenty
   and justice is trampled underfoot;
   when the poor get poorer
   and the world goes by uncaring –
   it's impossible not to ask yourself, day after day,
   why's it allowed to happen?
But he will come, I'm certain of it –
   not just because he promised to,
   though that's important, of course;
   not simply because he came back before,
   cheating death of its victory,
   triumphing over the grave,
   though that's more vital still;
   but because he *has* to return if anything is finally to make sense,
   if faith is to be anything more than a grand delusion.
And it *is* more;
   it *has* to be.
These goals we strive towards,
   this life revealed in Christ,
   the promises he made,
   the truths he taught,

everything he lived and died for –
they're real, I know that,
for they have turned my life around,
sustained me through my darkest moments,
lifted me beyond my highest thoughts,
and given me a joy that knows no bounds.
So though now we see but do not understand,
though faith is sometimes hard and Christ seems far away,
we'll hold fast to hope,
waiting for a time when there will be an end to tears and pain and death,
a time when God will live among his people
in a new and beautiful kingdom;
and we shall see him again, our Lord Jesus Christ,
crowned in glory and splendour,
King of kings,
Lord of lords,
all in all,
yet one with us!

Reading

Revelation 22:1-5, 20

Then the angel showed me the river of the water of life, bright as crystal, flowing from the throne of God and of the Lamb through the middle of the street of the city. On either side of the river is the tree of life with its twelve kinds of fruit, producing its fruit each month; and the leaves of the tree are for the healing of the nations. Nothing accursed will be found there any more. But the throne of God and of the Lamb will be in it, and his servants will worship him; they will see his face, and his name will be on their foreheads. And there will be no more night; they need no light of lamp or sun, for the Lord God will be their light, and they will reign for ever and ever.

The one who testifies to these things says, 'Surely I am coming soon.' Amen. Come, Lord Jesus!

Prayer

Gracious God,
we thank you for those extraordinary moments
we occasionally experience
which change our lives,
giving us joy and fulfilment
we never imagined possible.

We thank you especially
   for the great gift of your Holy Spirit –
   an experience which transformed
   the lives of the apostles,
   which has changed the lives
   of countless believers across the centuries,
   and which has power to reshape our lives
   here and now.
Open our hearts, our minds and our souls
   to your living presence
   so that we shall know your life-changing power
   for ourselves.
Amen.

Music   *Für Elise* Beethoven

Paul – Ambassador for Christ

Suggested visual material Jesus of Nazareth 3-6
The Life of Christ IV
St Paul
The Story of St Paul

MORNING SESSION

Music First movement of *'Moonlight' Sonata* Beethoven

Introduction Of all the people in the Scriptures apart from Jesus, few can capture the imagination as much as one man: the Apostle Paul. A man we meet first as Saul, an ardent Pharisee determined to stamp out the Christian Church and wipe away any mention of the name of Christ. Yet on the Damascus road all this is to change; having been an enemy of the Church Paul becomes its most celebrated champion. Here is a story of a life truly transformed by Christ, and it is a story which speaks to us of the change Jesus can make in our own life.

Prayer

Loving God,
 we are here today to reflect on one man –
 Jesus Christ.
But to do that we shall be thinking of another –
 the Apostle Paul –
 a man whose life you turned around,
 a man who you used
 in ways far beyond his expectations,
 a man you called to preach the Gospel,
 a man whose testimony still has power
 to move and challenge, even today.
Loving God,
 we may not have Paul's gifts, energy or vision,
 but you call us just the same.

And, as he discovered,
  you can use us
  in ways beyond our wildest imaginings.
Help us then, through this service,
  to learn from his experience,
  to hear your voice,
  and to make our response.
Amen.

Slides and music

Presto from *'Moonlight' Sonata* Beethoven
during which Acts 8:1-3, 9:1-2 is read

Meditation

So they claim he's alive, do they?
Back from the dead and offering new life to his followers?
Well, we'll see about that!
A few floggings,
  a few stonings,
  and we'll soon hear a different story.
What are they trying to prove, these people?
Do they really imagine we're going to swallow their nonsense?
He's dead, Jesus,
  nailed to the cross like a common criminal,
  and good riddance;
  so perish all blasphemers, that's what I say.
How can they still claim he's the Messiah?
I just don't understand it.
If he was, he'd hardly be dead now, would he?
And he definitely wouldn't have died in the way he did,
  humiliated,
  ridiculed,
  cursed,
  despised.
No, don't try telling me he's the Christ,
  I know better than that.
Product of the best Pharisaic education, that's me!
Acknowledged expert in the Law,
  got it all at my fingertips down to the last detail.
And I can assure you that this Jesus just does not fit the bill.
A jumped-up fanatic from Galilee,
  a misguided martyr from the sticks,

a good-for-nothing layabout looking to cause trouble.
I must say I thought we'd seen the last of him,
   we all did;
     but even in death he continues to spread his poison,
     duping his followers with his empty promises.
You have to admire their courage though, I'll give you that;
   after watching him die I expected they'd soon climb down,
   keep as far out of sight as possible.
And they did for a time –
   no sight or sound for many a week –
   until suddenly there they were,
   for no reason I can think of,
   not a care in the world apparently,
   heedless of the risk,
   carrying on where he'd left off.
Well, if that's what they want, that's what they're going to get –
   they can carry on all right,
   follow in his footsteps all the way to the cross;
   I'll be more than happy to oblige.
I don't know what changed them,
   and I don't care.
No, really, it's of no interest to me.
My duty is to destroy this cancer,
   wipe out this heresy
   before it does the same to us.
Bring them back begging for mercy,
   string up their ringleaders,
   and then we'll see whether they still claim he's alive –
   then we'll see what life he has to offer!

Slides and music

Qui tollis peccata mundi (Mass in C minor) Mozart
during which Acts 9:1-9 is read

Meditation

I was wrong,
   so terribly, totally wrong,
   and now I'm sick with shame.
To think that I, Paul, persecuted the Messiah;
   the one for whom we had waited so long,
   the one who we all longed to see.

I failed to recognise him,
    blinded by my own pride and bigotry.
I'd watched as his followers were killed,
    rejoicing in their deaths,
    glad to be associated with their destruction.
And then, when the opportunity finally came,
    I leapt at the chance to destroy them myself.
It was my mission,
    my great calling,
    and I pursued it gleefully,
    brutally,
    with unquenchable zeal.
They quaked at the sound of my voice, those Christians,
    and I gave glory to God.
They trembled as I approached,
    and I offered him my gratitude.
I have broken bodies,
    tormented minds,
    crushed spirits,
    all in the name of faith.
But then I saw it,
    there in the brightness,
    the face of Jesus,
    tears in his eyes.
I heard it,
    there in the silence,
    the voice of Jesus,
    'Why, Saul, why?'
And I knew then the awful, wonderful truth.
It was just as they had said –
    he was the Messiah,
    risen from the dead.
I know that now, but I wish I didn't,
    for I have become the one suffering,
    racked by guilt and sorrow.
Why did he spare me to endure this agony?
Why not finish me off there and then?
Or is this my punishment,
    his judgement on my foul, despicable crimes?
There's no way he can ever forgive me, I'm certain of that;
    not after all I've done.

And even if he did there's no way I could ever be accepted by his followers;
    they'd never believe someone like me could change that much.
So here I am,
    Paul, persecutor of Christ,
    grovelling in misery before him;
    Paul, exterminator of the Church,
    wishing I could be exterminated.
I was wrong, so terribly wrong.
But it's too late for excuses,
    too late for tears,
    too late to make amends,
    too late for anything.

Silent reflection

Slides and music
Sheep may safely graze J. S. Bach, during which Acts 9:10-19 is read

Meditation
Let's be honest, I was terrified,
    absolutely terrified.
We'd been trying to avoid him,
    hiding away for dear life
    our hearts trembling as we waited for the thud of footsteps
    that would spell the end.
So you can imagine,
    I thought I was dreaming –
    either that or off my head –
    when I felt this sudden urge to see him.
Saul! The very name sent shivers down our spines;
    avowed enemy of the Church,
    persecutor of all who followed Christ,
    determined to wipe out every last believer.
That's why he'd come to Damascus,
    to drag us back in irons,
    and he would have shown no mercy,
    we all knew that.
Yet somehow I couldn't get that voice out of my head:
    'Go and see him!'

I tried to fight it,
   told myself it was a trick of the mind,
   did my level best to think of something else,
   but it was no good;
   I knew God was calling me.
So I went,
   and I found him,
   and discovered that Jesus had found him first.
He was blind, you know,
   totally blind,
   yet he told me he had seen the light,
   that he was able to see more clearly than ever before,
   and as he spoke the tears poured down his face.
I knew what he meant, but I had my doubts at first;
   well, so would you, wouldn't you?
I thought it was a trap,
   some cunning plan to worm his way into our inner circle and catch us all.
I was waiting for him to suddenly leap up,
   eyes flashing hatred,
   ready to devour his prey.
But it didn't happen.
When I reached out and touched him,
   finally overcoming my fear,
   he looked at me for the first time,
   and there was only love.
I still remember that day so clearly.
I shall never forget the sheer terror
   as I stood outside his door,
   as I raised my hand to knock,
   as I set foot into the room and saw him.
But I shall never forget also
   that expression of his when he opened his eyes,
   the expression of a man who had found peace.
I'm so glad Jesus gave me the courage I needed.
He'd accepted Paul,
   he valued him,
   he loved him.
But he needed someone else to do the same.

Slides and music

Gloria ('Coronation' Mass) Mozart, during which Ephesians 3:7-13 is read

Meditation

It's incredible,
  quite astonishing!
To think that I, Paul,
  the man who hated Jesus and everything about him,
  should have come to love him so much.
I can still scarcely credit it.
When I look back and remember the man I used to be,
  so certain of my own righteousness,
  so determined to destroy his name,
  I wonder how I ever changed.
But I did,
  totally,
  not just in incidental details,
  not simply in outward allegiance,
  but in my heart and soul,
  right down to the very core of my being.
It's as though I'm a new person,
  created afresh in the image of my Saviour,
  my every thought and impulse different from what they used to be.
Not that I'm perfect, don't think I'm claiming that;
  I make my mistakes, all too often,
  sometimes despairing of ever being the person I would truly like to be.
Yet even then, at my lowest ebb,
  when I fail and fail again,
  I know he is with me,
  making me whole once more.
I'd have laughed at that once,
  greeted the idea with scorn
  and poured out more of my poison.
But then I met him,
  there on the Damascus road,
  and my life was turned upside down.
He called me to be an apostle,
  an ambassador in his service,
  and though I count myself the least of those who bear that name,
  it is my greatest joy
  and highest honour.
Not that it's been plain-sailing, mind you –
  I bear my scars
  and wear these chains.

And though I've done a lot, thanks to him,
　　more than I could have imagined possible –
　　building up his Church,
　　advancing his kingdom –
　　I know deep down I've barely started,
　　still so many yet to reach.
So I press on with one goal in mind –
　　to serve him more fully,
　　to love him more truly,
　　to know him more wholly,
　　until the day finally comes
　　when I shall see him
　　and know him completely,
　　face to face,
　　one to one.

Silent reflection

Slides and music

Für Elise Beethoven, during which Acts 17:22-34 is read

Meditation

He spoke with conviction, that man –
　　I'll give him that –
　　as though he totally believed what he was saying.
The arguments may have been weak sometimes,
　　not the same sophistication, the same subtlety, as our own philosophers;
　　and as an orator, to put it bluntly, I've heard better.
But he tried,
　　he really tried to get his message home,
　　more than anyone else I've ever met.
He'd done his homework too, that was clear,
　　speaking to us on our own ground in terms we would understand,
　　language we could immediately relate to.
And he wasn't just playing games,
　　out to prove some academic point or make his mark as a speaker.
You could see he was sincere,
　　desperate to get his message home.

One rarely hears that here, you know,
    here where ideas are two a penny
    and schools of thought vie together like brawling children,
    each resolved to win the day.
I've sat and listened many times
    while good and evil,
    life and death
    are toyed with in debate like a toddler's plaything –
    diverting,
    rewarding for a time,
    but then casually put aside until another day.
Not Paul though –
    he talked as one who had to speak,
    of things that burned within him,
    and when he spoke of Jesus,
    it was with eyes aflame and face aglow.
I won't say I'm convinced,
    not yet at least;
    I'll have to hear him further before I go that far.
But I'm intrigued,
    eager to find out more,
    for when he spoke of death and then of life,
    of Jesus rising from the tomb,
    he talked as one who knew,
    as one who'd seen,
    as one who had no doubts.
Well, if he's right and Jesus really is alive,
    if he spoke truth and this man really rose,
    then I want to meet him, see him for myself;
    not put my trust in another's faith
    but root it in my own.
Can it be true?
It seems impossible,
    too good for words.
Yet there's no denying it, despite what his critics may say –
    he spoke with conviction, that man,
    with a passion I have rarely heard,
    and a passion I would love to share.

Slides and music

I'm still standing Elton John, during which 2 Timothy 4:1-8 is read

Meditation

It's been hard sometimes,
   more hard than you will ever know.
I've run the race and kept the faith,
   glad to have played my part,
   but there've been times,
   all too many times,
   when I've wondered whether I could stay the course.
It's not just been the pain,
   though that's been cruel enough;
   flogged,
   stoned,
   set upon and beaten.
It's not just been the exhaustion
   though that's been crippling sometimes;
   limbs aching after yet another journey,
   mouth dry and stomach empty,
   weary to the point of death.
It's not just been the times in prison
   though they've been torment;
   deprived of freedom,
   held in chains,
   utterly alone in my cell.
They've all been costly, of course they have;
   but what's been hardest to bear,
   most difficult to endure,
   has been the bitterness,
   the sniping,
   even the hatred
   from those I counted my friends.
They've dogged my every step,
   opposed my every move,
   condemned my every success;
   not merely withholding praise
   but stirring up hostility,
   inciting persecution,
   all in the name of Christ.
It's a mystery to me for I have given so much to make him known,
   my only thought,
   my only goal,
   to share the faith and see his name be praised.
Was that so wrong? So false?

Yet still they thwart my work and do me down.
It's hurt me that, more than I can ever say,
   and often made me question whether I can carry on.
But I have, despite it all,
   and now, though you find me here in chains again,
   facing trial,
   facing death,
   I know that I shall run the race right to the very end.
For I have learned to look to Jesus and remember all that he endured,
   the pain,
   the grief,
   the loneliness,
   all for those like me who spat upon his name.
It's been hard sometimes,
   more hard than you will ever know,
   but then it was hard for him too,
   harder than for any of us.
Yet he saw it through faithfully, right to the very end.

Silent reflection

Prayer

Lord God,
   you know that life isn't always easy.
There are times when we feel exhausted,
   dismayed, frustrated, frightened, sick,
   trapped, overwhelmed, broken.
Yet as the apostle Paul understood,
   whatever we face it is nothing
   compared with what Jesus faced for us.
May that truth give us the strength to battle on,
   faithful to the last,
   in the knowledge that in life or death
   he will be sufficient for all our needs.
Amen.

Slides and music

First movement from *'Moonlight' Sonata* Beethoven

AFTERNOON SESSION

Music   First movement from *'Moonlight' Sonata* Beethoven

Prayer

Loving God,
  there are times in our lives when you call us
  to tasks that seem beyond us,
  tasks we would rather avoid.
We hear your voice
  but we do not feel up to the challenge;
  our natural inclination is to run away.
Yet if you ask us to do something
  you will give us the strength to do it.
Give us courage, then, to respond when you call,
  knowing that however things may seem
  you are always able to transform them
  in ways far beyond our expectations.

Slides and music

Allegro from *Winter (Four Seasons)* Vivaldi
during which Acts 26:1-2, 9-18, 24 is read

Meditation

He's out of his mind, that man,
  completely off his head.
I've heard a few tales in my time,
  but this one really takes the biscuit.
Jesus of Nazareth, risen from the dead,
  sending him out on his insane mission.
What does Paul take me for?
Some half-wit?
I know these Jews like to push their luck sometimes,
  but this fellow acts like I was born yesterday.
Fair enough, maybe Jesus was their long-awaited Messiah –
  I'm not qualified to dispute that –
  and maybe believing in him has changed Paul's life –
  that's his business –
  but all this rubbish about heavenly visions,
  meeting him on the road to Damascus,
  called to proclaim his message to the Gentiles –
  it's way over the top.

So what's he playing at – that's what I don't understand?
He's innocent of the charges against him – anyone can see that –
    misguided perhaps, but hardly undermining the empire.
There's no need to make up these pathetic stories.
And he's intelligent too – that's what makes it all the more puzzling;
    not your average fanatic, still less your typical villain.
He's well educated,
    well read,
    well travelled,
    well mannered.
In fact, I can't help but respect the man –
    there's something that sets him apart,
    marks him out from the rest,
    irresistibly attracts you.
Yet for all that he's off his rocker.
Too long locked up in prison perhaps,
    or too many hours spent filling his head with books.
It's a crying shame, for he could have gone far,
    really done something with his life,
    made a lasting contribution if only he hadn't become tangled up
    with those wretched Christians.
What can he see in them?
Why get involved with a bunch of nobodies,
    sacrificing health,
    money,
    even life itself,
    all for the sake of some crummy religion?
Yet he believes its been worth it;
    you only have to look at him to see that.
There's no question of going back,
    no hint of regret.
He's as passionate now,
    as committed now,
    as he's ever been.
It's a funny business,
    quite beyond me,
    but I have to admit, there's something about him,
    something about his expression when he talks of Jesus,
    that makes me wish that once,
    just once,
    I could have met Jesus for myself
        and found out what all the fuss is about.

Slides and music

O fortuna (Carmina Burana) Orff
during which Acts 25:23; 26:1, 12-19, 24-29 is read

Meditation

He won't get to me with that nonsense of his,
   I can tell you that right away.
All right, so maybe I am a Jew,
   and perhaps I do believe the prophets, in my own way,
   but that's my business, no one else's.
I've not got where I am today by bandying my religion around,
   that's for certain,
   and I've no intention of starting now.
It's hard enough being a Jew at the best of times,
   let alone getting mixed up with these Christians.
No, Paul, you can forget that;
   dig your own grave if you want to but keep me out of it!
To be honest I don't understand what he's playing at,
   why he's willing to risk everything,
   even his own life,
   for some fellow nailed to the cross years ago.
It just doesn't make sense to me.
What is it with this Jesus character that makes men lose their reason?
I've seen it happen time and again,
   sensible people with good prospects,
   so much to look forward to,
   throwing it all away on that so-called Messiah.
Why?
He must have been exceptional, I know that,
   and not just because so many chose to follow him.
I've heard the stories they tell –
   how he healed the sick,
   fed the multitude,
   raised the dead.
I've heard about his trial,
   how he stood there in silence,
   how he kept quiet as they flogged him, mocked him, killed him,
   how Pilate tried in vain to set him free, certain of his innocence.
I've heard of the empty tomb,
   how his followers claimed he was alive,
   made out they'd seen him,
   said he'd ascended into heaven.

Oh yes, I've heard all right, every little detail.
Not that I've taken much notice, of course,
    but it takes someone special for rumours like that to start about them.
'A king not of this world' — that's what he said he was.
Well, a nice thought certainly,
    a refreshing change in this greedy, grasping world;
    yet that's not the way things are, I'm afraid,
    and you have to make the best of what you're given.
If you don't help yourself, no one else will — isn't that what they say?
And look at Jesus: doesn't that just prove the point?
I've nothing against the man,
    quite admire him in fact, though keep that under your hat.
But, like I say, you have to be sensible, realistic,
    keep in with the right people if you want to survive in this world.
So I'm telling you again, he won't get to me with that nonsense of his,
    no way!
Just listen to him telling me what he thinks I believe!
The cheek of the man — I should clap him in irons for the sheer presumption!
But no need for that —
    there's only one end for Paul now and he knows it.
He's brave, you have to hand it to the fellow,
    even if he is a fool.
It's his choice: let him go the same way as his Jesus if that's what he wants;
    you'd almost think he counts the prospect an honour.
But me, no thank you — I'm looking after number one.

Silent reflection

Slides and music
Agnus Dei (Requiem) Mozart, during which 1 Corinthians 1:10-18 is read

Meditation
If he could see us now, what would he think?
It would break his heart, I'm sure of it,
    cause him as much pain, if not more, as those nails in his hands,
    that spear in his side.
How could they do this to him?
After all he said,
    all he did,
    all he tried to teach us!
I can't believe it's happening,
    that we could be so stupid.

But we can,
  and it is.
I've seen it,
  right here in Corinth;
  heard it with my own ears.
And what hurts most is that I'm involved;
  like it or not, I'm a part of it.
We're divided,
  split up into our own little factions,
  and it's happened without us even noticing it.
'I'm for Apollos,' says one;
  'I'm for Peter,'
  'I'm for Paul.'
And I know this is just the beginning,
  that there will be more –
  other leaders,
  other teachers,
  each with their own little band of followers.
What have we done?
And where do we go from here?
I'd like to say we can sort it out,
  bury our differences and get on with what really matters.
After all, we're all rooting for Christ, surely?
That's what it's all about,
  that's who we claim to follow –
  Christ crucified and risen!
Folly to some perhaps,
  nonsense to others,
  but to us the power and wisdom of God!
Yet it's not that simple, of course,
  I know that as well as any,
  for what does it actually mean –
  for me?
  for you?
  for others?
That's when the trouble starts,
  the rifts appear,
  for we're all different,
  each one of us –
  each with our own unique experiences,
  our individual way of looking at things,
  our particular quirks and foibles.

I soon found that out,
    stunned to find those I counted as brothers and sisters in Christ
    opposing my work,
    actually condemning my preaching to the Gentiles.
No, there are no easy answers,
    no magic solutions,
    and yet we have to work this thing out somehow;
    we can't just sit back and accept it,
    for I'm telling you, it would break his heart if he could see us now.
If!
What do I mean, *if?*
He *can* see it!
He *is* seeing it!
And every day it continues we carry on crucifying him —
    our divisions,
    our separation,
    pinning him to that cross in agony!

Slides and music

Love's Theme from *Midnight Express*
during which 1 Corinthians 13:1-13 is read

Meditation

He taught me the meaning of love,
    what it really means to say, 'I love you'.
Slowly,
    gently,
    he taught me.
Not through words,
    nor through gestures,
    but through showing me love in action.
I thought I'd understood,
    that I loved as much as the next man, maybe more.
Not perhaps as a husband loves his wife, or a father his children —
    there's not been time for that, sadly —
    but deeper,
    beyond such natural ties —
    my fellow apostles,
    my family in Christ,
    my fellow human beings.

And I did love in my own way, of course I did –
   my only goal,
   my single aim,
   to help them,
   serve them,
   reach them.
And yet, despite all that, I sometimes wondered if I'd ever loved at all,
   for deep down, in my heart of hearts, I knew it was all about me –
   my preaching, *my* striving, *my* loving;
   my efforts, *my* successes, *my* ambitions –
   all finally for my own satisfaction
   and even, I fear, my own glory as much as his.
It's human, I realise that, or so at least we tell ourselves,
   but is that true?
Or does it have to be?
For when I look at Jesus,
   all he did for me,
   I see a different truth,
   a different kind of love;
   patient, kind, humble;
   not serving self or seeking gain,
   but putting others first.
A love that knows me as I am,
   understands my faults,
   yet still believes in me.
A love which, though I turn away, accepts me,
   even dies for me!
That's what it means, this thing called love,
   seeing the worst, believing the best,
   asking nothing, and giving all.
I thought I'd understood, all those years ago,
   but I hadn't, hardly at all.
I'm still learning even now,
   still struggling to let go of self.
I can't do it alone,
   I've come to realise that at last;
   I need his help, his love flowing through me,
   and I'll carry on praying for that,
   striving for that,
   until my dying day,
   for I understand now that without love all else is nothing.

Prayer

Lord Jesus Christ,
   you summed up the Law in one simple word – 'love'.
Forgive us that we make the Gospel so complicated.
And forgive us that, though we talk so often about love,
   we all too rarely practise it.
Help us to look to you who showed us love in action –
   a love that bears all things, believes all things,
   hopes all things, endures all things.
And help us truly to realise that unless we have that
   then all our words, all our faith, and all our religion
   counts for nothing.
Amen.

Music   First movement from *'Moonlight' Sonata* Beethoven

Four Evangelists – One Gospel

Suggested visual material

Jesus of Nazareth 1-6
In the Beginning
Come, let us adore
The Life of Christ I-IV
Oberammergau 1990
He carries Our Cross

MORNING SESSION

Music

O thou that tellest good tidings (Messiah) Handel

Introduction

Matthew, Mark, Luke and John – four names we all recognise as the first books of the New Testament. But how much do we actually know about those Gospels? What is different about them? And why were they written? Obviously we cannot fully answer such questions on a day like this, but what we can do is get a taste of each of the Gospel writers, and in so doing perhaps glimpse a little of the distinctive nature of their message. In Matthew we hear about Old Testament prophecy fulfilled; in Mark we read the testimony of a follower of Jesus who saw first-hand at least something of his ministry, albeit from the sidelines; from Luke we receive an account based on the reminiscences of others; and from John come deep insights into the nature and purpose of Christ. Together they help us to capture a sense of the great wonder and mystery of the Gospel of Jesus Christ.

Prayer

Loving God,
    you have given us Good News,
    the Gospel of Jesus Christ.
And you have given us that news
    not simply through one person
    but through four,
    each in their own way testifying
    to what Jesus meant for them.

Loving God,
We come today to consider something of their stories,
  recognising that the Gospel writers
  were individuals like each of us,
  with their own needs, their own concerns,
  their own backgrounds, their own experiences.
Yet though they present their message
  in different ways,
  each one has something to say to us,
  something unique to contribute
  to our own journey of faith.
Speak to us through their testimony,
  so that we in turn may speak to others.
Amen.

Slides and music

Largo from *Spring (Four Seasons)* Vivaldi, during which Luke 1:1-4 is read

Meditation of Luke

I never knew him myself,
  not in the way the others did.
And yet I felt I had, such was the way Peter talked about him.
He was obviously quite a person, Jesus; that much is clear.
You can't make that sort of impression without being a bit special.
We used to sit, Peter and I, talking deep into the night,
  and as he spoke his face would come alive with pleasure.
He had so many memories –
  the day Jesus first called him, right out of the blue,
  the way he had healed the sick,
  cured the insane,
  fed the multitude,
  stilled the storm.
And then, of course, that final meal,
  the scene in the garden,
  the agony on the cross,
  the empty tomb.
So much to share, good and bad.
I was spellbound,
  completely hooked.
It wasn't just what he said
  but the way he said it.

He meant every word!
It was real for him,
   vital,
   as much good news after all that time as when it had first happened.
Not that he pulled any punches.
There was no glossing over the awkward episodes,
   no pretending it had all been easy.
He told me how he'd recognised Jesus was the Messiah,
   but also how he'd failed to understand what that meant.
He told me about the moment on the mountain top,
   but also that moment when the cock crowed.
He told me how he'd knelt at Jesus' feet,
   but how he refused to let Jesus kneel at his.
He knew he wasn't perfect,
   realised full well he still had much to learn,
   but he'd been changed for all that;
   through Jesus become a new man.
I wish I could have known Jesus like he did,
   heard him, seen him, met him for myself.
But, like I say, I never did.
Yet I do know him,
   personally,
   as my closest friend,
   and not just through what Peter said.
That was important, of course it was;
   it started there –
   my interest captured,
   my imagination aroused –
   but it's moved on since then,
   though I can't explain it.
I know it must sound crazy
   but I feel him with me day by day,
   I know he's always there by my side,
   I hear his voice,
   I see his hand,
   I experience his presence,
   and I honestly feel I know him as much as anyone could ever have done.

Slides and music

Comfort ye my people (Messiah) Handel
during which Matthew 2:1-6 is read

Meditation of Matthew

'It has been written.'
How often have I heard those words?
On the mouth of priest, rabbi, and Pharisee –
    time and time again, the same old refrain:
    'It has been written.'
And it's true of course.
It's there in black and white, just as they say;
    God's word to his people for us all to see –
    the sacred words of the Law,
    given to our fathers by God himself,
    spelling out his commandments.
The history of our people,
    the wisdom of the Teacher,
    the poetry of the psalms,
    the visions of the prophets,
    all that, and so much more,
    God's word to us!
Yes, it's there all right,
    but though I've always believed that,
    somehow it has never really touched me,
    not deep down in my heart where it matters.
I've accepted it, yes,
    but the words have never spoken to me in quite the way I hoped.
Now, though, it's different –
    astonishingly, incredibly, different –
    for I have only to think of Jesus to find myself saying,
    'It has been written!'
Why?
Well just listen to this.
    'You, Bethlehem, are by no means least among the rulers of Judah,
        for from you shall come a ruler
        who is to shepherd my people Israel.'
    'The virgin shall conceive and bear a son,
        and they shall name him Emmanuel.'
    'The people who sat in darkness have seen a great light,
        and for those who dwelt in the region and shadow of death
        light has dawned.'
    'For a child has been born for us,
        a son given to us;
        authority rests upon his shoulders;
        and he is named

Wonderful Counsellor,
Mighty God,
Everlasting Father,
Prince of Peace.'
Need I go on?
I don't think so.
It's all there in the prophets,
  foreshadowed in the Law,
  foretold from the very beginning.
And it happened –
  the prophecies fulfilled in a way I never for a moment expected,
  brought to life in Jesus Christ.
And now when I read the Scriptures
  I do not simply see words on a page;
  I see the Word made flesh,
  the one who alone makes sense of it all,
  God with us –
  'It has been written!'

Slides and music

Glory to God (Messiah) Handel, during which John 1:1-5, 9; 1:14, 18 is read

Meditation of John

There's only one word for it,
  one word that gets anywhere near the truth,
  that sums up the wonder of it all,
  and that's 'Jesus'.
Trust me, I know,
  for I've spent a lifetime trying to find the right words.
Since I followed Jesus all those years ago,
  since I sat with the apostles in that upper room,
  since we went out teaching and preaching in the Master's name,
  I've been looking for ways in which to describe my experience,
  and I've used words,
  masses of them,
  more than I can begin to count . . .
When I stood and preached to the multitudes,
  when I nurtured believers in their new-found faith,
  when I prayed for the sick,
  when I led times of worship,
  when I reminisced with friends,

when I witnessed to strangers,
    words, words, words.
But they've never been sufficient,
    never begun to express what I really want to say.
And now more than ever I find that's true,
    sitting here trying to record the good news
    as revealed to me.
I've written so much,
    page after page,
    my own words and his,
    woven together as best I can
    into a tapestry of his life.
I've told of the beginnings and the ends,
    of his signs,
    of his teaching,
    of his actions.
I've spoken of those lesser-known characters,
    the ones Matthew, Mark and Luke missed out,
    and I've given details of those private moments,
    when it was just us and Jesus together
    as the end drew near.
I've tried,
    I've really tried to get it across,
    to tell you what Jesus meant to me and to so many others.
But there's so much more I could still write,
    so much I've had to leave out.
I could go on to the end of time
    and still not do justice to all I want to tell you.
That's why I say there's only one word,
    one word that says it all,
    because Jesus was the fulfilment,
    the embodiment,
    the personification of God's word.
The Law and the Prophets spoke of him.
The wisdom of the teachers spoke of him.
The universe in all its glory speaks of him.
And if you want to listen,
    if you want to hear,
    if you want to understand what life is all about,
    then take my word for it,
    the only way is to know him for yourself,
    the word made flesh!

Silent reflection

Slides and music

Slow movement from *Pathetique Sonata* Beethoven
during which Matthew 9:9-13 is read

Meditation of Matthew

He had time for me,
    incredible, I know, but true.
He saw beneath the surface,
    beneath the greed, the selfishness and the corruption,
    and uncovered a person I didn't even know existed.
I groaned when I saw him coming, I won't pretend otherwise;
    another self-righteous prig coming to tell me my business,
    that's what I imagined.
And I'd had my fair share of those –
    well, nobody likes a tax collector, do they?
But I'd always given as good as I got.
I mean, it's not easy when you've a wife and kids at home to feed –
    we all have to earn a living somehow –
    and since the only people ready to give me a chance were the Romans
    what could I do?
Or did any of them really imagine I enjoyed working for them?
Anyway, someone had to do it, didn't they, so why not me?
I suppose Jesus understood that, for he didn't criticise or condemn –
    none of the two-faced hypocrisy of the Pharisees,
    none of the usual accusing glances or obscene gestures –
    just those two lovely words:
    'Follow me.'
You could have knocked me over.
It was the last thing I expected,
    took the wind right out of my sails.
But more than that I was excited,
    moved,
    fascinated,
    because he had time for me.
He hadn't written me off,
    he hadn't seen only the outside –
    he accepted me as I was,
    with all my sin sticking to me.
And the funny thing was, once he did that
    it was me who pointed to my faults,
    not him.

I felt ashamed,
   painfully aware of all that was wrong,
   longing to be different;
   yet at the same time set free,
   forgiven,
   offered a new beginning.
I followed, of course,
What else could I do?
Would you refuse a man like that?
Well, perhaps you would, but I'm glad I didn't,
   because despite everything since –
   the times I've let him down,
   the occasions I've misunderstood,
   the mistakes I've made,
   the faults I still have –
   he goes on accepting me day after day,
   not for what I might become,
   but for what I am!

Slides and music

And the glory of the Lord (Messiah) Handel
during which Mark 9:2-3 is read

Meditation of John

It was fantastic,
   extraordinary,
   mind-blowing;
   a once-in-a-lifetime experience,
   and I was lucky enough to be there –
   me, and Peter and James up on the mountain with Jesus.
We knew something was going to happen;
   we could see it from his manner when he asked us to join him,
   but we never dreamt of anything like that.
He seemed to change before our eyes,
   his clothes to glow,
   his face to shine.
And then – would you believe it –
   who did we see with him but Moses and Elijah!
Clear as day they were,
   chatting together like old friends.
We were struck dumb for a moment,
   lost for words,

and then dear old Peter got stuck in as usual.
'Can I do something?' he blurted out,
   'You will stay, won't you?'
And why not?
I mean, we were all enjoying ourselves,
   didn't want the moment to end,
   almost too good to be true!
But strangely, as soon as Peter finished speaking,
   the spell seemed to break.
The sky darkened as clouds came over
   and then, as a peal of thunder broke the silence,
   Moses and Elijah disappeared,
   leaving Jesus standing there alone,
   looking just as he always had,
   as ordinary as you or me.
Did we imagine it?
We've often asked ourselves that.
Or was it a vision,
   brought on perhaps by the heat
   or the altitude,
   or simply having one too many before we set off?
It must have been something like that, surely?
There's no other logical explanation.
Yet it's funny how we all saw the same thing,
   all down to the last detail.
I don't know what to make of it,
   but I wouldn't have missed it for the world.
It helped me understand what Peter had already begun to grasp,
   that Jesus was the Messiah,
   the answer to all our prayers,
   the fulfilment of the Law and the Prophets.
It was just a glimpse,
   a moment's wonderful insight
   which I thought at the time could never be repeated.
And that was true in a sense,
   for no one will ever witness quite what we saw in the way we saw it.
But we have all seen his glory now,
   not just the three of us,
   but Thomas, Andrew, Mary, Matthew, and so many others –
   the glory of the Father revealed in him.
We see it day after day after day,
   full of grace and truth,

And, believe me, that too is fantastic,
  extraordinary,
  unforgettable!

Silent reflection

Slides and music
Meditation Massenet, during which Matthew 26:17-20 is read

Meditation of Matthew

We were there to celebrate Passover,
  the twelve of us and Jesus, together in the upper room.
And I don't mind telling you
  our hearts were pounding,
  our pulses racing,
  our imaginations running riot.
I mean, the Passover!
You know the significance of that, surely?
A reminder of God delivering his people,
  setting them free from captivity,
  opening the way to a new and different life.
Well, what were we to expect?
Oh, it's easy now, looking back, to realise we were wrong,
  but at the time it seemed to all of us,
  all except Judas anyway,
  that this was it,
  the moment we'd been waiting for,
  the time when Jesus would pull the rabbit out of the hat,
  turn the tables on his enemies,
  show us he was in control after all.
Only then, whilst we were eating together,
  enjoying ourselves more than we had in a long time,
  he stood,
  quietly,
  solemnly,
  and we could see from the look in his eyes,
  the set of his face,
  that he had other ideas.
He took the bread,
  lifted it high,
  then broke it –

enough for all of us –
'This is my body, broken for you; do this in remembrance of me.'
And before we had time to argue,
    time even to take in what he was saying,
    he was holding the cup,
    passing it round –
'Take this and drink. This cup is the new covenant sealed in my blood.'
We were staggered,
    horrified,
    and to tell the truth more than a little shocked.
All right, so he'd talked of death before,
    often,
    too often,
    but we'd never actually believed it.
We thought he was exaggerating, I suppose,
    painting the blackest picture to keep us on our toes.
But here he was, if we'd heard him right, offering his own epitaph,
    saying his final farewells,
    preparing us for the end.
And he was of course, in a sense;
    it was the end of a chapter,
    the last page of the book.
Yet it wasn't over,
    by no means the end of the story;
    that had only just begun,
    and we, astonishingly, were part of it –
    his body, here on earth,
    the sequel to what he had started!
Well, we've done as he said,
    week after week,
    year after year,
    breaking bread and sharing wine,
    reminding ourselves of who he is and who we are,
    of what he has done and what we have still to do;
    and we'll go on sharing his supper,
    gladly,
    humbly,
    confidently,
    until he comes.

Silent reflection

Prayer

Lord Jesus Christ,
  we were not there at the stable like the shepherds;
  we were not one of the twelve you chose
  as your apostles;
  we were not able to see you heal the sick;
  we were not there as you broke bread
  in the upper room,
  as they pressed the crown of thorns on your head,
  as you suffered on the cross,
  as you appeared to the disciples
  following your resurrection,
  as you ascended into heaven.
Yet we can know you
  as much as any who were there,
  for you are with us now, with us always,
  here by our sides.
Lord Jesus Christ,
  we thank you for the daily reality
  of your living presence.
Amen.

Music   *He was despised (Messiah)* Handel

AFTERNOON SESSION

Music   Theme from *Symphony No 1* Elgar

Prayer

Gracious God,
  we thank you for the gift of words
  through which we are able to express so much.
We thank you for the words of Scripture
  that speak so powerfully of your love.
But most of all we thank you
  for putting your words in action,
  making them come alive in the person of Jesus.
Help us in our turn not simply to use words
  but to act upon them,
  not just to talk about faith
  but to live it day by day.
Amen.

Slides and music

Rhapsody on a theme of Paganini Rachmaninov
during which John 17:1, 6-17 is read

Meditation of John

We were there in the upper room,
   just us and Jesus,
   the night drawing in,
   the end drawing near.
We knew it,
   he knew it.
There could be no doubt any more, not for any of us;
   no question of a last-minute reprieve.
We'd seen Judas sneaking out, darkness in his eyes,
   and we knew it wouldn't be long before the vultures descended,
   hungry to devour their prey.
We wanted him to run for it;
   back to Nazareth,
   back to Galilee,
   back to the safety of the wilderness,
   anywhere but there in Jerusalem.
But he wouldn't listen, of course,
   wouldn't even consider it.
So we stayed with him,
   nervous,
   fearful,
   one eye over our shoulders, but determined to do our best for him.
He was under no illusions;
   he knew full well what was coming –
   an ugly, agonising death.
And it was getting to him,
   eating away inside,
   that much we could all see.
When he broke bread, he was trembling,
   clearly petrified about what lay ahead;
   and as he shared the wine, there was a sob in his voice,
   a tear in his eye.
Yet then he spoke,
   softly,
   gently,
   almost as if in a dream,
   and we realised he was praying –

not for himself,
  but for us!
Not for his own life,
  but for the life of the world!
Yes, I know that sounds hard to believe, but it's true, honestly.
I was there, remember;
  I heard him.
It wasn't his death that was troubling him,
  it was the fear that we wouldn't stay together,
  that somehow we'd become divided,
  even end up fighting among ourselves.
God knows why he thought that,
  but you could see how worried he was,
  how much our unity meant to him.
It was his dying wish in a way,
  his last request –
  that we should stay together:
  one people,
  one faith,
  one God.
I'm sure he needn't have worried, least of all at a time like that.
All right, so we've had our differences since then, I admit it –
  we don't always see things the same way,
  and maybe once in a while we might even have fallen out –
  but I honestly can't imagine anything major coming between us, can you,
  not in the long run?
After all, we're his disciples, aren't we, each one of us?
All called by him,
  all confessing the same Lord,
  and what could ever be more important than that?

Slides and music

Nimrod (Enigma Variations) Elgar, during which Matthew 26:36-46 is read

Meditation of Matthew

He was scared, that much is certain.
I've never seen him like it before.
He'd always seemed so sure,
  so confident,
  so at ease with himself,
  even when he talked about death
  and he'd done that often enough.

I really thought it didn't worry him, the way he'd spoken,
    but this time it was different,
    so different.
We'd just finished supper,
    and he'd seemed strangely preoccupied throughout,
    so we weren't surprised when he suggested going out for a little air –
    a stroll to clear our heads, that's what we expected.
But then he asked us to pray for him,
    and off he went alone into the darkness.
Gone for ages it seemed,
    and when he came back you should have seen him.
Shaking like a leaf he was,
    eyes wide with fear,
    sweating buckets,
    a right old state.
We were shocked, I can tell you.
It made us nervous just to look at him.
And the tone of voice he used with us,
    just because we'd dozed off for a few minutes.
I know he was hurt, but I ask you, it was past midnight!
Three times he went off,
    and each time he came back the same –
    terrified.
He was scared, make no mistake.
It wasn't as easy as we all thought.
Not easy at all.

Slides and music

Violin Romance No 2 in F major Beethoven
during which Mark 14:50-52 is read

Meditation of Mark

Was that really me, all those years ago,
    running naked from the garden?
I've heard the story so many times;
    how they'd been with Jesus sharing the Last Supper,
    how they broke bread and drunk wine,
    how they followed him into the garden, and fell asleep,
    how Judas betrayed him with a kiss –
    yes, I'd heard it all, and shed tears with the best of them.
But it's that young man who always fascinated me –
    the one they so nearly collared,

so nearly dragged with Jesus before Caiaphas –
because that was me.
I'd been there all evening, hoping to catch sight of the Master,
   hiding quietly in the bushes,
  and when he came out my heart leapt.
He was there, alone,
   just a few yards away,
   the rest of his disciples waiting at a distance,
   and he so near I could almost touch him,
   so close I could hear his every word.
But delight turned to horror as the soldiers arrived,
   dark figures silhouetted against the flames of their torches,
   like demons emerging out of hell.
I was paralysed with fear,
   realising I too was in danger.
And eventually it was too much for me.
I broke cover and ran for it,
   heard the shouts,
   felt their hands grasp my clothing,
   but kept on running, desperate to get away.
And somehow I made it, running naked and tearful into my mother's arms.
It's a long time ago now, of course,
   many years,
   yet do you know what?
Nobody knows that boy was me;
   it's been my guilty secret all this while,
   my skeleton in the cupboard,
   the ghost which I've never had the courage to exorcise.
I should have told them, had done with it like Peter did,
   but he had no choice did he?
That's the difference – they knew about *him*,
   he couldn't hide.
My failure was unknown to anyone but myself,
   and as the time went by I wanted to keep it that way.
It's become harder to tell, harder to face,
   and so much easier to keep locked away.
Yet it's not been easy, not really,
   for it's always there,
   my secret shame, my private pain.
They trust me now, that's the trouble,
   respect me, look to me for guidance and leadership,
   but I can't help asking myself, 'What if they knew? What then?'

Yet Jesus knows, and he's accepted me all this time.
It's no good: I have to tell them,
  for until I'm honest with others I'm not being honest with him
  or myself.

Slides and music

Behold the lamb of God (Messiah) Handel
during which Mark 15:22-26, 33-34 is read

Meditation of Mark

He was groaning,
  a sound like I'd never heard before,
  a sound I never want to hear again –
  awful,
  stomach-churning,
  indescribable –
  the sound of unimaginable pain,
  of overwhelming sorrow,
  of utter isolation.
And I could watch it no longer.
I thought I was ready for it,
  prepared for the worst,
  for I knew he had to die.
But I wasn't ready,
  not for this;
  I never realised people could suffer so much,
  that anything could be quite so terrible.
But I know now,
  and I'm telling you straight,
  I'd have felt sorry for anyone facing that –
  a robber,
  a mugger,
  even a murderer!
My heart would still have bled for them.
But to see Jesus there,
  a man of such gentleness and compassion,
  a man who had always loved and never hated,
  a man who had brought healing to the sick
  and wholeness to the broken,
  it all but finished me.
What had he done to deserve this?

What crime had he committed?
What was it about him that aroused such passion,
   such devotion,
   yet such loathing?
I prayed that God would finish it,
   put him out of his misery,
   but still the torment continued,
   still they mocked him, delighting in his pain.
I knew he was suffering, but even then didn't realise how much,
   not until he lifted his head and I saw the despair in his eyes,
   not until he spoke and I heard the wretchedness in his voice:
   'My God, my God, why have you forsaken me?'
Then I realised,
   and my blood ran cold.
He felt alone,
   totally alone,
   abandoned by everyone he'd loved and trusted,
   even by God himself.
He could cope with the rest –
   he'd even expected it –
   but God?
It was the final torture,
   the ultimate agony,
   a pain beyond words.
He was groaning, a sound like I'd never heard before,
   a sound which suddenly I understood,
   and a sound I could listen to no longer.

Slides and music

Valse Brilliante in E flat major Chopin, during which Acts 4:1-3 is read

Meditation of John

We just can't help ourselves.
I know that sounds foolish,
   that we're risking our lives carrying on,
   that we'd be better off keeping our heads down;
   but it's no good,
   we have to speak,
   have to tell what God has done for us.
It's not that we're looking for trouble,
   don't think that;
   we value our lives as much as anyone.

It's not that we want to make a name for ourselves;
   believe me we'd both be happier out of the limelight.
And it's not that we're simply full of our own ideas,
   too self-opinionated to know when to keep quiet.
At least I don't think that's true, though we may be wrong.
No, the fact is we have no choice.
Despite ourselves,
   against our better judgement,
   we find the words just keep on coming.
When we're there in the synagogue listening to the Scriptures
   we have to tell what it means.
When we're out in the market-place, the crowds thronging about us,
   we have to share the Good News.
When the lame come for healing,
   the poor for help,
   the lonely for friendship,
   the lost for guidance,
   we have to speak of the faith we have found in Jesus,
   the way, the truth, and the life we have discovered through him.
Honestly, we've no interest in banging our own drum,
   no desire to get up on our soap-box;
   we simply have to testify to everything he's done for us,
   and everything he can do for them.
That's why we're here today waiting to appear before the Council,
   back in hot water once again and about to get another roasting.
We don't enjoy it – of course we don't –
   in fact we're terrified,
   paranoid about what they might do to us,
   unable to forget what happened to Jesus.
Oh no, we're under no illusions;
   we know full well what the cost might be
   and the prospect makes us sick with fear.
They've been lenient so far but they won't keep on the kid-gloves for ever.
Yet it makes no difference –
   we have to speak of what we've seen and heard.
How can we do anything less when Jesus did so much for us?
It's our duty,
   our privilege,
   our responsibility,
   the very least we owe to him,
   the very least we owe to them.

Don't get us wrong;
  we're not going to stick our necks out for the sake of it,
  but when God gives us the words to speak
  we simply can't keep silent.

Silent reflection

Slides and music

But who may abide? (Messiah) Handel
during which Matthew 25:31-33 is read

Meditation of Matthew

He told us he would come again,
  that as he had departed so he would return.
And we believed him,
  totally,
  without reserve or hesitation.
It was what kept us going, that promise,
  the one thing that gave us strength to battle on through thick and thin.
Yet sometimes,
  just occasionally,
  I catch myself wondering whether we should look forward;
  whether it will all be so cosy,
  so comfortable,
  as we sometimes seem to imagine.
You see, I can't help remembering those words of his,
  about the sheep and the goats,
  about the final judgement –
  so simple,
  so straightforward,
  yet so chilling in their implications:
  'I was hungry, and you fed me,
  Thirsty, and you gave me a drink,
  A stranger and you welcomed me,
  Naked, sick, imprisoned, and you were there to help.'
That's what he said –
  through serving these,
  even the very least of them,
  you serve me.
It sounds good, doesn't it?

The sort of message we like to hear.
Yet sometimes those words disturb me,
   for I can't help asking, 'Which am I?'
Oh, I know which I'd like to be, stands to reason!
And I know which I should be, all too well.
But if I'm honest,
   really truthful with myself,
   I fear I'm more often a goat than a sheep.
I saw the plight of the hungry,
   but it was me I worried about feeding.
I heard the cry of the thirsty,
   but it was my own need I satisfied.
I spotted the loneliness of the stranger,
   but wasn't sure I could trust them.
I was told about the naked,
   but it was I who got the new clothes.
I glimpsed the despair of the sick,
   but was afraid to risk infection.
I knew some were denied their freedom,
   but was reluctant to get involved.
Not now, I told them;
   next time I'll do something,
   next time I'll help –
   God will understand.
But will he, that's the question?
I've been good at talking,
   good at preaching,
   good at praying,
   and in faithfulness at worship I have few peers.
Yet when I recall those words of Jesus
   and measure them against his life,
   sometimes I find myself almost hoping he doesn't come back,
   for if he does and judgement comes,
   even though I've called him Lord,
   it may be me at whom he points the finger,
   and me he says he never even knew.

Slides and music

Ode to Joy from *Symphony No 9* Beethoven
during which John 1:1-5, 9-14, 16-18 is read

Meditation of John

He lived among us,
   flesh and blood like you and me,
   walking our earth,
   sharing our humanity,
   fully part of this bruised and battered world of ours.
He knew our joys
   and felt our sorrows,
   shared our laughter,
   shed our tears.
Have you thought about that –
   ever really stopped to consider what it means?
The Word of God,
   creator of the universe,
   beginning and end of all,
   here among us –
   weak,
   frail,
   vulnerable –
   God not just telling us about love
   but showing us!
I didn't realise it, I must confess,
   not in all those three years I followed him, memorable though they were.
He was just a man – that's the way I saw it –
   and I'd followed him expecting nothing more –
   attracted by his teaching, sure,
   spellbound by his charisma,
   but it was always him down here
   and God out there –
   distant,
   remote,
   far off.
I was looking to Jesus for guidance, that's all;
   some way to bridge the gap,
   make God seem closer.
And he did too,
   day after day bringing faith to life in a way I'd never thought possible.
But the thing that's surprised me,
   made me think again about this man I followed,
   is that he's still doing it,
   after all this time,
   as much as he ever was!

Every moment I learn something more,
   every second God becomes more real –
   so much that he's a part of me and I of him.
It's been a long job, but slowly,
   piece by piece,
   the jigsaw has come together,
   the penny dropped,
   the truth sunk home.
'He who has seen me,' he told us, 'has seen the Father.
   The Father and I are one.'
I understand now,
   at long last I do see!
And I marvel,
   a shiver of wonder running up my spine,
   for I realise that in Jesus of Nazareth –
   the child born in the manger,
   the man who walked among us,
   the one who continues to change my life –
   God himself has met me,
   the Word made flesh!

Slides and music

Rex Tremendae (Requiem) Mozart, during which Revelation 21:1-4 is read

Meditation of John

One day we'll see him again.
Don't ask me when,
   don't ask me how,
   but one day
   when all this struggle is over –
   all the pain,
   all the grief,
   all the fear,
   all the doubt –
   then he will return to establish his kingdom.
I know that's hard to believe sometimes.
When you keep on battling against the odds and nothing seems to change,
   when you stand up for what is good yet evil seems to triumph,
   when love is met with hatred,
   gentleness with violence,
   truth with falsehood –
   of course you start to wonder.

When you're faced with suffering,
   sickness,
   death;
   when greed and corruption are rewarded with plenty
   and justice is trampled underfoot;
   when the poor get poorer
   and the world goes by uncaring –
   it's impossible not to ask yourself, day after day,
   why's it allowed to happen?
But he will come, I'm certain of it –
   not just because he promised to,
   though that's important, of course;
   not simply because he came back before,
   cheating death of its victory,
   triumphing over the grave,
   though that's more vital still;
   but because he *has* to return if anything is finally to make sense,
   if faith is to be anything more than a grand delusion.
And it *is* more;
   it *has* to be.
These goals we strive towards,
   this life revealed in Christ,
   the promises he made,
   the truths he taught,
   everything he lived and died for –
   they're real, I know that,
   for they have turned my life around,
   sustained me through my darkest moments,
   lifted me beyond my highest thoughts,
   and given me a joy that knows no bounds.
So though now we see but do not understand,
   though faith is sometimes hard and Christ seems far away,
   we'll hold fast to hope,
   waiting for a time when there will be an end to tears and pain and death,
   a time when God will live among his people
   in a new and beautiful kingdom;
   and we shall see him again, our Lord Jesus Christ,
   crowned in glory and splendour,
   King of kings,
   Lord of lords,
   all in all,
   yet one with us!

Reading

Revelation 22:1-5, 20

Then the angel showed me the river of the water of life, bright as crystal, flowing from the throne of God and of the Lamb through the middle of the street of the city. On either side of the river is the tree of life with its twelve kinds of fruit, producing its fruit each month; and the leaves of the tree are for the healing of the nations. Nothing accursed will be found there any more. But the throne of God and of the Lamb will be in it, and his servants will worship him; they will see his face, and his name will be on their foreheads. And there will be no more night; they need no light of lamp or sun, for the Lord God will be their light, and they will reign for ever and ever.

The one who testifies to these things says, 'Surely I am coming soon.'
Amen. Come, Lord Jesus!

Silent reflection

Blessing

Gracious God,
  we thank you for the gift of words
  through which we are able to express so much.
We thank you for the words of Scripture
  that speak so powerfully of your love.
But most of all we thank you
  for putting your words in action,
  making them come alive in the person of Jesus.
Help us in our turn not simply to use words
  but to act upon them,
  not just to talk about faith
  but to live it day by day.

Music   *For unto us a child is born (Messiah)* Handel

New Beginnings

Suggested visual material	Jesus of Nazareth 2, 3, 4, 5 and 6 The Life of Christ IV St Paul The Story of Saint Paul In the Beginning

MORNING SESSION

Music	*Since by man came death (Messiah)* Handel
Introduction	How often have you wished you could have another go at something? When an opportunity is missed or a chance wasted there is nothing we would like more than to turn the clock back and have another bite of the cherry. Sadly, of course, that is impossible. We may, on occasions, be allowed a second crack at what we failed to capitalise on first time round, but the legacy of the past will always in some way be with us. Except, that is, when it comes to Christ, for in him the offer is always there of a fresh start, a clean break, a new beginning. That is a truth we see time and again throughout the Gospels, lives which had apparently come to the end of the road, people who had come to the end of their tether, suddenly finding a new chapter opening up before them full of promise. Whatever had happened before, it was over and done with, its power to tie them down broken for ever! Here in a nutshell is the good news of Jesus Christ, and it is that which we shall be exploring today through the experience of some of those who were touched by his ministry. But we start at perhaps the greatest new beginning of all – the birth of Jesus Christ, the Word made flesh, and the birth of life itself at the dawn of time which that same Word brought into being.

Prayer

Loving God,
    we thank you for this new day,
    rich with opportunity,
    full of promise.
Speak to us through it of the newness of life
    you offer through Jesus Christ –
    how, through him,
    you are able to take any moment,
    any situation,
    any person,
    and give the opportunity to begin again.
Keep us looking to the future with confidence,
    and so help us to greet this and every day
    with a sense of anticipation,
    inspired by the knowledge of your love,
    and the assurance of your renewing power;
    through Jesus Christ our Lord.
Amen.

Slides and music

Gloria (Missa Ouer natus est nobis) Tallis
during which John 1:1-5, 10-14 is read

Meditation of John

'Where did it all start?' they ask me.
'Tell us the story again.'
And I know just what they want to hear –
    about the inn and the stable,
    the baby lying in a manger,
    shepherds out in the fields by night,
    and wise men travelling from afar.
I know why they ask, of course I do,
    for which of us hasn't thrilled to those marvellous events,
    that astonishing day when the Word became flesh,
    dwelling here on earth amongst us?
Yet wonderful though that all is, it's not where it started,
    and if we stop there, then we see only a fraction of the picture,
    the merest glimpse of everything God has done for us in Christ.
We have got to go right back to see more –
    before Bethlehem,

before the prophets
before the Law,
before time itself, would you believe? –
for that's where it started:
literally 'in the beginning'.
Yes, even there the saving purpose of God was at work,
his creating, redeeming Word
bringing light and love into the world,
shaping not just the heavens and the earth
but the lives of all,
every man, woman and child.
That's the mind-boggling wonder of it –
the fact not just that God made us,
but that through Christ he was determined from the outset
to share our lives,
to take on our flesh,
to identify himself totally with the joys and sorrows,
the beauty and the ugliness of humankind.
It defies belief, doesn't it?
Yet it's true –
God wanting us to know him not as his creatures
but as his children,
not as puppets forced to dance to his tune
but as people responding freely to his love,
and to achieve that he patiently and painstakingly prepared the way,
revealing year after year a little more of his purpose,
a glimpse more of his kingdom,
until at last,
in the fullness of time,
the Word became flesh and lived among us,
full of grace and truth.
It wasn't an afterthought, the incarnation,
a last-ditch attempt to make the best of a bad job –
it was planned from the dawn of time.
So next time you hear the story of the stable and the manger,
of the shepherds gazing in wonder
and the magi kneeling in homage,
stop for a moment
and reflect on everything which made it all possible,
the eternal purpose which so carefully prepared the way of Christ,
and then ask yourself this:
are you prepared to respond to his coming?

Prayer

Gracious God,
   despite our repeated disobedience
   your love continues undiminished,
   reaching out to us every moment of every day.
Despite the rejection of the world
   still you go on seeking to draw it to yourself,
   until every broken relationship with you is mended.
So it is now and so it has always been,
   from the beginning of time your nature always to have mercy.
Help us to appreciate the enormity of your faithfulness,
   and to use this season of Advent
   to open our hearts more fully to your grace;
   through Jesus Christ our Lord.
Amen.

Silence

Slides and music

El Rorro Traditional Mexican Carol, during which Luke 2:1-7 is read

Meditation of Mary, mother of Jesus

He looked so tiny lying there,
   so vulnerable –
   like a little china doll,
   like thistledown swaying in the breeze –
   and I wanted simply to hold him in my arms
   and protect him from the world outside.
Could this be God's Son, I asked,
   the one destined to be great,
   the Prince of Peace,
   a ruler over Israel?
Surely not!
It had been hard enough to believe at the start,
   when the angel first broke the news –
   to think that I, Mary, had been chosen above all others,
   singled out to bear in my womb the Messiah –
   but now, as I gazed down into the manger,
   and saw those little arms waving,
   that sweet innocent face wrinkled up in sleep,

and those eyes so tightly shut,
   it seemed doubly impossible,
   out of the question,
   a foolish fancy of my fevered imagination.
Be sensible, I told myself,
   there's no way God could take such a gamble,
   no possibility, if the fate of the world truly hung in the balance,
   that he would stake it all on a helpless child,
   least of all one born where we found ourselves –
   a stable of all places!
And, as if to prove the point, that very moment Jesus awoke,
   tears filling his eyes,
   a scream of protest on his lips,
   and I realised he was hungry,
   well past his usual feed.
It dawned on me then, the staggering implications –
   he needed me, this child,
   not just for food, or warmth, or protection,
   but for everything,
   his very future in my hands.
Would God allow that?
Could he ever need *us* as much as *we* need him?
No, there had to be some mistake –
   it just couldn't be, could it?
Could it?

Prayer

Gracious God,
   you came to our world in fulfilment of your promises of old,
   your word embodied in a child lying in a manger.
You loved us so much
   that you staked everything
   to break down the barriers that keep us from you.
You shared our humanity from birth to death,
   so that with you we might share your eternity,
   life in all its fullness.
You became God with us,
   so that we might become one with *you*.
Teach us that, as you needed Mary's response then,
   you need *our* response now;
   our willingness to accept your mercy
   and experience the blessings you so long to give us.

Come again now and be born in our hearts,
    so that we may truly love you
    and joyfully serve you, this and every day;
    through Jesus Christ our Lord.
Amen.

Silence

Slides and music

Come to me (Fountain of Life) Rizza
during which Mark 5:21-24, 35-43 is read

Meditation of Jairus

I can't tell you how awful it was,
    how devastated I felt
    when my servants burst through the crowd to break the news.
There was no need for them to speak;
    one look at their faces said it all –
    she was dead,
    my beautiful, precious daughter lost to me for ever –
    and it was as though my whole world fell apart in that moment.
I'd dared to hope, you see;
    I'd actually believed that this man Jesus
    might yet save her where all others had failed,
    and when he agreed to come, my heart had missed a beat,
    skipping in anticipation
    at the promise of that awful cloud lifting at last.
But I knew now it was all over –
    and, quite simply, I was overcome,
    nothing and no one seeming to matter any more;
    not even Jesus.
To be honest I'd forgotten he was still there,
    his presence past significance beside the intensity of my grief –
    until suddenly I heard his voice,
    felt his hand upon my shoulder,
    and I realised *he'd* not forgotten *me*,
    his concern anything but at an end.
'Do not fear,' he told me, 'only believe.'
As simple as that –
    no embellishment,

no explanation,
   just that quiet, unruffled instruction.
Well, I didn't know what to think!
Hadn't the man been listening?
My daughter was dead,
   all hope extinguished,
   nothing now anyone could do, not even him.
Yet there was something about his presence
   which made it impossible to argue,
   so we walked on together,
   and, to be truthful, I was glad of his company –
   the calmness,
   the peace,
   and the sense of purpose which radiated from him,
   somehow giving solace in my hour of despair.
He'd discover what had happened soon enough,
   and, who could tell, maybe even then
   he might have some crumb of comfort to offer.
But when we got back home –
   the family sobbing their hearts out,
   my wife just about inconsolable –
   then, as if I didn't have enough on my plate,
   his attitude really began to trouble me,
   for he carried on as if nothing had happened,
   as if it were all fussing over a storm in a teacup.
'Why all the commotion?' he asked, 'She's only sleeping.'
Sleeping!
I could hardly believe my ears!
What was wrong with the fellow?
Could he really not see it, even now?
Little wonder the neighbours laughed at him.
Yet somehow I didn't have the heart to argue –
   it just didn't seem worth the hassle –
   so I let him usher everyone out of the house,
   everyone but myself and the family,
   and then we went in to where she was lying,
   just where I'd left her a short time before,
   but so white now,
   so still,
   so cold.
I watched in a daze as he reached out,
   scarcely able to see with the tears running down my face,
   and then I heard a voice,

his voice,
   gentle but firm,
   'Little girl, get up!'
And, believe it or not, she did!
She opened her eyes and walked towards us,
   for all the world as though she'd simply been sleeping after all!
I can't make sense of it, no –
   what he did or how he did it is beyond my ability to fathom –
   but I tell you this,
   my daughter was dead,
   and he brought her back to life,
   my heart was broken,
   and he filled it again with joy,
   and if he can do that, then, quite honestly, what can't he do?
It seems to me nothing is beyond him!

Prayer

Lord Jesus Christ,
   you promise new life to those who follow you –
   not just a different quality of life here and now,
   though that is a part of it,
   but life beyond the grave; life eternal.
We thank you for the way you foreshadowed that promise
   during your earthly ministry,
   demonstrating your sovereign, life-giving power.
You raised Lazarus,
   you raised the daughter of Jairus,
   you raised the son of a widow,
   and finally, after three days in the tomb,
   you rose yourself!
Through word and deed you have given us the assurance
   that nothing in life or in death
   can ever separate us from your love.
Lord Jesus Christ, the resurrection and the life,
   we praise you.
Amen.

Silence

Slides and music

Silent, surrendered (Fountain of Life) Rizza
during which Mark 5:25-34 is read

Meditation of the woman who touched Jesus' cloak

I was sick –
    sick of body,
    sick of mind,
    sick of spirit –
    fed up with having my hopes raised only to be dashed again,
    fed up with everything.
I'd suffered for so long,
    my strength failing,
    my fears multiplying,
    and I was ready to give up,
    to say goodbye to it all,
    to curl up in some dark corner and let life slip away.
But then suddenly I saw him, just a few yards in front of me,
    the man they were all talking about –
    Jesus of Nazareth,
    prophet,
    teacher,
    worker of miracles –
    and it took only one glance to convince me
    he was the answer to my prayers.
Yes, I was desperate, admittedly,
    ready to believe anything, clutch at any straw,
    but there was more to it than that,
    for I could see immediately that this man was unique,
    everything about him proclaiming his love for others.
So I pushed my way through the crowds
    and I reached out and touched him,
    just the faintest of contacts, that's all,
    yet immediately I felt whole again,
    a knowledge deep within that I was well.
But before I had time to celebrate I froze in horror,
    for he stopped,
    and turned,
    and looked around curiously,
    eyes sweeping over the crowd.
Goodness knows how he'd felt my touch amongst so many,
    but he had,
    and I realised then the awfulness of what I'd done,
    breaking every commandment in the book
    by touching him in my condition.

I waited for the rebuke,
   the explosion of anger which would shatter my illusions,
   yet it never came;
   just that one simple question:
   'Who touched me?'
There was no escape.
Much as I longed to melt away into the crowd,
   I knew there could be no deceiving this man,
   so I shambled forward and blurted out the whole story,
   pleading for forgiveness,
   begging him to make allowances.
I still feared the worst,
   but finally I dared to meet his eyes,
   and there he was,
   gently returning my gaze,
   a look of love and understanding which I shall never forget.
'Daughter,' he said, 'your faith has made you well.
   Go in peace, and be healed of your disease.'
It was true, the disease had gone,
   but there was more than that,
   much, much more.
I'd found new meaning, new hope, new purpose,
   strength which I'd never known before,
   peace such as I'd never imagined possible.
He sensed my need that day before I even expressed it,
   responding instinctively to my silent plea;
   and I'm whole now –
   whole in body,
   whole in mind,
   whole in spirit –
   ready for whatever life might bring,
   ready for anything!

Prayer

Lord Jesus Christ,
   you touched the sick and made them well;
   you touched the lepers and made them clean;
   you touched the blind and made them see;
   you touched the lame and made them walk.
In these and so many other ways you brought healing
   but, more wonderful still, you brought wholeness,
   a health of body, mind and spirit.

Reach out to all who suffer today,
     and work through all those
     to whom you have entrusted the ministry of healing
     in all its many forms.
Grant your renewing, restoring touch through them,
     and grant also the blessing which you alone can bring,
     your strength and inner peace
     which nothing we may face can finally destroy.
In your name we ask it.
Amen.

Silence

Music   *Chanson de Matin* Elgar

AFTERNOON SESSION

Music   *Spring Song in A* Mendelssohn

Prayer

Lord Jesus Christ,
     you are the same yesterday, today and tomorrow,
     always loving,
     always ready to show mercy,
     always waiting to lead us forward.
Because of your constancy
     we know that you will be with us
     in whatever we face,
     for you are Lord of past, present and future.
Take, then, what has been,
     work in what is,
     and direct what shall yet be,
     to the glory of your name.
Amen.

Slides and music

Adagio (Piano Sonata K332) Mozart, during which Luke 7:1-10 is read

Meditation of the Roman centurion

They thought I was mad when I sent for him like that,
    a small deputation meekly appealing for help.
Why ask, they said, when you can command?
Why waste time with polite requests
    when you have only to say the word and it is done?
And, of course, they had a point,
    for I had the power, had I wished to use it,
    to compel Jesus to come,
    whether he wanted to or not.
I was a Roman soldier, remember,
    and a centurion to boot,
    one of the ruling elite,
    a man of authority,
    used to having my own way.
Yet it wasn't that simple, not this time.
I knew it even before I met the man
    from all the accounts I heard of him.
I could command my men,
    win their trust, their respect, their allegiance,
    but I couldn't win their souls,
    not as Jesus had won the heart and soul of the multitude.
I could fight with the best of them,
    no battle too fierce for me,
    no enemy too strong,
    but I couldn't take on the forces of evil,
    the powers of darkness,
    still less hope to rout them as he was doing.
I could build up or tear down, keep peace or make war,
    but I couldn't restore the broken-hearted,
    heal the sick or raise the dead as he had done.
He spoke with an authority I could never hope to equal,
    acted with a power no person alive could ever begin to match,
    and, to be honest, I was in awe of him –
    there's no other word for it –
    conscious that he was no ordinary man
    but one sent by God,
    before whom and beside whom I was as nothing.
I had no claim on his mercy,
    no reason to expect his help.
It was all down to him –
    his goodness,
    his grace –

and he didn't disappoint me,
   my servant restored to health even as we spoke.
Was my faith so very special?
It didn't feel like it at the time, despite what he said.
But if you think it was, let me tell you its source,
   for there's no secret.
I saw what *I* could do,
   I saw what *he* had done,
   I saw what needed doing,
   and I put them together, as simple as that.
The rest was down to him.

Prayer

Sovereign God,
   there are things we can do ourselves
   and things only you can do;
   there are times when we have the resources in ourselves
   to cope with a situation
   and times when we depend utterly on you for help.
Teach us to know the difference,
   and help us to remember
   that, though our own reserves may run dry,
   yours never will.
Give us an appreciation of our own abilities
   and of yours,
   and help us to get the balance right;
   through Jesus Christ our Lord.
Amen.

Silence

Slides and music

O Lord, my heart is not proud (Fountain of Life) Rizza
during which Luke 8:26-39 is read

Meditation of Legion

You just can't imagine what it was like –
   the turmoil, the agony, the confusion I went through,
   day after day,
   year after year,

my tortured mind hell-bent, so it seemed,
on self-destruction.
It would have been less painful, perhaps,
had my reason gone completely;
at least then the nightmare world I lived in
would have been the only one I knew.
But it wasn't like that –
I was still cursed with those occasional lucid moments,
those awful interludes when sanity briefly returned
and I witnessed the man I'd become –
like a wild beast, scavenging in the wilds,
an outcast from Hades, skulking there among the tombs.
I could have wept with the shame of it,
the torment I felt so dreadful that words can't describe it,
and, yes, there were times
when I'd have gladly hurled myself from the cliff-top,
dashed my head against the rocks,
anything to escape that degradation to which I'd sunk.
Believe me, I came close on many occasions,
but then the madness would take hold again,
its horrors almost welcome after that awful glimpse of reality.
To cap it all, there were crowds sometimes
who came to watch me, do you realise that? –
gawping, giggling groups of sightseers
queuing to see this freak everyone was talking about.
Can you imagine how it felt,
listening to their gasps of incredulity,
watching as their eyes widened in disbelief,
sensing their revulsion, their pity, their disgust?
I expected more of the same that day Jesus came by –
yet another dose of humiliation to endure,
but when he kept on coming
instead of keeping his distance,
when he looked me eye to eye
with no trace of fear or repugnance,
suddenly I knew this man was different from the usual visitors –
and it threw me completely.
I didn't know if I was afraid or excited,
and perhaps that explains what happened next,
for suddenly it was as though all the demons in my head
were let loose at once,
a thousand voices clamouring for attention,

yelling,
shrieking,
cursing,
screaming,
my mind torn now this way, now that,
sensing both threat and hope,
the prospect of rebuke and the promise of redemption.
I begged him to go – can you believe that? –
even though I longed for him to stay.
I actually implored him to leave me in 'peace',
though he alone could bring that greatest of gifts
which I craved so desperately.
Had it been anyone else they'd have been off like a shot,
no further reason needed for leaving me to my fate.
But not Jesus.
There was still no sign of rejection from him,
just a calm, unshakable authority,
and an inner quietness which I longed to share.
Don't ask me what happened next –
I still can't make sense of it and I don't think I ever will –
but the next moment it was as though all hell broke lose,
noise, chaos, confusion everywhere,
and then . . .
suddenly . . .
all was still . . .
not just the world outside,
but the world within,
body, mind and spirit,
a tranquillity such as I'd never even dared to imagine!
It was over,
the whole ghastly business put behind me,
and I've learned to forget over the years,
to let go and start again.
But one thing I won't forget, as long as I live,
is what Jesus did for me that day –
the way he reached out to me in my need and set me free,
the way he touched me with his peace
and brought rest to my soul!

Prayer

Lord,
>   we talk of peace but all too rarely find it,
>   for our minds are full of a multitude of concerns
>   which pull us this way and that
>   until we feel bewildered and confused.

We hear your still, small voice bidding us to let go and rest,
>   but always there is another call,
>   another demand on our attention pressing in upon us,
>   and, before we know it, your word is drowned
>   in the noisy bustle of life.

Lord, we cannot ignore the world
>   or our responsibilities within it,
>   and we would not want to,
>   for there is so much you have given us there which is good,
>   but help us always to make time for you within it,
>   so that, even when chaos seems to reign,
>   your quietness may fill our souls,
>   bringing an inner calm which cannot be shaken.

Amen.

Silence

Slides and music

Libera me Domine (Requiem) Verdi, during which John 8:2-11 is read

Meditation of the woman caught in adultery

I expected him to condemn me like all the rest,
>   to shake his head in disgust and send me to my death.

Just another self-righteous busybody, that's what I thought –
>   you know the sort,
>   the kind always up on their soap box,
>   sounding off about something or other,
>   telling folk how they ought to live their lives.

Not that it mattered much this time who he was,
>   for there was no getting away from it, I'd broken the law,
>   caught, as they say, well and truly in the act –
>   no way anyone could get me out of that one,
>   even if they'd wished to.

And you could see from the smug look of the Pharisees
    that they felt the same –
    lips twisted with contempt,
    eyes glittering with hatred,
    their hands positively itching to pick up the first stone
    and strike me down.
It was just a matter of time,
    a question of completing the necessary formalities
    before the verdict was given.
So I cowered there trembling,
    waiting for the fateful signal for them to begin,
    expecting each moment to be my last.
I waited . . .
    and I waited . . .
    sweat trickling down my brow,
    limbs shaking in terror . . .
But it didn't happen,
    no word,
    no sign,
    nothing.
What could it mean?
A reprieve?
Surely not.
But what then?
Some heartless trick to prolong my agony,
    an unforeseen last-minute technicality,
    or simply a pause while they gathered the rocks to stone me?
There was only one way to find out,
    so I looked up,
    tense,
    fearful . . .
    then stopped,
    transfixed,
    catching my breath in astonishment,
    for we were alone,
    just the two of us,
    me and Jesus,
    not another soul to be seen.
I thought I was dreaming for a moment,
    either that or the stoning had despatched me
    unbeknown to another life.

But then he spoke,
   his eyes gentle yet piercing as he voiced my unspoken question:
   'Woman, where are your accusers?'
They were gone, each one of them,
   none able, apparently, to throw the first stone;
   and even as I struggled to take it in, he spoke again,
   those marvellous, memorable words:
   'Neither do I condemn you.'
I should have danced for joy, shouldn't I? –
   whooped with delight,
   laughed in exultation –
   for I was free,
   not simply reprieved but forgiven,
   invited to go back and start again.
But I didn't laugh.
I broke down in tears,
   the sobs convulsing my body,
   tears streaming down my face,
   for suddenly, faced by this astonishing man,
   I saw myself as I really was . . .
   and became my own accuser.
I'd expected death, and been given life,
   feared judgement, and been shown mercy;
   what had seemed the end was suddenly a new beginning –
   and it was all too much to take in!
Not any more, though.
I understand now what he's done for me,
   and I look back still to that day with wonder,
   my whole being throbbing with praise,
   for he met me in my need and made me whole,
   he saw me at my worst,
   and dared to believe the best!

Prayer
Lord Jesus Christ,
   you did not come to judge or condemn the world,
   but in order to save it.
Where others saw the bad in people,
   you saw the good.
You recognised the value in everyone,
   and instilled in all a sense of worth.
Such was your willingness to show acceptance to the unacceptable
   that many were scandalised by your behaviour.

Forgive us that we too can be equally self-righteous,
  more concerned with judgement than mercy.
Forgive us for failing to see in ourselves
  the evil which we are so ready to see in others.
Teach us to look at the world with your eyes,
  and to deal graciously in all our relationships,
  just as you have dealt graciously with us.
Amen.

Silence

Slides and music

Gloria (Coronation Mass) Mozart, during which Luke 24:36-43 is read

Meditation of Peter

He was back!
Back in the land of the living,
  just when we'd given up hope!
Three days it had been,
  three days of dark despair as slowly the truth sank home –
  our Lord, laid in a tomb,
  dead and buried,
  never to walk this earth again.
We couldn't believe it at first,
  none of us,
  even though we'd seen it for ourselves.
We expected to wake up any moment to find it was all a dream,
  a dreadful mistake that had somehow taken us in.
But as the numbness passed, so the reality hit us,
  and the pain began in earnest.
It was an end to everything –
  our plans,
  our hopes,
  our dreams.
There was nothing left to live for,
  that's how we felt –
  we'd pinned our hopes on him,
  and he was gone.
Only he wasn't!
He was there,
  meeting Mary in the garden as her heart broke beside the tomb.

He was there,
  on the Emmaus road as two followers trudged slowly home,
  their world in tatters.
He was there,
  speaking to Thomas, breaking through his disbelief!
He was there,
  standing among us in the upper room!
He was back in the land of the living,
  and suddenly so were we –
  faith rekindled,
  hope renewed,
  joy reborn,
  life beginning again!

Prayer

Lord Jesus Christ,
  just when it looked all over,
  when the world had written you off
  and even your disciples had given up on you,
  you came back – defeat revealed as victory.
Teach us what that means for us today;
  not only the promise of eternal life,
  but good news for life here and now.
Help us to understand that, whatever tragedies we may suffer,
  whatever obstacles we may face,
  whatever disappointments we may experience,
  we can bounce back from them with your help,
  for you are a God able to transform even the darkest moments
  and lead us through them into the light of your love.
Gladly, then, we put our hand in yours,
  knowing that in life or death
  you will never fail us or forsake us.
Amen.

Silence

Slides and music

Adagio (Cello Concerto) Haydn, during which Acts 15:36-41 is read

Meditation of John Mark

Was I hurt by Paul's attitude,
    his refusal to let me share again in his ministry?
Not really, no,
    for I knew that I'd let him down when he needed me most,
    walked away when I couldn't stand the heat.
I hadn't been well, admittedly,
    the demands of our journey having told on me
    more than I'd anticipated –
    not just the physical toll, though that was testing enough,
    but the mental and spiritual exhaustion,
    the pressure of constantly giving out
    with scarcely a moment's respite –
    yet whatever strain *I* was under,
    Paul was wrestling with far worse,
    only he never once complained,
    the idea of taking a break
    not even crossing his mind for a moment.
He had a mission to fulfil,
    a calling to honour,
    and he wasn't going to rest until he'd completed it,
    however much it cost him.
Me, I took the first opportunity to cut and run.
So no, I couldn't blame him –
    I'd made my bed,
    now I could lie on it.
Yet thankfully that wasn't the end of the story,
    for, though I didn't deserve it,
    there was someone else ready to give me another chance –
    good old Barnabas.
It was typical of the man, really –
    no wonder we'd called him 'son of encouragement' –
    always ready to see the best,
    to make allowances,
    to draw out the good instead of dwell on the bad.
He may not have made the headlines like the others did,
    but to many of us he was the star of the show,
    his gentle prompting the secret behind so much of our success.
It was true for me, that's for sure –
    while some like Paul were writing me off,
    he stepped in with a word of welcome,
    and I needed no second bidding –
    this time I would not fail.

w on a life of service,
␣nent in the cause of the kingdom,
␣from the bottom of my heart
who made it possible,
Barnabas.
C. ␣never ceases to tell me, it isn't him I owe it to,
n␣ ␣nally;
it's Christ,
the one who is always there, however much we've failed,
however little we deserve it,
ready to put the past behind us
and help us start again!

Prayer

Lord,
   it's not easy to give someone a second chance,
   especially when they've let us down personally.
It's hard to overcome our feelings of hurt and anger,
   and harder still to trust that person in the way we used to.
Yet you go on giving us another chance day after day,
   and despite our repeated failure
   you are willing still to entrust us
   with the work of your kingdom.
Teach us, then,
   instead of finding fault to look for strengths,
   and instead of putting people down to lift them up.
Help us to forgive others as you forgive us,
   and so may we offer a ministry of encouragement
   to all we meet;
   through Jesus Christ our Lord.
Amen.

Silence

Blessing

Music   *Jesu, joy of man's desiring* J. S. Bach

The Cost of Discipleship

Suggested visual material	Jesus of Nazareth 3 and 4 The Life of Christ IV Man of the Cross

MORNING SESSION

Music   *Come to me (Fountain of Life)* Rizza

Introduction   'If any want to become my followers, let them deny themselves and take up their cross and follow me' (Mark 8:34b). Words of Jesus which, in the euphoria of Christian celebration, we can sometimes forget, yet which lie at the heart of Christian discipleship. The life of service involves cost as well as reward; a price to pay as well as a blessing to receive. Lose sight of that and we are in danger of presenting a lop-sided and ultimately false gospel. Alongside what we get out of faith we must always remember what Jesus asks us to put in; his call to deny ourselves and put others first, to seek treasures in heaven rather than riches on earth, to be last rather than first, to face trials now in order to help build his kingdom to come. If we expect the Christian life to be plain sailing, then we have not understood the call or listened to the words of the one who called us. Responding in faith will inevitably bring times of challenge, just as it has done to those before us, but, if we are willing to meet the cost, then, like them, we will find the price worth paying, for we will discover life as God intends it to be. 'Those who want to save their life will lose it, and those who lose their life for the sake of the gospel, will save it' (Mark 8:35).

Prayer

Lord Jesus Christ,
    you gave your all so that we might have life.
You counted yourself as nothing
    so that we might rejoice
    in the wonder of your love.
You endured agony of body, mind and spirit,
    so that we might receive mercy
    and know the peace which only you can give.
Help us today to recognise more clearly
    everything you did for us,
    and so inspire us
    to give a little of ourselves in return.
Teach us to walk the way of the cross,
    and to bear the cost gladly
    for the joy set before us,
    knowing that you will be with us,
    each step of the way,
    whatever we may face.
Amen.

Slides and music

Canticle de Jean Racine Fauré, during which Luke 7:18b-19, 21-23 is read

Meditation of John the Baptist

Shall I tell you something strange?
Almost funny you might call it, were it not so sad.
It's about me,
    the voice in the wilderness,
    the baptiser in the Jordan,
    the one sent to prepare the way of the Lord.
Well, I managed that, didn't I?
Or at least so they'll tell you –
    I made straight a path in the wilderness,
    I paved the way for his coming,
    and, yes, I have to say I made a good job of it,
    too good in a sense,
    for, much to my embarrassment, many were so impressed
    they followed me instead of him.
But it wasn't just them who got it wrong,
    it was me,
    for when Jesus finally came I was as unprepared as any.

Oh, I didn't realise it at the time,
    far from it –
    in fact, I thought I was an example to them all,
    the one who, more than any other,
    understood who he was and what he came to do.
'Behold the lamb of God!' I told them,
    'the one who comes to take away the sin of the world.'
A good speech, wouldn't you say?
But it was just words,
    sounding impressive,
    but belying the truth beneath.
And it wasn't long after –
    when his ministry had begun and mine ended,
    when he was travelling the byways of Judah
    and I was rotting in prison –
    that I found myself questioning everything.
'Could he be the Messiah?' I asked,
    'the one we'd so long waited for?'
If he was, then why was so little happening –
    why so little evidence of his kingdom getting closer?
I should have known different, of course I should,
    and, yes, you may well say a hint of jealousy
    coloured my judgement.
But, honestly, how would you have felt in my position,
    knowing that, having given your all,
    more would be asked,
    even life itself?
It won't be long now before they come for me,
    I'm under no illusions.
There's no escape,
    no possibility of a last-minute reprieve;
    that wife of Herod's won't rest
    until she sees me dead and buried,
    the voice in the wilderness silenced for ever.
I wasn't prepared for that when I started,
    and I still wouldn't have been, just a day ago.
But thank God he's given me time to think,
    to hear what Jesus is doing,
    to understand what it's all leading up to,
    and I'm ready now,
    at last I'm ready,
    prepared for anything
    prepared for everything!

Prayer

Gracious God,
   there are times when, like John the Baptist,
   we find ourselves in the wilderness of doubt and despair.
We look at our lives, at the world, even at you,
   and we are overwhelmed by a sense of hopelessness,
   by questions as to why you do not act to establish your kingdom
   or respond to us in our time of need.
Help us at such moments when all seems dark
   to put our faith in you,
   trusting that your light will finally shine again.
Inspire us with the knowledge that time and again
   it has been in the wilderness experiences of people's lives
   that you have been supremely at work –
   challenging, deepening and strengthening their faith,
   equipping them for new avenues of service,
   and opening the way to a richer experience of your love.
In that assurance, lead us forward;
   through Jesus Christ our Lord.
Amen.

Silence

Slides and music

Adagietto from L'Arlésienne (Suite No. 1) Bizet
during which Luke 18:18-25 is read

Meditation of the rich ruler

It was a lot to ask, wasn't it,
   too much to expect of anyone?
I was ready to do my bit, after all,
   happy to be more than generous if that's what he wanted;
   but to give up everything,
   to leave it all behind so that I could follow him,
   well, quite simply, it wasn't on.
So I left,
   disappointed,
   disillusioned,
   preferring the riches I could handle now
   to the promise of treasure in heaven.

It was a shame though –
  had he asked for a quarter,
  a half,
  even the bulk of my wealth,
  I'd have said yes, happily enough,
  for he had something I didn't,
  a tranquillity, an assurance, a sense of purpose beyond price,
  more precious than anything money can buy,
  and I wanted to share it,
  to be part of something which really mattered,
  to grasp hold of a prize which would never fade,
  never perish.
Did I have my regrets?
Of course I did,
  and I prayed many times for help to accept his challenge,
  yet somehow, though I longed to respond,
  the resolve was never quite there.
Until today, that is,
  for I arrived here in Jerusalem for the Passover,
  and I saw a crowd gathering in the streets,
  and, there among them, a man struggling under a cross,
  collapsing in exhaustion,
  writhing in agony as they nailed him up to die,
  and do you know what? – it was Jesus.
Don't ask how it could happen, for I'll never know –
  how anyone could kill a man like that just makes no sense –
  yet I understood one thing.
He'd given his all,
  everything,
  precisely what he'd asked of me,
  and more besides!
And suddenly,
  as I watched him suffer,
  as I heard his groans,
  as I saw him take his final breath,
  his words came flooding back,
  cutting deep into my soul:
  'Sell all that you own and distribute the money to the poor,
  and you will have treasure in heaven;
  then come, follow me.'
It wasn't much to ask, was it?

Prayer

Gracious God,
    no one can ever give us more than you have given,
    for you have blessed us with life itself –
    life overflowing with good things, life eternal –
    and to make that gift possible you gave of yourself,
    not just a little but all.
You bore the limitations of our flesh;
    you endured rejection, humiliation
    and finally death on a cross;
    and, most awesome of all,
    through Christ you took on yourself
    the dreadful burden of human sinfulness,
    experiencing the despair and isolation that brings.
Forgive us that, despite all this,
    we give so grudgingly in return.
Forgive us that though our words say one thing,
    our lives say another.
Forgive us that so often our thoughts are little for you,
    none for others
    and all for ourselves.
Help us to catch again a glimpse into the wonder of your love
    which you have freely given,
    and so may we spontaneously give something back
    in joyful and heartfelt thanksgiving;
    through Jesus Christ our Lord.
Amen.

Silence

Slides and music

Kyrie eleison (Fountain of Life) Rizza, during which Luke 21:1-4 is read

Meditation of the widow at the treasury

I was ashamed, if I'm truthful,
    desperately praying that no one would notice me,
    for what would they think
    when they saw those two miserable coins of mine;
    what sort of person would they take me for?
They seemed little short of an insult,
    worse, in some ways, than bringing nothing at all,

and believe me, I'd toyed seriously
    with staying away altogether to spare my blushes.
It had been different once,
    when my husband was alive –
    then I could hold my head up in any company,
    my gifts, if not extravagant, were more than generous.
But times were hard,
    a matter of getting through from one day to the next
    as best I could;
    life's little luxuries a thing of the past,
    and many of its necessities too.
Yet there was one thing I was resolved to do, come what may,
    even if it meant going short,
    and that was to continue offering something to God.
So there I was, that day in the temple,
    surreptitiously bringing my feeble gift.
It wasn't much, I know,
    not in the eyes of the world, anyway,
    but to me it was a small fortune,
    the last thing I had in the world.
Well, you can imagine my horror when I arrived there
    to find this crowd with Jesus watching.
It was my worst nightmare come true,
    my pathetic offering exposed to the full glare of public scrutiny,
    and I felt certain I would die of shame,
    waiting with weary resignation
    for the inevitable howl of laughter or snort of disgust.
And when Jesus nodded towards me
    I could feel the colour rising to my cheeks,
    skin crawling with embarrassment.
Yet then, he spoke,
    his words, would you believe, not of condemnation but praise,
    singling me out as an example to follow
    rather than an object of ridicule.
It's the thought which counts, we sometimes say,
    and Jesus understood that.
Somehow he knew how much that gift had cost me,
    and to him those small pieces of copper
    were like nuggets of gold!
I went out that morning with my heart singing,
    head held high after all,
    and I brought my offering from then on

without any hesitation or any sense of unworthiness,
for I understood that God sees things differently from us,
that he measures the gift not by how much it's worth,
but by how much it means!

Prayer

Gracious God,
   you give to us out of love,
   more and more blessings poured out upon us day after day.
Forgive us for so often giving to you out of habit or duty.
We make our offering in worship
   because it is expected of us.
We make time for personal devotion
   because we feel we ought to.
We make time for others
   because our conscience pricks us.
The end result may seem worthy,
   but the true value is small.
Teach us instead to give joyfully,
   not because we must but because we may.
Teach us to offer our money, our worship and our service
   as a gesture of love and an expression of our appreciation.
Help us to understand that it is not the gift that matters so much
   as the spirit in which it is given,
   and may that awareness inspire all we offer to you;
   through Jesus Christ our Lord.
Amen.

Silence

Slides and music

Jesus, you are the way (Fountain of Life) Rizza
during which Mark 14:3-9 is read

Meditation of the woman who anointed Jesus' head

Was it guilt that made them turn on me?
I couldn't help but wonder,
   for there were some there who'd welcomed me very differently
   the last time I saw them,
   eager not only to share my company but my bed as well.
Oh yes, there were a few skeletons in the cupboard that day,
   enough to wreck many a career and destroy many a family.

Is that what they thought –
    that I'd come to tell all,
    expose them for the hypocrites they were?
It would have served them right if I had.
But no, they had nothing to fear,
    such revelations were the last thing on my mind.
I wanted to see Jesus, that's all,
    for I'd come to recognise that here was a man
    different from any I'd known before,
    concerned not for himself but for others,
    his only desire, it seemed, to bring a little light
    into the darkness of this world.
I'd taken some convincing, mind you –
    the kind of man I was used to made cynicism come easy –
    but I'd watched him talking with the multitude,
    healing the sick, comforting the distressed;
    I'd seen him welcoming the poor, embracing the little children,
    accepting the unacceptable;
    and I knew then, beyond all doubt,
    that he was genuine through and through,
    offering a glimpse of the way life could and should be.
Quite simply I was entranced,
    captivated,
    longing to discover that life for myself.
I had no right to be there, I knew that,
    but I wanted to respond,
    to show him that he'd touched me
    in a way no one else had ever done –
    not my body but my soul –
    so I burst in with my perfume,
    ignoring the gasps, the protests, the cries of outrage,
    and in a wild impulsive gesture I poured it over his head,
    anointing him with love.
You should have seen their faces!
I actually think some thought I was making a pass at him.
But not Jesus –
    he understood –
    the compassion in his eyes as he looked up at me,
    the concern, the welcome,
    sending a tingle down my spine,
    for these told me in a way words never could
    that he had time for me,

time for the person I was
   as much as the person I could become.
It cost me something that day,
   not just the perfume but my career,
   for there was no way I could carry on selling my body
   after that encounter,
   but I've this horrible feeling that Jesus is going to pay far more
   for the love he has for us,
   for as he leapt to my defence that day he said the strangest of things,
   words which have troubled me ever since –
   something about anointing his body for burial.
Could he really have meant it?
He's too good for this world, I've always said that,
   but surely no one could want to remove him from it,
   not even his enemies.
No one would want to do that –
   would they?

Prayer

Lord,
   there are many ready to sneer at faith.
'Who do they think they are?'
'What makes them so special?'
We've all heard the kind of thing people throw at us.
Yet we know that you love us
   not because we deserve it
   but solely through your grace.
We recognise our faults, we acknowledge our sinfulness,
   and we realise full well that we will never be perfect,
   but we ask you to help us live more authentically as your disciples
   and to offer our lives as best we can
   as a joyful outpouring of thanksgiving
   and a spontaneous expression of praise.
Amen.

Silence

Music   *Pié Jesu (Requiem)* Andrew Lloyd Weber

AFTERNOON SESSION

Music   *Adagio (Oboe Concerto)* Marcello

Prayer

Loving God,
  we talk of serving others
  but so often we live for ourselves,
  we speak of self-sacrifice
  but practise self-interest.
Forgive us for failing to follow Jesus,
  and for distorting the Gospel
  to serve our own purposes.
Remind us afresh
  of the great love you have shown in Christ.
Inspire us through those who responded faithfully
  to his call,
  and so help us in turn to give as well as receive,
  to bear willingly the cost of discipleship,
  for his name's sake.
Amen.

Slides and music

Adagio un poco mosso (Piano Concerto No. 5) Beethoven
during which John 3:1-6; 19:38-42 is read

Meditation of Nicodemus

It was dark when I went to him that first time,
  the middle of the night when all was quiet –
  and can you blame me?
It just wouldn't have done, would it,
  a man in my position to be seen associating with Jesus?
Even a hint of involvement
  and my fellow Pharisees would have lynched me on the spot!
He was the enemy,
  the blasphemer,
  the one who threatened everything we stood for –
  not just misguided,
  but dangerous,
  evil –

a threat to our society,
    a challenge to the very heart of our religion.
I knew all that,
    or at least I knew the theory,
    and, yes, I'd been as shocked as any
    by some of the things he'd said,
    not to mention the things he'd done.
Yet I couldn't get him out of my mind, try as I might.
I can't say why exactly,
    for it wasn't any one word or deed that hooked me –
    it was all of them together,
    the way each reinforced the other,
    combining to make him the person he was.
He spoke of love,
    and he showed what love was all about.
He talked of forgiveness,
    and I simply haven't met a more forgiving man.
He talked of life,
    and there was a quality to his own life that I couldn't help but envy.
He talked of God,
    and I could see God was more real,
    more personal,
    more special to him,
    than I'd ever have dreamed possible for anyone.
So I went
    and I talked.
I listened
    and I learned.
Nervous, true,
    hesitant,
    strictly incognito,
    and so very, very slow to understand.
Yet, little by little, the truth broke through my confusion,
    a ray of light in the darkness,
    new birth for my parched and barren soul.
It was dark when I went again,
    a night far blacker than that first night,
    for they'd taken their revenge by then, as I knew they would,
    done him to death on the cross.
And as he hung there in agony,
    his gasps piercing the air,
    suddenly the sun vanished and darkness fell.

That had them worried, you can well imagine,
    more than a few scuttling off in panic.
But not me,
    for I had seen the truth he spoke of
    and found the life he promised.
So, while others stumbled blindly in the darkness,
    for me it was lighter than the lightest day,
    and brighter than the brightest sunshine.

Prayer

Lord Jesus Christ,
    you tell us to walk in the light,
    and to be witnesses to it through the things we do
    and the people we are.
You call us to let your light shine through us
    so that others might see the good works we do
    and give glory to God.
Forgive us that all too often we do the opposite,
    hiding our light under a bushel,
    even sometimes to the point of secret discipleship.
Afraid of what others might think
    and concerned that admitting faith in you
    may prejudice our standing in this world,
    we keep our beliefs private,
    imagining they can be kept between us and you.
Forgive us the feebleness of our commitment
    and the weakness of our love.
Help us to recognise everything you have done for us
    while we still walked in darkness,
    and so teach us to acknowledge you proudly
    as the light of our lives,
    whatever the cost might be.
In your name we pray.
Amen.

Silence

Slides and music

Lesson 1 for Maundy Thursday Palestrina
during which Luke 22:39-46 is read

Meditation of Peter

He was unsure of himself,
    for the first time in his life
    unsure of his ability to face the future,
    and it hurt him more than the pain he was finally to suffer.
You see, there'd never been any doubt until then,
    never even the slightest suggestion of hesitation.
Despite the hostility, the resentment, the abuse from so many,
    he'd set his face resolutely towards Jerusalem,
    knowing from the very beginning where it would all end.
He understood it all,
    the pain and humiliation he must suffer,
    conscious of it even way back
    in those heady days of his baptism,
    yet he'd carried on willingly,
    the prospect seeming to hold no fear for him,
    and we'd marvelled at the faith, the love,
    the courage of the man,
    the sheer commitment
    which gave him such awesome strength and inner purpose.
But suddenly, that evening, it was all so very different,
    a shadow blotting out the light which had shone so brightly.
I saw despair in his eyes rather than hope,
    fear rather than laughter,
    sorrow rather than joy,
    and, most terrible of all, that desperate look of uncertainty,
    so alien,
    so devastating,
    so crushing a burden.
It was all suddenly too real,
    no longer theory but fact –
    the agony and the isolation he was about to face –
    and, like any of us would in his place, he wanted to back away,
    find an easier course,
    a less dreadful option.
It struck me then, as never before,
    that he didn't know what lay beyond death
    any more than I did.
He'd always believed,
    always trusted,
    but he had no more certainty than you and me –
    only the assurance of faith,

the conviction borne of trust,
and there in the darkness,
as the chill of night took hold,
it all hung on a thread
as he wrestled with the torment of doubt.
I know what I'd have done had I been him –
quite simply, I wouldn't have stopped running
until Jerusalem was just a memory!
But not Jesus.
He stayed quietly in the garden, as I knew he would,
and he offered not just his *faith* but his *doubt* to God –
'not *my* will but *yours* be done'.
Well, he was sure of one thing after that –
there was no way back,
death now a cast-iron certainty;
but it wasn't dying itself that was the problem for him,
it was not knowing whether it would all be worth it,
whether it could actually make a difference
to this world we live in,
and there was no way of answering that for certain
this side of eternity.
He was unsure –
of himself,
of his faith,
of his ability to face the future –
but despite it all he risked everything,
offering life itself,
so that we might know the truth,
and be free from death –
free for all eternity!

Prayer

Loving God,
you call us to live by faith, not by sight,
to put our faith in things unseen rather than seen,
and most of the time we are able to do that.
But occasionally we are faced by circumstances
which cause us to doubt,
throwing a shadow over everything we believe.
We question our ability to keep going,
we wonder what is happening to us,
and though we look to you for assurance, we do not find it.

Help us when such moments come
   to know that you have been there before us in Christ
   and that you understand what we are facing.
Inspire us through the faith and courage he showed,
   and so help us to trust in your purpose
   even when we cannot see the way ahead.
In his name we pray.
Amen.

Silence

Slides and music

Agnus Dei J. S. Bach, during which Mark 15:33-36, 40-41 is read

Meditation of Mary Magdalene

He was gasping,
   his breath coming short and sharp,
   his body contorted in agony,
   and I could scarcely bring myself to watch.
It's a dreadful business, crucifixion, at the best of times,
   even when the poor wretch up there deserves to die,
   but when it's a friend,
   a loved one,
   somebody who's been special to you,
   then, I'm telling you, it's indescribable.
To stand by helpless as the pain takes hold,
   as the muscles tear and the tendons snap,
   as life ebbs out of the body –
   to see the misery,
   the torment,
   the despair,
   and to know it must get worse
   before finally, in the sweet embrace of death, it gets better;
   you just can't imagine what that feels like,
   not unless you've been there.
And we *were* there, more's the pity,
   each one of us enduring our own private hell.
We wanted to run, God knows! –
   to close our eyes and pretend it wasn't happening.
But we couldn't, could we?

For he needed us then more than ever,
    simply to know we were there,
    that we cared,
    that he wasn't alone.
It wasn't much, I grant you,
    the few of us huddled together,
    watching nervously from the shadows,
    fearful of recognition,
    but it was enough,
    one ray of sunshine in a wilderness of darkness;
    for he knew that despite our faults,
    the weakness of our faith and feebleness of our commitment,
    we were risking something,
    sticking our necks out for love of him.
He was gasping,
    and we prayed it wouldn't be much longer
    before release finally came.
But however long it took,
    and whatever it might cost us,
    we were resolved to stay to the bitter end –
    it was the very least we could do.

Prayer

Lord Jesus Christ,
        we know we can never repay
        the love you showed us on the cross,
        however we might try,
        but what we *can* do is show how much it means to us.
And we can do that most of all through staying close to you,
        seeking your will and obeying your voice.
It is this which will breathe life into our faith and worship;
        this which will prove the words on our lips
        through the light in our lives –
        your purpose guiding our footsteps,
        your love shining from our hearts.
Lord Jesus Christ, it may not be easy,
        it may even be costly,
        but help us to stay true to you,
        just as you stayed true to us.
Amen.

Silence

Slides and music

Jesu, joy of man's desiring J. S. Bach
during which Philippians 4:4-7, 10-12 is read

Meditation of Paul

Was I happy with my lot?
Well, as a matter of fact, I wasn't,
   not at first, anyway.
Oh, I gave thanks, don't get me wrong –
   I marvelled each day at the love of Christ
   and rejoiced constantly at the awesome grace he'd shown to me,
   but for all that there was much I found difficult,
   far more than I'd ever bargained for.
It wasn't the weariness,
   the endless travel,
   the days, weeks, even months without a rest –
   I could cope with those, despite my infirmities.
But when the hostility began,
   the beatings,
   the stone-throwing,
   the interminable hours rotting in a prison cell,
   that's when it became hard to bear,
   when I began to wonder just what I'd got myself into.
You wouldn't believe the things I endured,
   the hunger,
   the pain,
   the privations –
   enough to break anyone,
   crush the strongest of spirits.
And yet, somehow, they weren't able to do that,
   for in my darkest moments I always found the strength I needed –
   a word of encouragement,
   a sign of hope,
   a light dawning –
   and I knew that Christ was with me even there,
   especially there,
   in my time of need.
I may have been hungry,
   but I had food in plenty for my soul.
I may have been broken in body,
   but my spirit had been made whole.

I may have been poor in the things of this world,
     but I was rich in the things of God.
It didn't take away the pain, I can't claim that –
     the hardship, the fear and the suffering were just as real,
     just as terrible –
     but it changed the way I saw them,
     my perspective on life, on death, on everything
     transformed for ever.
I had joy in my heart,
     peace which passed all understanding,
     and the promise of treasure in heaven –
     whatever else might be taken from me,
     nothing could take away those.
It was enough, and more than enough!

Prayer

Loving God,
     you do not promise those who follow you
     a life in which everything will go smoothly.
You do not guarantee success or prosperity,
     nor do you offer immunity from the trials
     and tribulations of this world.
Indeed, true service may involve us in sacrifice and self-denial,
     more demands rather than *less*,
     greater and more testing challenges
     than we may ever have faced without you.
But what you *do* promise us is fulfilment in Christ.
Through him you are able to satisfy our spiritual hunger and thirst,
     to meet our deepest needs,
     to give us inner peace and an enduring contentment
     in each and every circumstance.
Such peace does not come overnight –
     it matures gradually as day by day we learn to let go
     and put our trust in you.
Reach out then, and draw us ever closer to your side,
     so that we may learn the secret
     of being content with whatever we have;
     through Jesus Christ our Lord.
Amen.

Silence

Slides and music

Pilgrims' Chorus (Tannhäuser) Wagner
during which Hebrews 11:32-12:2 is read

Meditation of the writer to the Hebrews

I was ready to give up, if I'm honest,
   tired, scared, disillusioned.
We all were, every last one of us,
   just about ready to call it a day.
You ask why?
Well, you wouldn't have if you'd been there with us,
   if you'd heard the screams as we did,
   the cries for mercy,
   the gasps of agony,
   the sobs of desolation as yet more martyrs went to their death.
It was hard, I can tell you,
   and, worse still, we knew that at any moment
   our turn might come –
   the axe,
   the sword,
   the stones,
   the lions,
   all waiting for another victim to satisfy their hunger.
We'd lost hundreds,
   good honest men and women,
   honest,
   devout,
   dedicated,
   led like lambs to the slaughter,
   nothing and no one able to save them,
   not even our prayers.
What could I say to bring hope in such times?
What possible message of reassurance could I give
   when I was troubled and confused myself?
It was a crisis for me as well as them,
   every one of us struggling to make sense
   of such dreadful carnage,
   such appalling suffering,
   but there seemed nothing to say,
   no words which offered any hope or comfort.

Until suddenly I thought of Jesus,
   the pain he endured for us –
   gasping as the lash tore into his flesh,
   as the thorns pierced his head,
   as the nails smashed through his hands and feet;
   groaning as the cramps convulsed his body
   and the lifeblood seeped away.
He need not have faced it,
   but he'd done so willingly,
   faithful to the last for our sake.
And I knew then that, whatever might be asked of us,
   whatever we might suffer,
   it could never be worse than the agony he endured,
   the terrible total desolation he was asked to bear.
It wasn't an answer, of course, I can't claim that –
   it simply rephrased the question –
   but it was enough,
   for I knew then, and I could say then with confidence,
   that God is with us in our suffering,
   by our sides, whatever we might face.

Prayer

   Living Lord,
   as well as the good times, life brings the bad –
   moments of pain, fear, sorrow and suffering.
Most of the time we are able to get by,
   tested but not pushed to the limit,
   but occasionally we question our ability to continue,
   so great are the problems we face.
We feel crushed, overwhelmed,
   our strength sapped and our spirits exhausted,
   even our faith hanging by a thread.
Be with us in such moments
   and give us courage to persevere despite everything.
Though the present seems bleak and the future looks hopeless,
   though our burdens seem many and our resources few,
   help us still to walk the way of Christ,
   knowing that he has gone before us
   and is waiting to meet us at our journey's end.
Take our hand and lead us forward,
   for his name's sake.
Amen.

Silence

Blessing

Music   *Jesus, you are the way (Fountain of Life)* Rizza

Peter – Journey of Discovery

Suggested visual   Jesus of Nazareth 5 and 6
material   The Life of Christ IV
    Man of the Cross

MORNING SESSION

Music   *Träumerei* Schumann

Introduction   For Simon Peter, the last days in the earthly ministry of Jesus must have looked very much as though they were the last days of his own discipleship. He had come far from the time when Jesus first called him, and going into that final week he believed his faith was able to face anything thrown at it, but, of course, events were to prove otherwise. Three times he was to deny the man he had so confidently promised to follow, and the experience was to all but break him. Yet the journey wasn't over; in fact, it had barely begun. Today, then, we begin with the events of that last week and we explore how Jesus was to take Peter forward into new horizons previously undreamt of. His story brings hope to us all, for it reminds us that no matter how hopeless the future may seem, the grace of God is always there, waiting to lead us forward.

Prayer

Lord Jesus Christ,
    you have called us to faith
    and we long to respond,
    to live as your people
    and offer our lives in joyful service,
    but the reality is that all too often we fail,
    the spirit willing but the flesh weak,
    and it is hard at such times not to lose heart.
Speak to us today
    and assure us of your grace
    which never gives up on us,

however weak our faith may be,
however often we may let you down.
Teach us to let go of the past
   and to look forward to the future,
   confident that your purpose continues
   and that you are able to use us
   in ways beyond our imagining,
In your name we pray.
Amen.

Slides and music

Adagio (Oboe Concerto) Marcello, during which Luke 22:7-13 is read

Meditation

It was ready for us, just as he'd said it would be,
   everything arranged,
   everything in its place,
   down to the very last detail,
   as if our arrival there had been planned long before;
   yet – can you believe it? – still the penny didn't drop!
It was only later –
   after we'd shared supper together,
   after his enemies had come for him in the garden,
   after they'd beaten him, broken him,
   nailed him to the cross –
   it was only then that the awesome truth suddenly hit us:
   he *had* planned it! –
   every move, every step, meticulously prepared,
   weeks, months, even years beforehand –
   and our minds reeled at the enormity of it all.
When we'd walked by his side,
   blissfully unaware of anything untoward,
   he'd known that death was waiting for him,
   lurking greedily around the corner.
When we watched as he healed the sick and comforted the distressed,
   his thoughts all for others rather than himself,
   he was aware, nonetheless, of the awful fate in store for him,
   the horror, the hurt, the humiliation.
When we'd accompanied him proudly as he entered Jerusalem,
   basking in his reflected glory,
   revelling in the adulation,
   he'd had one eye already fixed on the days ahead –

on this last meal we would share together,
on the darkness to come in Gethsemane,
on the torture of crucifixion.
Suddenly it all made sense –
how that stranger had been waiting to meet us inside the city,
how we'd only to say 'The teacher asks . . .'
and it was done,
how we were shown upstairs to that little room
without any need for explanation.
He'd realised, all along,
probably from the very beginning,
that this moment would come,
that the path he had chosen would lead to suffering and death,
yet still he carried on,
undeterred,
undaunted.
And as that truth dawned on me, a lump came to my throat,
for he'd done it, willingly, for people like me.
He'd known I would deny him,
that we'd all fail him in our own way,
yet it didn't matter,
still he cared enough to die for us.
He saw us at our worst,
recognising our deepest weaknesses,
yet still he walked the way of the cross,
faithful to the last.
I can't believe it, even now –
that anyone could love us that much –
but it's true,
I saw the proof for myself.
We deserved nothing, as he well knew,
yet he went to the cross
and gave everything.

Prayer

Lord Jesus Christ,
you didn't just accept death for our sakes;
you chose it.
You didn't simply let things happen;
you planned them in advance,
knowing the way you would take,
down to that final agony on the cross.

The only thing you couldn't guarantee was resurrection –
    that had to be taken on trust.
You staked all, you gave all,
    and you did it willingly for our sakes.
Such love is too wonderful to comprehend,
    but we thank you for it from the bottom of our hearts.
Lord Jesus Christ, receive our praise.
Amen.

Silence

Slides and music

Lesson 1 for Maundy Thursday Palestrina
during which Luke 22:39-46 is read

Meditation

He was unsure of himself,
    for the first time in his life
    unsure of his ability to face the future,
    and it hurt him more than the pain he was finally to suffer.
You see, there'd never been any doubt until then,
    never even the slightest suggestion of hesitation.
Despite the hostility, the resentment, the abuse from so many,
    he'd set his face resolutely towards Jerusalem,
    knowing from the very beginning where it would all end.
He understood it all,
    the pain and humiliation he must suffer,
    conscious of it even way back
    in those heady days of his baptism,
    yet he'd carried on willingly,
    the prospect seeming to hold no fear for him,
    and we'd marvelled at the faith, the love,
    the courage of the man,
    the sheer commitment
    which gave him such awesome strength and inner purpose.
But suddenly, that evening, it was all so very different,
    a shadow blotting out the light which had shone so brightly.
I saw despair in his eyes rather than hope,
    fear rather than laughter,
    sorrow rather than joy,
    and, most terrible of all, that desperate look of uncertainty,

so alien,
so devastating,
so crushing a burden.
It was all suddenly too real,
no longer theory but fact –
the agony and the isolation he was about to face –
and, like any of us would in his place, he wanted to back away,
find an easier course,
a less dreadful option.
It struck me then, as never before,
that he didn't know what lay beyond death
any more than I did.
He'd always believed,
always trusted,
but he had no more certainty than you and me –
only the assurance of faith,
the conviction borne of trust,
and there in the darkness,
as the chill of night took hold,
it all hung on a thread
as he wrestled with the torment of doubt.
I know what I'd have done had I been him –
quite simply, I wouldn't have stopped running
until Jerusalem was just a memory!
But not Jesus.
He stayed quietly in the garden, as I knew he would,
and he offered not just his *faith* but his *doubt* to God –
'not *my* will but *yours* be done'.
Well, he was sure of one thing after that –
there was no way back,
death now a cast-iron certainty;
but it wasn't dying itself that was the problem for him,
it was not knowing whether it would all be worth it,
whether it could actually make a difference
to this world we live in,
and there was no way of answering that for certain
this side of eternity.
He was unsure –
of himself,
of his faith,
of his ability to face the future –
but despite it all he risked everything,

offering life itself,
so that we might know the truth,
and be free from death –
free for all eternity!

Prayer

Loving God,
you call us to live by faith, not by sight,
to put our faith in things unseen rather than seen,
and most of the time we are able to do that.
But occasionally we are faced by circumstances
which cause us to doubt,
throwing a shadow over everything we believe.
We question our ability to keep going,
we wonder what is happening to us,
and though we look to you for assurance, we do not find it.
Help us when such moments come
to know that you have been there before us in Christ
and that you understand what we are facing.
Inspire us through the faith and courage he showed,
and so help us to trust in your purpose
even when we cannot see the way ahead.
In his name we pray.
Amen.

Silence

Slides and music

Gloria (Coronation Mass) Mozart, during which Luke 24:36-43 is read

Meditation

He was back!
Back in the land of the living,
just when we'd given up hope!
Three days it had been,
three days of dark despair as slowly the truth sank home –
our Lord, laid in a tomb,
dead and buried,
never to walk this earth again.
We couldn't believe it at first,
none of us,
even though we'd seen it for ourselves.

We expected to wake up any moment to find it was all a dream,
    a dreadful mistake that had somehow taken us in.
But as the numbness passed, so the reality hit us,
    and the pain began in earnest.
It was an end to everything –
    our plans,
    our hopes,
    our dreams.
There was nothing left to live for,
    that's how we felt –
    we'd pinned our hopes on him,
    and he was gone.
Only he wasn't!
He was there,
    meeting Mary in the garden as her heart broke beside the tomb.
He was there,
    on the Emmaus road as two followers trudged slowly home,
    their world in tatters.
He was there,
    speaking to Thomas, breaking through his disbelief!
He was there,
    standing among us in the upper room!
He was back in the land of the living,
    and suddenly so were we –
    faith rekindled,
    hope renewed,
    joy reborn,
    life beginning again!

Prayer

Lord Jesus Christ,
    just when it looked all over,
    when the world had written you off
    and even your disciples had given up on you,
    you came back – defeat revealed as victory.
Teach us what that means for us today;
    not only the promise of eternal life,
    but good news for life here and now.
Help us to understand that, whatever tragedies we may suffer,
    whatever obstacles we may face,
    whatever disappointments we may experience,

we can bounce back from them with your help,
   for you are a God able to transform even the darkest moments
   and lead us through them into the light of your love.
Gladly, then, we put our hand in yours,
   knowing that in life or death
   you will never fail us or forsake us.
Amen.

Silence

Music   *On wings of song* Mendelssohn

AFTERNOON SESSION

Music   *Spring Song in A* Mendelssohn

Prayer
Loving God,
   you call us to a journey of faith,
   but sometimes that journey grinds to a halt.
We get stuck in a rut,
   closed to new directions,
   bogged down by the past,
   or reluctant to step into an unfamiliar future,
   preferring the view we know
   to horizons which may stretch and challenge us.
Move within us through your Holy Spirit,
   meet with us through the risen Christ,
   and so give light to our path
   that we may step forward in faith,
   and travel onwards wherever you might lead,
   through Jesus Christ our Lord.
Amen.

Slides and music
Send forth your spirit, Lord (Fountain of Life) Rizza
during which Acts 2:1-21 is read

Meditation

I don't know who was the more surprised,
   us, or them?
They were bewildered, certainly,
   unable to make head or tail of what was going on,
   amazed to hear us speaking to them in their own language
   and wondering what on earth it all could mean.
But if anything, our astonishment was the greater,
   each of us scarcely able to believe what was happening.
Yes, I know we'd been told to expect it,
   the promise given by Christ himself,
   but as to what it meant,
   what it actually involved,
   we'd no idea until that incredible moment
   when the Spirit came.
No warning,
   no tell-tale signs,
   just bang! –
   and our lives were changed for ever.
Truthfully, I never thought I had it in me,
   to get out there and speak fearlessly for Christ –
   and as for sharing in his ministry,
   continuing where he had left off,
   the very idea seemed ridiculous.
Only that's what happened –
   gifts beyond our wildest imagining,
   power beyond our most fantastic dreams,
   a joy that burned unquenchably within us
   and a sense of purpose which nothing could contain.
We were no longer on our own, gazing wistfully to the heavens –
   Christ was with us,
   and in a way more wonderful than he'd ever been before;
   not just by our side,
   but in our hearts,
   filling our whole being with his presence.
It was more than we'd ever expected,
   more than any of us had dared hope for,
   and we had to pinch ourselves to be sure it was true.
But it was,
   and I tell you what,
   impossible though it seems,
   I shouldn't wonder if God has more yet in store,

new experiences of his love,
new expressions of his purpose,
not just for us but for everyone,
his Spirit poured out on all, just as the prophet said –
nothing will surprise us now!

Prayer

Gracious God,
we are reminded today
of the renewing, transforming power of your Holy Spirit,
through which you have fired
ordinary people like us across the years
to live and work for you
in joyful faith and fearless service.
Help us to know today, through that same Spirit,
that you are able to take any person, any place,
any moment, any situation,
and achieve within each one things far more wonderful
than we can ever begin to imagine.
In Christ's name we pray.
Amen.

Silence

Slides and music

Gavotte (Holberg Suite) Grieg
during which Acts 10:1-6, 9-20, 23a, 24-28, 34b-35, 44-48 is read

Meditation

You must be joking, Lord!
That's what I told him,
and I was deadly serious,
for the very idea of eating such unclean gentile food
filled me with revulsion,
my stomach heaving at the prospect.
Even if I'd been starving I wouldn't have touched it –
no way!
Yet this voice went on and on, ringing in my ears:
'Get up, Peter. Kill and eat.'
And each time afterwards, despite my protestations,
the same message:
'What God has made clean, you must not call profane.'

I was thankful to wake up and find it was all a dream,
    yet my relief was short-lived
    for the picture still haunted me,
    hovering in my mind's eye,
    and, try as I might, I could not remove it.
I was baffled,
    mystified,
    and a touch ashamed at even entertaining such thoughts,
    for they went against everything I believed,
    everything I'd been taught from my mother's arms.
But there was no time for brooding
    for suddenly these strangers appeared, calling my name,
    and to their voices was added another –
    that voice of my dream:
    'Get up,
    go down,
    go with them.'
So I went,
    and found that God had gone before me –
    a man waiting there expectantly,
    a Roman centurion,
    and all at once, it made sense,
    the mystery resolved.
He was a Gentile, you see,
    according to our law unclean, impure,
    someone I was bound, as a Jew, to refuse –
    and just a day earlier I'd have done just that,
    the alternative unthinkable.
Only that was yesterday,
    this was today –
    God had shown me different,
    his love open to any,
    whatever their culture, colour or creed.
I left him rejoicing,
    singing God's praises and filled with the Holy Spirit,
    that man I'd have passed by without a thought,
    impervious to his pleas.
But while *I* saw the barriers which kept us apart,
    God through his love brought us together,
    and at last, for the first time in my life,
    I saw not the outside but the person within,
    the life beneath –

the child of God for whom Christ died,
as he died for you,
for me,
for everyone!

Prayer

Mighty God,
we imagine that we are open to those around us,
but in reality we are not.
Our attitudes are coloured by a host of preconceptions
which subconsciously create deep-rooted prejudices within us.
We pass judgement without even realising it
and close our minds to anyone or anything
which dares to challenge our narrow horizons.
Forgive us,
and help us to realise that truth is far bigger
than any one of us can grasp alone.
Teach us to be open to all the ways you are at work
and everything we can learn from the experiences
and insights of others.
Sweep away the bias and bigotry
which can so easily come to dominate our lives,
and so may we grasp the height, length, depth and breadth
of your purpose which transcends all our expectations;
through Jesus Christ our Lord.
Amen.

Silence

Blessing

Music   *Jesu, joy of man's desiring* J. S. Bach

John the Apostle – Witness to the Light

Suggested visual material
In the Beginning
Jesus of Nazareth 1, 3, 4 and 6
The Life of Christ IV

MORNING SESSION

Music
Intermezzo Mascagni

Introduction
'There was a man sent from God, whose name was John. He came as a witness to testify to the light, so that all might believe through him. He himself was not the light, but he came to testify to the light.' Words written by the Apostle John concerning his namesake John the Baptist, but they could just as well have been written about himself, for in the words of his Gospel we have one of the best-loved accounts of the life and ministry of Jesus, and a testimony of faith which over the years must have led countless others to a personal experience of the love of Christ. There is, of course, no way in a time as short as we have to do justice to either the extent or the depth of his writings, and we make no attempt in this Quiet Day to do so. The aim, rather, is to give us a flavour of the faith which sustained John, the convictions that he held, and the experience of Christ which lay behind it all. To do so, we dip briefly into his Gospel and the first of his epistles, supplementing this with a description of his preaching ministry taken from the book of Acts. Finally, we turn to the book of Revelation, a book which, according to some, was written by one of John's successors in the Church, carrying on the Apostle's ministry where he had left off. The voice of John has spoken powerfully to innumerable people across the years. What does it have to say to us today?

Prayer

Gracious God,
   we thank you for the testimony of Scripture
   to your love revealed in Christ;
   and, above all, we thank you today
   for all the experiences of your grace
   and goodness which lie behind the testimonies of the Evangelists.
They wrote to preserve a record
   of his love and ministry,
   they wrote to set down their understanding of the story,
   but, most of all, they wrote to communicate their faith,
   so that others in turn might come to see and believe for themselves.
Speak to us now as we share together,
   as we listen to your word,
   and reflect on the nature of Jesus.
May all that we hear and see
   come alive in our hearts,
   so that our faith may grow
   and our love for you be enriched.
In the name of Christ we pray.
Amen.

Slides and music

Gloria (Missa Ouer natus est nobis) Tallis
during which John 1:1-5, 10-14 is read

Meditation

'Where did it all start?' they ask me.
'Tell us the story again.'
And I know just what they want to hear –
   about the inn and the stable,
   the baby lying in a manger,
   shepherds out in the fields by night,
   and wise men travelling from afar.
I know why they ask, of course I do,
   for which of us hasn't thrilled to those marvellous events,
   that astonishing day when the Word became flesh,
   dwelling here on earth amongst us?
Yet wonderful though that all is, it's not where it started,
   and if we stop there, then we see only a fraction of the picture,
   the merest glimpse of everything God has done for us in Christ.

We have got to go right back to see more –
   before Bethlehem,
   before the prophets
   before the Law,
   before time itself, would you believe? –
   for that's where it started:
   literally 'in the beginning'.
Yes, even there the saving purpose of God was at work,
   his creating, redeeming Word
   bringing light and love into the world,
   shaping not just the heavens and the earth
   but the lives of all,
   every man, woman and child.
That's the mind-boggling wonder of it –
   the fact not just that God made us,
   but that through Christ he was determined from the outset
   to share our lives,
   to take on our flesh,
   to identify himself totally with the joys and sorrows,
   the beauty and the ugliness of humankind.
It defies belief, doesn't it?
Yet it's true –
   God wanting us to know him not as his creatures
   but as his children,
   not as puppets forced to dance to his tune
   but as people responding freely to his love,
   and to achieve that he patiently and painstakingly prepared the way,
   revealing year after year a little more of his purpose,
   a glimpse more of his kingdom,
   until at last,
   in the fullness of time,
   the Word became flesh and lived among us,
   full of grace and truth.
It wasn't an afterthought, the incarnation,
   a last-ditch attempt to make the best of a bad job –
   it was planned from the dawn of time.
So next time you hear the story of the stable and the manger,
   of the shepherds gazing in wonder
   and the magi kneeling in homage,
   stop for a moment
   and reflect on everything which made it all possible,

the eternal purpose which so carefully prepared the way of Christ,
and then ask yourself this:
are you prepared to respond to his coming?

Prayer

Gracious God,
  despite our repeated disobedience
  your love continues undiminished,
  reaching out to us every moment of every day.
Despite the rejection of the world
  still you go on seeking to draw it to yourself,
  until every broken relationship with you is mended.
So it is now and so it has always been,
  from the beginning of time your nature always to have mercy.
Help us to appreciate the enormity of your faithfulness,
  and to use this season of Advent
  to open our hearts more fully to your grace;
  through Jesus Christ our Lord.
Amen.

Silence

Slides and music

Alleluia (Exsultate, Jubilate) Mozart, during which John 20:1-10 is read

Meditation

One look, that's all it took!
One look,
  and I knew beyond all doubt that God was at work,
  that Jesus was alive!
I should have known it sooner, of course,
  for he'd told us what to expect often enough,
  but when the hammer blow fell
  we simply couldn't see beyond it,
  tears blinding our minds as well as our eyes.
It was when Mary came bursting in,
  beside herself with excitement,
  that the mist started to clear,
  that his words about death and resurrection
  came flooding back,
  rekindling a flame that had all but been extinguished.

I ran then as I've never run before,
   hope lending wings to my feet,
   heart pounding within me,
   not just from the exertion
   but from the emotion that had taken hold of me,
   the curious mixture of fear and exhilaration.
I wanted so much to believe it was true,
   only I was afraid it might be some cruel hoax
   or fancy of the imagination,
   a trick of the mind or, worse still, of our enemies.
But when I went in to the tomb
   and found the abandoned grave clothes,
   then I knew,
   and my spirit soared in jubilation.
He was not there:
   he had risen just as he promised,
   death not able to have the final word.
And suddenly everything fitted into place,
   the heartache, the hurt, the humiliation –
   it was all meant to be,
   all a part of God's sovereign purpose!
Where we had seen darkness, he had brought light!
Where there had been death, now there was life!
Everything was turned around,
   transformed,
   renewed,
   sharing in the wonder of resurrection.
One look, that's all it took –
   one look, and life was changed for ever!

Prayer

Gracious God,
   we thank you that our faith
   is not founded on theory or speculation –
   on the ideas of theologians or the musings of philosophers.
It is rooted in what individuals have seen and heard,
   in the living testimony of ordinary people like us,
   in the testimony of countless generations of believers
   who have encountered the risen Christ for themselves
   through his Spirit.
In him, you came, you lived, you died, you rose again,
   making yourself known through the concrete events of history.

For all who saw for themselves and passed the message on,
   receive our thanks.
And for all that we experience today
   of your continuing love and your life-giving purpose,
   we give you our praise in joyful worship;
   through Jesus Christ, our risen, victorious Saviour.
Amen.

Silence

Slides and music

Veni, lumen cordium (Fountain of Life) Rizza
during which Acts 1:1-5, 8, 12-14 is read

Meditation

'You will be my witnesses
   in Jerusalem,
   in all Judea and Samaria,
   and to the ends of the earth.'
Quite a picture, isn't it,
   a prospect to stir the heart and fire the imagination.
But I tell you what,
   huddled there together in that upper room,
   those words seemed a long way off,
   a beautiful but rapidly fading memory.
We were terrified of going out, if the truth be told,
   despite our prayers,
   despite his promise,
   scared stiff our enemies would come for us
   as they'd come for him,
   and send us off to some equally ghastly death.
We wished it were different, of course we did –
   we longed for courage to get out there
   and proclaim the good news,
   to tell the world what Christ had done,
   but, even if we had found that courage,
   it wouldn't have counted for much,
   for we had no idea what to say or how to say it.
We were twelve men with a mission –
   and none of us had the first idea where to start,
   let alone where it all might finish!

So we just sat there,
   and waited,
   and hoped,
   longing to believe it might be true
   but in our heart of hearts wondering if it ever could be –
   for who were we,
   ordinary folk like us,
   to set the world on fire?
It was an unlikely prospect, to say the least.
Only, suddenly, out of the blue, it happened,
   a sound like a mighty rushing wind filling the room,
   tongues of fire leaping and dancing upon us,
   and, all at once, an ecstasy beyond words,
   a peace, a joy and a confidence that defied description.
No more fear or doubt,
   no more hesitation –
   our mouths were opened and we spoke boldly,
   moving out among the multitude that had gathered,
   the words flowing freely as we needed them,
   and each heard us,
   amazed,
   bewildered to hear us speaking in their own tongue.
A one-minute wonder?
Don't you believe it!
It was the beginning of an astonishing adventure,
   a lifetime of witness,
   an incredible journey of discipleship,
   out into Jerusalem,
   on to Judea and Samaria,
   and beyond to the ends of the earth.
As I say, quite a picture, isn't it?
One to stir even the coldest heart
   and fire the poorest of imaginations.
At least I hope it does,
   for the job's not over, not by a long way,
   nor, praise God, is the promise.
The call is there, and the offer is there,
   for you and anyone who believes –
   the promise of power to be witnesses to the risen Christ.
Wait patiently,
   trust in the promise of the Father,
   and you, like us, will receive.

Prayer

Lord,
  it is hard to share our faith with a few,
  let alone many.
When we listen to your call
  to be witnesses to the ends of the earth
  we feel that the task is hopelessly beyond us,
  our resources feebly inadequate to meet the challenge.
Yet that is to view things from our perspective
  rather than yours,
  for you do not leave us dependent on our strength
  but rather equip us with the power of the Holy Spirit
  who is able to work in ways far exceeding our expectations.
Move within us,
  as you have moved in your people across the centuries,
  and teach us to trust you for the help we need,
  when we need it.
In the name of Christ we pray.
Amen.

Silence

Music   *Adagio sostenuto (Moonlight Sonata)* Beethoven

AFTERNOON SESSION

Music   *Grave/Allegro di molto e con brio (Pathétique Sonata)*
          Beethoven

Prayer

Lord Jesus Christ,
  we have considered your ministry
  during your earthly life,
  from your birth to your death
  to your resurrection.
Now we think of your continuing ministry
  through your Holy Spirit;
  a Spirit and a ministry in which we share.

Open again your word to us,
   so that we may learn
   from all who have gone before us,
   and so live in such a way
   as to be an example for those who will follow,
   for your name's sake.
Amen.

Slides and music

The Mirror of the Trinity (Magnificat) Praetorius
during which John 15:12-27 is read

Meditation

I didn't know what he was on about at the time,
   not the faintest idea,
   despite the way I nodded
   and attempted to smile in the right places.
The Advocate?
The Son who comes from the Father?
What did it all mean?
We believed he was sent by God, yes –
   called to reveal his will,
   build his kingdom –
   but was he saying more,
   pointing to a closer relationship?
It seemed so,
   yet, try as we might, we just couldn't get our heads round it.
'The Lord our God is one' –
   isn't that what we'd always been told?
Indeed, he said it himself,
   made no bones about it,
   so how could he also tell us, 'He who has seen me
   has seen the Father'?
We were baffled, there's no other word for it,
   and when he went on to talk about the Spirit of truth,
   the one his Father would send in his name,
   quite simply, by then, we were reeling,
   unable to make head or tail of what he was getting at.
'Do we understand now, though?' you ask.

Well, no, we don't actually –
    funnily enough if we try to explain it
    we still struggle as much as ever;
    the more we try, the worse the knots we tie ourselves in.
Yet, strange though it may sound, it makes sense despite that –
    for day after day, year after year, we've tasted the truth,
    the reality of Father, Son and Holy Spirit.
We look up,
    to the stars and the sky,
    the wonder of the heavens,
    and God is there, enthroned in splendour,
    sovereign over all.
We look around,
    at the world he's given –
    its awesome beauty,
    its endless interest,
    its bountiful provision –
    and he is there,
    stretching out his hand in love,
    inviting us to share in its wonder.
We look nearby,
    at family and friends,
    beyond, to the nameless faces of the multitude,
    and he is there,
    giving and receiving,
    waiting to feed and to be fed.
We look within,
    at our aching souls,
    our pleading hearts,
    and he is there,
    breathing new life,
    new purpose within us.
One God, yes,
    but a God we meet in different guises,
    different ways,
    three in one and one in three.
It sounds odd, I know,
    and take it from me, you'll never explain it,
    no matter how you try,
    yet don't worry, for what finally matters is this:
    though words may fail you, the experience never will!

Prayer

Almighty God,
　there are no words able to sum up your nature,
　to say everything about you that needs to be said.
We do our best to express our faith,
　but inevitably we fall short,
　for you are greater than our minds can fathom,
　ultimately defying human understanding.
Yet we experience your love day after day
　in a multitude of ways:
　we glimpse your glory in the wonder of the heavens
　and the beauty of the earth;
　we see everything we believe to be true about you
　revealed in Jesus Christ,
　his life, death and resurrection;
　and we feel your power at work deep within us
　through what we call your Spirit.
Each reveals different aspects of your character,
　yet it is only when we take them together,
　recognising them as facets of one being, one truth,
　that we begin to understand something of your wonder.
Our intellects reel at the mystery of it all,
　yet in our heart and soul we know that you are with us,
　and we rejoice.
Almighty God, Father, Son and Holy Spirit,
　receive our praise.
Amen!

Silence

Slides and music

Salut d'Amour Elgar, during which 1 John 4:7-21 is read

Meditation

Sentimental rubbish, that's what some will accuse me of,
　another airy-fairy spiel about 'love',
　whatever that's supposed to mean.
And I can see their point,
　for we do use the word loosely,
　enough sometimes to cover a multitude of sins.
Yet I'm sorry, but when it comes to God
　there's no other word that will do,
　for God *is* love!

It's as simple,
   as straightforward,
   as uncomplicated as that –
   the one description that says it all,
   and if you lose that simple truth, you lose everything.
Not that you'd think it, mind you, to hear some people talk,
   the picture they paint altogether different.
A God of wrath, they say,
   of justice, righteousness, punishment,
   sometimes jealous,
   often forbidding,
   remote, holy, set apart.
He *is* those, of course –
   or at least he can be when necessary –
   but never out of malice,
   only in love.
He longs to bless, not punish,
   to give, rather than take away;
   his nature is always to have mercy,
   to show kindness,
   to fill our lives with good things.
If you see him otherwise,
   as some vengeful ogre intent on destroying you,
   then you don't know him,
   for I tell you, God *is* love –
   all the law,
   all the commandments,
   all our faith summed up in that small but wonderful word.
And though I can't put it into words,
   you'll understand what I mean if you *do* know him,
   for his love will flow in you, through you and from you,
   touching every part of your life.
No, we don't deserve such goodness,
   not for a moment,
   for we'll continue to fail him,
   our love always imperfect;
   but isn't that just the point,
   the thing which makes love so special?
It *does* cover a multitude of sins! –
   cleansing,
   renewing,
   restoring,

forgiving –
refusing to let go come what may.
That's the God we serve,
   the sort of being he is –
   and if that isn't love, I don't know what is!

Prayer

Lord God,
   we use many words to describe you,
   many terms in an attempt sum up all you are
   and all you mean.
We speak of your power, your might, your majesty
   as we try to express your greatness.
We call you eternal, everlasting, infinite
   in an effort to convey your timelessness.
We speak of your justice, righteousness and holiness
   as we strive to give voice to your otherness.
We call you Creator, Father, Redeemer
   as we seek to articulate your goodness.
Yet always our words fall short,
   pointing to part but not all of the truth.
But we praise you that there is one word that says it all,
   which is able to encapsulate your mystery and wonder,
   your sovereignty and transcendence,
   your mercy and faithfulness –
   that little word 'love'.
Overworked, misapplied, misunderstood we know it to be,
   but with you it says it all,
   for it is your whole nature, your whole purpose
   and your whole being.
In that knowledge may we live each day,
   assured that, whatever may be, your love will always enfold us
   until it finally conquers all.
Lord God, we praise you,
   through Jesus Christ our Lord.
Amen.

Silence

Slides and music

Come, Lord (Fountain of Life) Rizza
during which Revelation 21:1-4; 22:5 is read

Meditation

I had a dream last night,
   a wonderful, astonishing dream –
   so real,
   so vivid,
   that it will live with me for the rest of my days.
I caught a glimpse of God,
   enthroned in majesty,
   encircled by the great company of heaven,
   and there at his right hand,
   exalted,
   lifted up in splendour,
   our Lord Jesus Christ,
   King of kings and Lord of lords!
It was wonderful,
   breathtaking,
   indescribable.
Yet I have to share it with you somehow –
   clutching at metaphors,
   searching for the right words,
   but at least giving you some idea of what I saw.
Why? I hear you say.
What does it matter if it was only a dream?
And I take your point.
Yet I have this feeling, deep within,
   no – more than just a feeling – this certainty,
   that God was speaking to me through that dream;
   speaking to *me*,
   to *you*,
   to everyone with ears to hear and a mind to listen.
He was telling us that in all the chaos of this humdrum world;
   all the changes and chances of this uncertain life;
   despite all the pain,
   all the suffering,
   all the evil,
   all the sorrow,
   everything that seems to fight against him,
   God is there,
   slowly but surely working out his purpose.
And one day,
   in the fullness of time,
   his kingdom will come
   and his will shall be done.

Don't ask me when, for I can't tell you that.
But though we may not see it
and though we may not feel it,
I am assured that he will triumph.
Joy will take the place of sorrow.
Life will follow death.
Love will be victorious!

Prayer

Eternal and sovereign God,
you have promised that one day there will be an end
to everything that frustrates your will and denies your love.
You promise us a kingdom
in which there will be no more hatred,
no more sorrow and no more suffering;
a kingdom of everlasting peace
filled with light and love and happiness.
You promise that death itself shall be overcome
and we shall be raised to life eternal,
one with all your people from every place and time,
and one with you.
That great picture seems like a dream sometimes,
faced by the cold realities of life now,
and yet we know that what you have promised shall be done.
So may that vision burn bright in our hearts –
a constant source of comfort and inspiration
as we journey in faith towards that final goal.
Walk with us and see us safely through,
until that time when your word is fulfilled,
your will is done
and your kingdom comes in all its glory;
through Jesus Christ our Lord.
Amen.

Silence

Blessing

Music   *God so loved the world (The Crucifixion)* Stainer

Paul – The Man and the Message

Suggested visual material

In the Beginning
Jesus of Nazareth 3, 4 and 6
The Life of Christ IV
St Paul
The Story of Saint Paul

MORNING SESSION

Music

Pilgrims' Chorus (Tannhäuser) Wagner

Introduction

Few people, besides Jesus himself, have had such an impact on the Church or the Christian faith as the Apostle Paul. It is to his vision, energy and enthusiasm that we owe the transformation of Christianity from a branch of Judaism to a world-wide faith which still today continues to grow. Yet few people could have seemed more unlikely candidates for such a job, given Paul's hatred for anything to do with Jesus, unparalleled in his time. Admittedly he had many ideally suited gifts which God was able to make use of, but there were equally as many characteristics totally unsuited to the demands of his calling, not least his poor health, his unimposing presence and his so-called 'thorn in the flesh', whatever that might have been. Yet not only was he used uniquely by God in those early days; he continues to speak equally powerfully today, his letters together making up a substantial portion of the New Testament. Today, then, we stop to consider both the man himself and the message he preached. What can we learn from the way Jesus changed Paul's life? What lessons can we draw from his experiences? And what does he have to say concerning our own faith and discipleship? If we are willing to explore such questions we will find the voice of Paul speaking to us here and now and, through that, the voice of God himself.

Prayer

Sovereign God,
  we thank you for the way
  you have spoken across the centuries,
  the way you have repeatedly changed people
  and transformed situations in a manner
  which, to human eyes, looked impossible.
Inspire us today
  as we reflect upon one such example
  of your renewing power,
  and help us through that
  to understand more clearly
  everything you are able to do in our own lives
  and the world today,
  through Jesus Christ our Lord.
Amen.

Slides and music

First Movement (Holberg Suite) Grieg, during which Acts 9:1-9 is read

Meditation

Jesus? The very name filled me with fury –
  not just anger but a blind, all-consuming rage.
To think that some were calling him the Messiah,
  this man who had wilfully flouted the law,
  desecrated the temple,
  blasphemed against God himself,
  and finally suffered the fate due to all his kind,
  death on a cross –
  how could anyone look up to a person like that?
Yet there were plenty only too willing,
  and as if that weren't enough,
  they actually claimed he was alive,
  that somehow he'd cheated death itself
  and risen from the tomb.
Ridiculous!
Well, they could swallow such nonsense if they wanted to,
  but not me, you could be sure of that.

I knew exactly what I stood for,
   precisely what I believed,
   and no one was going to shake me from it,
   least of all some misguided crank from Galilee.
But if I was secure, others weren't,
   and it was my duty to protect them from possible contagion,
   so I set about his followers with a vengeance,
   determined to wipe away every last trace of their heresy
   by whatever means necessary.
Let Jesus show himself now, I sneered!
Only that's where I came unstuck,
   for he did,
   there on the Damascus road –
   a blinding flash and a voice from heaven:
   'Saul, Saul, why do you persecute me?'
It couldn't be, I thought, surely?
But it was,
   the man I believed dead and buried, all too clearly alive!
I expected immediate retribution,
   to be struck down on the spot as a lesson to all –
   let's be clear, I deserved it.
But, instead, something very different and completely unexpected –
   the call to service,
   to carry his name to the Gentiles,
   to help build his kingdom.
Me! Paul!
I couldn't believe it,
   nor anyone else, come to that,
   the last thing anyone would have imagined possible
   in their wildest dreams.
Yet that's how it worked out,
   the results there to be seen by anyone who cares to question.
God, in his mercy, saw fit to use me,
   the greatest of sinners,
   the least of disciples,
   to proclaim the good news of Christ crucified and risen.
I thought I knew just where I stood,
   that I understood precisely who I was and what I was doing,
   but I learned that day a truth which still fills me with wonder:
   the fact that Jesus knew me better than I knew myself,
   and still loved me, despite it all!

Prayer

Gracious God,
   you are under no illusions about us.
You do not imagine we are better than we really are,
   nor are you taken in by the mask we wear for the world.
You see us in all our shabbiness and shame,
   and you reach out in love.
But you are under no illusions either about our unworthiness.
You do not consider that we are worse than we really are,
   nor are you swayed
   by the way we can sometimes do ourselves down.
You see us in all our potential and all our weakness,
   and you find a place in your heart for both.
You see the bad *and* the good,
   the worst *and* the best,
   and you recognise not only what we are
   but what we might become through your grace.
Come to us now, as we come to you,
   and use us for your glory,
   in the name of Jesus Christ our Lord.
Amen.

Silence

Slides and music

The Swan (Carnival of the Animals) Saint-Saens
during which Romans 7:14-25 is read

Meditation

Have you ever tried turning over a new leaf?
I have,
   again,
   and again,
   and again.
Every morning I wake up and say,
   'Today is going to be different!'
And every night I lie down with the knowledge that is wasn't.

For all my good intentions
    I make the same mistakes I've always made,
    display the same old weaknesses,
    succumb to the same old temptations –
    a constant cycle of failure.
Why does it happen?
I just can't work it out,
    for I want so much to be faithful –
    more than anything else in the world –
    yet somehow, before I know it, I find I've fallen again,
    unable to do even my own will,
    let alone God's.
It's as though there are two selves at war within me,
    one intent on good and the other on evil,
    and you don't need me to tell you which one emerges the victor.
Can it ever change?
I'd like to think so,
    but I honestly don't think it will,
    for though the spirit is willing, the flesh is weak,
    rushing, like a moth before a candle,
    towards its own destruction.
Do you wonder that I despair sometimes?
It's impossible not to.
Yet I shouldn't lose heart,
    because despite it all God still loves me,
    not for what one day I might be,
    but for what I am now,
    with all my sin sticking to me.
That's why he sent his Son into the world –
    not to save the righteous,
    but to rescue people like you and me,
    weak, foolish, faithless,
    unable to help ourselves.
It doesn't mean I'll stop trying,
    I'll never do that until my dying day.
But it *does* mean, however many times I fail,
    however often he finds me lying in the gutter,
    he'll be there to pick me up and set me on my way again,
    cleansed, restored, forgiven,
    the slate wiped clean, ready to start afresh –
    through his grace, a new creation!

Prayer

Merciful God,
  unlike us you don't dwell on our failures.
Instead, you invite us to acknowledge them openly before you,
  to receive your pardon and then to move on.
Teach us to do just that –
  to accept your offer for what it is
  and, rather than wallow in our guilt,
  to rejoice in your mercy.
Help us not simply to *talk* about new life
  but to *live* it joyfully,
  receiving each moment as your gracious gift;
  through Jesus Christ our Lord.
Amen.

Silence

Slides and music

The trumpet shall sound (Messiah) Handel
during which 1 Corinthians 15:12-22, 35-36, 42-44a, 50-57 is read

Meditation

'What will it be like?' they ask me.
  'What sort of body will we have?
  What sort of clothes?
  What sort of food?'
And then, as if that weren't enough,
  'When will it be?
  Where will we go?
  How will it happen?'
As if *I* should know!
All right, so maybe I did catch a glimpse of life outside the body,
  but that doesn't make me an expert, does it –
  an authority on the life to come?
Yet admit that to some people
  and they start to question everything,
  as though the whole idea of resurrection
  hinges on our ability to understand it.
I know why they ask, of course I do,
  for it's not easy living with mystery,
  accepting claims one cannot fathom or even begin to picture;
  yet is that really anything new

when it comes to the things of God?
'My thoughts are not your thoughts,
    nor are your ways my ways' –
    isn't that what he told us,
    so why presume they are?
I realised long ago just because we don't understand something
    doesn't mean it isn't true.
The trouble is we start in the wrong place,
    looking to what's yet to be rather than what's been already,
    but it's there that our faith rests –
    in the wonder of the empty tomb, the folded grave clothes,
    the risen Lord,
    in the glorious message of his victory over death,
    his final triumph over evil.
Isn't that enough for you?
It is for me.
I can't explain how it happened, but I know it's real,
    for I've met him myself,
    experienced his presence,
    died, through his power, to the old self and risen to the new.
Take away that, and you take away everything.
We'd all like to know more, I accept that,
    to end, once and for all, the guessing and speculation,
    but we wouldn't understand even if it was spelt out for us,
    for the things God has in store
    are beyond the human eye to see or heart to conceive.
So no more brooding about the future –
    what *may* be,
    what *could* be.
Think rather of Christ –
    what he's *done*,
    what he's *doing*,
    and then you will learn to take on trust
    the things he's yet to do,
    and the life which yet *shall* be.

Prayer

Sovereign God,
    you do not ask us to base our faith on what might be
    but on what *has* been and what *is*.
You came to our world in Christ and lived among us,
    demonstrating your commitment to humankind.

Through him you suffered and died on a cross,
  but in triumph you rose again,
  testifying to your victory over death.
And now, through that same Jesus,
  we experience the daily reality of your presence
  and the constant wonder of your love.
May all you have done and continue to do
  inspire us to trust in the future you hold for us,
  confident that as you are with us now
  so you shall be for all eternity;
  through Jesus Christ our Lord.
Amen.

Silence

Music *I know that my redeemer liveth (Messiah)* Handel

AFTERNOON SESSION

Music *Pié Jesu (Requiem)* Andrew Lloyd Weber

Prayer
Gracious God,
  you are able to do in our lives
  far more than we can even begin to imagine.
Forgive us for losing sight of that fact –
  for being content to muddle along,
  frustrating your will and quenching your Spirit
  through the narrowness of our vision.
Give us today a new sense of all you want to achieve,
  and of the way you are able to use us in achieving it.
Stir our imaginations,
  and send us out renewed in faith,
  to live and work for your glory;
  through Jesus Christ our Lord.
Amen.

Slides and music
Etude in E Chopin, during which 2 Corinthians 12:7b-10 is read

Meditation

I could think about nothing else at the time
    but that affliction of mine,
    that thorn in the flesh, as I finally came to call it.
It dominated my whole life, and very nearly destroyed me,
    sapping my strength,
    destroying my confidence,
    eating into the very fabric of my faith.
Try as I might, I just couldn't get it out of my head –
    it was always there,
    preying on my mind,
    lurking in the shadows,
    waiting to devour me.
When I woke up in the morning it was waiting to meet me,
    a constant reminder of my weakness.
When I walked in the street it pursued me,
    striking me down when I least expected.
When I talked with friends it was there too,
    breaking into our conversation.
When I turned to God in prayer, even there it turned up,
    insinuating itself between us.
And I was getting desperate,
    sucked ever deeper into a dark pit of despair,
    the laughter, the love, the life being drained from me.
Why? I asked.
Why me?
What sin had I committed?
What penance did I have to do
    before God would have pity and set me free?
I'd make it worth it, I told him,
    not just for me but for both our sakes.
I could do so much more,
    serve him so much better,
    if only he'd hear my prayer.
But there was no answer,
    no release,
    nothing.
I begged him again,
    angry,
    disappointed,
    resentful.
But it made no difference –
    still nothing.

So I left off for a while,
    until my patience could take it no longer,
    the frustration too much to bear.
And then once more I asked,
    grovelling this time,
    begging,
    pleading.
But yet again, nothing,
    just a blank, empty silence.
Or so I thought,
    until suddenly this picture of Jesus came to me,
    his eyes filled with pain, his body broken,
    and on his head a crown of thorns;
    the blood trickling down his tortured face,
    the hands outstretched in agony –
    and all at once I knew I was wrong.
He'd heard me all right,
    and answered,
    only I hadn't been ready to listen.
For it was there,
    in the sorrow and suffering of the Cross,
    that God fulfilled his eternal purpose;
    there,
    in what the world counts weakness,
    that God showed us true greatness!
So have I finally come to terms with this problem of mine,
    exorcised the demon that's haunted me for so long?
No, I can't claim that,
    for I still have my moments,
    still sometimes ask why,
    and still hope some day it might be different.
But when I catch myself feeling like that
    I stop and think of Jesus,
    and I realise again
    that in my weakness is God's strength.

Prayer

Loving God,
    we do not like living with weakness.
We want to feel strong, in control of our destiny,
    able to stand up against whatever life might throw at us,
    and we resent anything which threatens that sense of security.

Yet time and again across the years
   you have turned this world's expectations upside-down,
   your values totally different from our own.
You humble the proud, you bring down the mighty,
   you reduce the powerful to nothing,
   choosing instead to work through those
   who seem insignificant and vulnerable.
Teach us, then, when we find our weaknesses hard to accept,
   to recognise that you are able to use them
   in ways beyond our imagining,
   and to understand that in those very weaknesses
   your strength is most perfectly seen;
   through Jesus Christ our Lord.
Amen.

Silence

Slides and music

Jesu, joy of man's desiring J. S. Bach
during which Philippians 4:4-7, 10-12 is read

Meditation

Was I happy with my lot?
Well, as a matter of fact, I wasn't,
   not at first, anyway.
Oh, I gave thanks, don't get me wrong –
   I marvelled each day at the love of Christ
   and rejoiced constantly at the awesome grace he'd shown to me,
   but for all that there was much I found difficult,
   far more than I'd ever bargained for.
It wasn't the weariness,
   the endless travel,
   the days, weeks, even months without a rest –
   I could cope with those, despite my infirmities.
But when the hostility began,
   the beatings,
   the stone-throwing,
   the interminable hours rotting in a prison cell,
   that's when it became hard to bear,
   when I began to wonder just what I'd got myself into.
You wouldn't believe the things I endured,
   the hunger,

the pain,
the privations –
enough to break anyone,
crush the strongest of spirits.
And yet, somehow, they weren't able to do that,
for in my darkest moments I always found the strength I needed –
a word of encouragement,
a sign of hope,
a light dawning –
and I knew that Christ was with me even there,
especially there,
in my time of need.
I may have been hungry,
but I had food in plenty for my soul.
I may have been broken in body,
but my spirit had been made whole.
I may have been poor in the things of this world,
but I was rich in the things of God.
It didn't take away the pain, I can't claim that –
the hardship, the fear and the suffering were just as real,
just as terrible –
but it changed the way I saw them,
my perspective on life, on death, on everything
transformed for ever.
I had joy in my heart,
peace which passed all understanding,
and the promise of treasure in heaven –
whatever else might be taken from me,
nothing could take away those.
It was enough, and more than enough!

Prayer

Loving God,
you do not promise those who follow you
a life in which everything will go smoothly.
You do not guarantee success or prosperity,
nor do you offer immunity from the trials
and tribulations of this world.
Indeed, true service may involve us in sacrifice and self-denial,
more demands rather than *less*,
greater and more testing challenges
than we may ever have faced without you.

But what you *do* promise us is fulfilment in Christ.
Through him you are able to satisfy our spiritual hunger and thirst,
    to meet our deepest needs,
    to give us inner peace and an enduring contentment
    in each and every circumstance.
Such peace does not come overnight –
    it matures gradually as day by day we learn to let go
    and put our trust in you.
Reach out then, and draw us ever closer to your side,
    so that we may learn the secret
    of being content with whatever we have;
    through Jesus Christ our Lord.
Amen.

Silence

Slides and music

Moderato (Serenade for strings in E minor) Dvořák
during which Galatians 1:13-24 is read

Meditation

It looked impossible at the beginning,
    utterly beyond me.
And I don't mind confessing there were many times
    when I felt like giving up,
    throwing in the towel and cutting my losses.
Surprised?
You shouldn't be.
After all, just look what I was up against –
    me, Paul, called to take the gospel beyond Jerusalem,
    beyond Judea,
    out to the ends of the earth!
It was a tall order by anyone's reckoning,
    and when you remember how the Jews felt about the Gentiles,
    and how the Gentiles felt in return,
    well, you can begin to understand the scale of the problem, can't you!
I was up against it from the very start,
    doing my best to keep a foot in both camps to avoid causing offence,
    trying to share the good news,
    but forever keeping one eye over my shoulder,
    knowing the snipers wouldn't be far away.

It didn't help I suppose, with my own people anyway,
  me being a Jew myself,
  schooled as a Pharisee and expert in the law to boot!
They thought I was betraying my roots,
  reneging on my convictions,
  denying the faith of our fathers.
And as for the Gentiles, many simply wondered what I was doing,
  pushing my nose into their affairs.
So, yes, I had my doubts, to put it mildly!
Wouldn't you have felt the same?
Who was I to overcome that sort of prejudice,
  to break down the barriers between us,
  to bring people of such contrasting backgrounds together
  into one family of humankind?
Who was I to talk of a new way of thinking,
  of building a different sort of kingdom,
  of sharing a different sort of love?
Someone else perhaps – but me?
No way!
And yet the mystery is, I did!
Somehow, in a way I'll never understand,
  I found the strength and the words I needed
  when I needed them most.
I found energy to begin new tasks,
  courage to meet new people,
  faith to dream new dreams.
I unearthed reserves I never knew existed,
  and achieved results I never imagined possible –
  all kinds of people
  in all kinds of ways,
  discovering the joy of sharing and working together,
  discovering a faith that answered their deepest needs –
  a faith to live by.
It looked impossible, you can't argue with that –
  wonderful yet altogether ridiculous.
But it wasn't,
  for I've discovered since then,
  much to my amazement,
  much to my relief,
  that I can do all things
  through him who strengthens me.
Thanks be to God!

Prayer

Sovereign God,
  the challenges you set before us may be very modest
  compared with those faced by others over the years,
  but they can seem daunting nonetheless.
We feel inadequate to meet the task,
  acutely conscious of our lack of faith,
  the limitations of our gifts
  and our inability to serve you as we would wish.
Yet time and again throughout history
  you have taken the most unpromising of material
  and used it in ways defying all expectations.
You have turned doubt into faith,
  weakness into strength,
  timid service into fearless discipleship,
  and you go on doing that today
  through the power of your Holy Spirit.
Give us, then, the faith to respond to your call,
  trusting that, whatever you ask of us,
  you will be by our side to help us see it through,
  to the glory of your name.
Amen.

Silence

Slides and music

Nocturne No 2 in E flat Chopin, during which Philippians 1:3-8 is read

Meditation

It's been good to share with you,
  more than you'll ever know.
The times we've been through,
  the experiences we've faced,
  they've gone together,
  little by little,
  bit by bit,
  to weave a web between us –
  our lives inextricably entwined.
I've preached the word to you,
  led your prayers and guided your thoughts.

I've visited your homes,
   heard your problems,
   witnessed your joys.
But more than that,
   we've laughed together,
   learned together,
   grieved together,
   grown together –
   this time that's passed as much about your ministry to me
   as mine to you.
And they will live with me, the moments we've shared –
   the good times,
   the bad,
   the times of joy,
   the times of sorrow –
   remembered or unremembered, they have all been special,
   every one of them –
   a part of the person I am,
   a symbol of all that we have been together.
It's been good to share,
   more than words can quite express;
   and it's hard to part,
   more difficult that you may ever think.
But it's not goodbye,
   not for us or anyone who holds dear the name of Christ –
   simply farewell, until that day we meet again,
   in this life or the next.
Whatever the future,
   whatever we face,
   come rain or sunshine,
   pleasure or pain,
   we are one with each other, always,
   through being one together in him.

Prayer

Lord Jesus Christ,
   we thank you for all those
   with whom we have walked on the journey of faith,
   those who have been part of our family in Jesus Christ.
We praise you for the gift of fellowship
   which continues to mean so much to us –
   for all the strength and support we receive through it;

the love, comfort, inspiration and encouragement it brings us
in such abundance.
You do not leave us to travel alone
but bind us together through your Spirit,
granting us a unity of faith and purpose
which transcends those things which keep us apart.
Forgive us those times we have failed to share as we ought to,
neglecting each other's needs
and forgetting our mutual responsibilities.
Forgive us the divisions we have allowed to come between us;
the thoughtless words and careless actions
which have broken your body.
Teach us to open our hearts to one another,
to grow together in love
and to celebrate the privilege of belonging to your people;
through Jesus Christ our Lord.
Amen.

Silence

Blessing

Music   *Pilgrims' Chorus (Tannhäuser)* Wagner

Living with Doubt

Suggested visual material	Jesus of Nazareth 1, 2, 3, 4, 5 and 6 The Life of Christ IV Man of the Cross

MORNING SESSION

Music	*Credo in unum Deum (Mass in C minor)* Mozart
Introduction	'I believe in God, the Father Almighty, creator of heaven and earth. I believe in Jesus Christ, his only Son, our Lord.' The opening words of the Apostles' Creed, which across the centuries have been accepted and repeated as a summary of the faith of the Church, the essentials of Christian belief. And probably most of us most of the time would be happy to add our voices alongside those who have gone before us. Most, but not all, of the time – because for virtually every one of us there are times when we find ourselves wrestling with doubts; a multitude of questions which unexpectedly thrust themselves upon us, disturbing our peace and even threatening to undermine our faith completely. To make things worse, such moments are often compounded by a sense of guilt, a feeling that we are wrong and even sinful to entertain such thoughts. The result can be a lonely struggle in the wilderness, crushed by a sense of isolation, failure and shame. Yet if we look at the Scriptures we see there that doubt is not as uncommon as we might at first imagine. Alongside the glowing testimonies of faith, there are also several examples of those whose faith was tested to the limit; those who were not quite so sure and who found themselves struggling to keep going. Who can forget the words of the father who came to Jesus seeking help for his son: 'I believe; help my unbelief'; or the words of Thomas: 'Unless I see the mark of the nails in his hands, and put my

finger in the mark of the nails and my hand in his side, I will not believe.' Even Jesus himself apparently faced a time when for a moment he seemed to question his ability to continue: 'Father, if you are willing, remove this cup from me; yet, not my will but yours be done.' Doubt may come to us all, however secure in faith we appear to be. Do not fear it, for it is not something to be ashamed of. Believe, rather, that God is able to take and use your questions to lead you into a deeper understanding of his purpose and a richer sense of his love. Do that, and you will discover that doubt is not the opposite of faith, but for many of us an essential part of the journey of discipleship.

Prayer

Gracious God,
    we come today confessing our faith
    in your love,
    your goodness,
    your purpose.
We acknowledge your greatness,
    we rejoice in your mercy,
    and we thank you for the many blessings
    you have showered upon us.
But we come today also confessing our doubt –
    the many things we don't understand,
    the statements of faith which don't make sense,
    the events of life which seem to contradict
    everything we believe about you.
Gracious God,
    there are times when we are sure
    and times when we are uncertain;
    times when we feel ready to take on the world
    and times when faith hangs by a thread.
Give us sufficient trust in you
    to acknowledge all such feelings openly,
    and sufficient humility
    to offer each to you honestly in prayer.
Save us from taking refuge
    in hollow words or empty ritual,
    but teach us to face the challenges life brings

and to work through our faith
in the light of them,
so that, having been tested,
it may grow the stronger,
able to face all and still to stand,
through Jesus Christ our Lord.
Amen.

Slides and music

Il riposo – per il Santissimo Natale (Concerto for strings) Vivaldi
during which Isaiah 9:2, 6-7 is read

Meditation of a resident of Jerusalem

'The people who walked in darkness have seen a great light.'
Do you remember those words?
Of course you do – it's hard not to, isn't it?
But do you think they mean anything?
Do you actually believe that things will change,
    that the Messiah will come
    and finally establish his kingdom?
I used to, once.
I used to read that passage time and again,
    a warm glow stealing over me
    until I tingled with anticipation,
    convinced that God would soon transform this world of ours.
Any day now, I thought,
    it can't be long –
    surely.
But another day, another month, another year came and went,
    and, with each one, faith lost a little of its sparkle,
    until finally the lustre is just about gone,
    no more than a dull gleam left
    where once that confidence shone so brightly.
What happened?
Did I misunderstand something,
    or did the prophet get it wrong,
    his vision not the glorious promise I thought it was
    but an empty illusory dream?
Believe me, I want to think otherwise,
    my spirit still crying out to be proved wrong,
    but just look around you –
    at the sin,

the suffering,
the sorrow,
the squalor –
and then tell me honestly
where God is in all this.
Can you see that light he promised?
I can't.
I've waited, as so many have waited before me,
   telling myself that evil can't have the last word,
   that good must finally triumph,
   but there's still no sign,
   nothing to give grounds for optimism,
   and it's all I can do not to lose heart completely.
Yet I must hope;
   somehow, despite it all, I must keep faith,
   for if there's really nothing else in this world than what you see,
   then God help us!
I may have my doubts,
   and it may not be easy,
   but so long as there's even the merest spark of faith left,
   the tiniest, faintest flicker,
   I'm going to go on hoping,
   and go on praying:
   come, Lord,
   come!

Prayer

Gracious God,
   we talk of light shining in the darkness,
   yet sometimes the reality appears very different.
There is so much injustice and oppression in our world;
   so much greed and envy,
   pride, prejudice, hatred and evil.
We are besieged each day
   by stories of poverty, sickness, sorrow and suffering –
   some far afield,
   some on our very own doorstep.
Lord, we try to trust in your purpose,
   but there is so much that seems to belie your love
   and contradict our faith.
Reach out, we ask, wherever there is darkness,
   bringing help and healing, hope and wholeness.

Come again to our world,
   and may the light of your love shine in our hearts
   and in the hearts of all,
   to the glory of your name.
Amen.

Silence

Slides and music

Ovysen and Kolyada Procession (Christmas Eve Suite) Rimsky-Korsakov
during which Luke 1:5-20 is read

Meditation of Zechariah

I wanted to believe it, honestly!
After all those years trying,
   all those false hopes and crushing disappointments,
   there was nothing I wanted to believe more.
A child!
A son!
At our time of life!
Wonderful!
But that was the trouble –
   we were too old,
   not just *over* the hill but well down the other side,
   and we'd both accepted we just weren't meant to be parents.
It hurt, of course it did,
   but little by little we'd come to terms with it,
   the pain easing as we threw ourselves into what was left us.
So why suddenly this strange vision,
   this sense of God speaking to me
   in a way so real and powerful
   it was as though an angel was there in person,
   spelling out the message word for word?
To be frank I felt we could do without it, both of us,
   and, whatever else, there was no way I intended
   to go running back to Elizabeth,
   opening up old wounds.
So I just laughed it off,
   shrugged my shoulders and carried on
   as though nothing had happened.
Let's face it, I reasoned,

a few more years and we'd be pushing up the daisies,
    an end to life's mysteries once and for all.
Well, I couldn't have been more wrong, could I?
For it happened,
    every last word of it,
    down to the final detail!
How did I feel?
Well, you can imagine.
Ecstatic!
Just about beside myself with joy!
It was the proudest and most wonderful moment of my life,
    and for a time after the birth I could think of nothing else,
    every moment too precious to waste.
Yet I've been thinking recently
    about those words spoken by the angel,
    for when he spoke of John's coming,
    he talked also of the role he was destined to fulfil:
    'He will turn many of the people of Israel to the Lord their God.
    With the spirit and power of Elijah he will go before him,
    to make ready a people prepared for the Lord.'
I forgot that afterwards in all the excitement,
    too much else going on to give it a second thought.
But do you think it could possibly mean what I think it does?
God's promised Messiah, coming at last?
A child, born to *me*, *that* was wonderful!
But for us *all*,
    a child to change the world –
    could that really be?

Prayer
Loving God,
    for all our faith
    there are some things we consider beyond us
    and beyond you.
Belief says one thing but realism another,
    and in consequence we set limits
    to the way you are able to work in our lives.
Yet time and again you have overturned human expectations,
    demonstrating that all things are possible
    for those who love you.
Teach us, then,
    to look beyond the obvious and immediate,

and to live rather in the light of your sovereign grace
which is able to do far more
than we can ever ask or imagine;
through Jesus Christ our Lord.
Amen.

Silence

Slides and music
Intermezzo (Carmen, Suite No. 1) Bizet
during which Matthew 6:31-33; 7:7-11 is read

Meditation of a listener to the Sermon on the Mount
'Ask,' he said, 'and you will receive.'
Just like that,
    or so at least it sounded.
As though all we have to do is put in our request,
    place our order,
    and at the drop of a hat it will be there before us,
    served up on a plate,
    exactly to our requirements.
Do you believe that?
I'm not sure I do.
And I'm not sure I want to either,
    for if he really meant that,
    then where would it all end,
    when could we ever stop asking?
We couldn't, could we?
Not while there's still suffering in the world,
    still need,
    sorrow,
    hunger,
    disease,
    despair.
It wouldn't be right –
    a dereliction of duty, you might call it.
And anyway, even if we could wipe those out,
    rid the world of its many ills,
    that wouldn't be the end of it, not by a long way,
    for there would always be something else to ask for –
    a gift we know we lack,
    a dream still unfulfilled,

a person we long to reach –
always just one more favour
before we could be completely satisfied.
It would end up with God at our beck and call,
bowing to our every whim,
dancing to our tune, instead of us responding to his.
So no, he couldn't have meant that, could he?
But what then?
What was Jesus getting at
with that weird but wonderful promise?
I've wrestled with that day after day,
and I've begun to wonder
if maybe we're looking at it the wrong way round,
too much at self and too little at Jesus.
'Do not worry about your life,' he told us,
'what you will eat or what you will drink,
or about your body, what you will wear.
Strive first for the kingdom of God and his righteousness,
and all these things will be given to you as well.'
Ask for what matters, isn't that what he was saying –
for those things in life which can bring you lasting happiness –
treasures in heaven rather than pleasure on earth?
It's not that this life was unimportant to him.
He cared about the world's suffering
more than anyone I've ever known.
But he came to tackle not simply the symptoms but the cause,
not just the way things look but the way they are –
the way we think,
the way we speak,
the way we act,
each transformed deep inside.
I may be wrong, of course,
but I think that's what he meant;
something like it anyway.
Ask God for guidance, strength, faith, renewal.
Ask him to teach, use, shape, forgive you.
Ask for these things,
earnestly,
honestly –
the gifts of his kingdom –
and you *will* receive
until your cup runs over!

Prayer

Loving God,
　you long to shower us with blessings,
　to fill our lives with good things,
　yet there are times when, through our weakness of faith,
　we frustrate your gracious purpose
　and deprive ourselves of the inexpressible riches you so freely offer.
We do not seek, so we do not find.
We do not ask, so we do not receive.
We concern ourselves with the fleeting pleasures of the moment
　and so fail to grasp treasures which endure for eternity.
Forgive us the shallowness of our values
　and the limitations of our understanding.
Teach us to set our hearts
　on those things which truly have the power to satisfy,
　which you so yearn to share with us.
In Christ's name.
Amen.

Silence

Slides and music

Credo (Mass in B minor) J. S. Bach, during which Mark 9:14-24 is read

Meditation of the father of the epileptic boy

Lord, I do believe,
　truly.
Despite my doubts,
　despite my questions,
　I do believe.
Not that my faith is perfect, I'm not saying that –
　there's still much that puzzles me,
　much I'd like to ask you about further, given the chance.
But I believe you're different,
　that you can change lives in a way others can't,
　that you can bring hope where there's despair,
　joy where there's sorrow,
　peace where there's turmoil,
　love where there's hate.
And I need those things now as never before,
　not for myself, but for my son.

He's suffering, you see,
    troubled in body and mind,
    day after day thrown into terrible convulsions.
And, Lord, I'm afraid of what might happen,
    what he might do to himself when the fits come upon him.
It's breaking my heart seeing him like this,
    having to stand by helpless as he writhes and groans.
Yet I've tried everything –
    every doctor,
    every healer,
    even your own disciples,
    all to no avail.
Not one has been able to help,
    none able to provide the answer I long to find.
So I've come finally to you,
    my last throw of the dice,
    and I'm begging you, Lord:
    help!
Oh, I know I don't deserve it –
    I'm not pretending otherwise.
I have my doubts, all too many –
    barely understanding half of what you teach,
    and even what does make sense is hard to accept.
I don't have the makings of a disciple, I realise that,
    all kinds of things wrong in my life –
    ask anyone.
And though I want to change,
    to become the person you would have me be,
    I'm not sure I can come anywhere near it.
In fact, though I say I believe,
    I'm not even certain of that,
    for I'm torn in two,
    half of me sure, half of me not,
    my faith and doubt warring together,
    each battling for the upper hand,
    each ebbing and flowing as the mood takes me.
Yet I've seen what you've been able to do for others,
    I've heard about the wonders you perform,
    and I'm sure that if anyone can help me, then it's you.
So you see, I do believe a little,
    not as much as I'd like,
    not as much as I should,

but I do believe,
   and I'm trying so hard to believe more.
In the meantime, I'm begging you, Lord,
   on bended knee, I'm begging you:
   help my unbelief.

Prayer

Lord,
   you know our faith isn't perfect.
There is much that we don't understand,
   much that we question,
   and much that is not all it ought to be.
Despite our love for you,
   we find it difficult to trust as we know we should,
   the things we don't believe
   triumphing over the things we do.
Yet, for all its weakness,
   you know that our faith is real,
   and you know that we long to serve you better.
Take, then, what we are and what we offer,
   and, through your grace, provide what we lack
   until the faith we profess with our lips
   may be echoed in our lives,
   and our faith be made complete.
Amen.

Silence

Slides and music

Lesson 1 for Maundy Thursday Palestrina
during which Luke 22:39-46 is read

Meditation of Peter

He was unsure of himself,
   for the first time in his life
   unsure of his ability to face the future,
   and it hurt him more than the pain he was finally to suffer.
You see, there'd never been any doubt until then,
   never even the slightest suggestion of hesitation.
Despite the hostility, the resentment, the abuse from so many,
   he'd set his face resolutely towards Jerusalem,
   knowing from the very beginning where it would all end.

He understood it all,
  the pain and humiliation he must suffer,
  conscious of it even way back
  in those heady days of his baptism,
  yet he'd carried on willingly,
  the prospect seeming to hold no fear for him,
  and we'd marvelled at the faith, the love,
  the courage of the man,
  the sheer commitment
  which gave him such awesome strength and inner purpose.
But suddenly, that evening, it was all so very different,
  a shadow blotting out the light which had shone so brightly.
I saw despair in his eyes rather than hope,
  fear rather than laughter,
  sorrow rather than joy,
  and, most terrible of all, that desperate look of uncertainty,
  so alien,
  so devastating,
  so crushing a burden.
It was all suddenly too real,
  no longer theory but fact –
  the agony and the isolation he was about to face –
  and, like any of us would in his place, he wanted to back away,
  find an easier course,
  a less dreadful option.
It struck me then, as never before,
  that he didn't know what lay beyond death
  any more than I did.
He'd always believed,
  always trusted,
  but he had no more certainty than you and me –
  only the assurance of faith,
  the conviction borne of trust,
  and there in the darkness,
  as the chill of night took hold,
  it all hung on a thread
  as he wrestled with the torment of doubt.
I know what I'd have done had I been him –
  quite simply, I wouldn't have stopped running
  until Jerusalem was just a memory!
But not Jesus.
He stayed quietly in the garden, as I knew he would,
  and he offered not just his *faith* but his *doubt* to God –
  'not *my* will but *yours* be done'.

Well, he was sure of one thing after that –
    there was no way back,
    death now a cast-iron certainty;
    but it wasn't dying itself that was the problem for him,
    it was not knowing whether it would all be worth it,
    whether it could actually make a difference
    to this world we live in,
    and there was no way of answering that for certain
    this side of eternity.
He was unsure –
    of himself,
    of his faith,
    of his ability to face the future –
    but despite it all he risked everything,
    offering life itself,
    so that we might know the truth,
    and be free from death –
    free for all eternity!

Prayer

Loving God,
    you call us to live by faith, not by sight,
    to put our faith in things unseen rather than seen,
    and most of the time we are able to do that.
But occasionally we are faced by circumstances
    which cause us to doubt,
    throwing a shadow over everything we believe.
We question our ability to keep going,
    we wonder what is happening to us,
    and though we look to you for assurance, we do not find it.
Help us when such moments come
    to know that you have been there before us in Christ
    and that you understand what we are facing.
Inspire us through the faith and courage he showed,
    and so help us to trust in your purpose
    even when we cannot see the way ahead.
In his name we pray.
Amen.

Silence

Music   *Silent, surrendered (Fountain of Life)* Rizza

AFTERNOON SESSION

Music   *O Lord, my heart is not proud (Fountain of Life)* Rizza

Prayer
Gracious God,
    we come to you just as we are,
    with all our strengths and weaknesses,
    our faith and our doubt.
Open your heart to us and respond to our need.
Nurture our faith,
    strengthen our love,
    and enrich our understanding of your grace.
Draw close to us so that we may draw closer to you,
    today and every day,
    through Jesus Christ our Lord.
Amen.

Slides and music
Gloria (Mass in B minor) J. S. Bach, during which John 20:19-29 is read

Meditation of Thomas
I wanted to know, that's all,
    to see for myself if it could possibly be true –
    was that so awful?
Remember, we'd *all* doubted at first,
    when the women came back that morning,
    dismissing their story of the empty tomb as so much nonsense,
    so why point the finger at me,
    as though *I* questioned and *they* didn't?
All right, the situation had changed since then, I accept that,
    for they all claimed to have seen him in the meantime,
    and not just them, but others,
    each adamant the Lord had risen,
    yet as much as I wanted to believe it, I simply couldn't,
    not unless the proof was spelt out for me in black and white.
That was me all over, I'm afraid,
    the way I'd been since a boy,
    struggling to accept anything I couldn't touch for myself

or see with my own eyes,
   and I'd said as much to Jesus before he died,
   that day he spoke about his Father's house,
   and his going there to prepare a place for us.
'Believe in God,' he'd said,
   'believe also in me.'
A wonderful promise, yes,
   only to me he was talking in riddles,
   and I made no bones about it:
   'Lord, we do not know where you are going.
   How can we know the way?'
He wasn't angry with me,
   though he could have been,
   for after all that time, all he'd said, I should have known,
   just as I should have understood
   he would rise from the tomb and return among us.
He'd spoken of it, often enough,
   done his best to prepare us not simply for his death
   but his resurrection to follow,
   but, as so often happens, we dwelt on the bad
   and forgot the good,
   unable to see beyond the demands of the present moment.
So despite it all I refused to believe,
   convinced there were still too many questions
   and not enough answers.
And I'd be doing that still,
   still wondering if it ever could be,
   but for his grace.
For suddenly he was there again, standing among us,
   arms outstretched in welcome,
   those pierced hands reaching out to me, Thomas,
   and I knew I'd been wrong –
   he was alive, just as they'd said,
   risen and victorious –
   and I knelt down in worship,
   my heart overflowing with thanksgiving,
   for he'd come, despite me,
   despite my lack of faith –
   though I had doubted him,
   still he believed in me!

Prayer

Loving God,
  you call us to live by faith, not by sight,
  to put our faith in things unseen rather than seen,
  and most of the time we are able to do that.
But occasionally we are faced by circumstances
  which cause us to doubt,
  throwing a shadow over everything we believe.
We question our ability to keep going,
  we wonder what is happening to us,
  and though we look to you for assurance, we do not find it.
Help us when such moments come
  to know that you have been there before us in Christ
  and that you understand what we are facing.
Inspire us through the faith and courage he showed,
  and so help us to trust in your purpose
  even when we cannot see the way ahead.
In his name we pray.
Amen.

Silence

Slides and music

The Gadfly Shostakovich, during which Acts 12:1-17 is read

Meditation of Mary, the mother of John Mark

Our prayers were answered that night,
  wonderfully, sensationally answered –
  and you could have knocked us over with a feather.
We never expected it, you see –
  despite everything God had done among us,
  the astonishing signs,
  the awesome wonders,
  not one of us believed our prayers would make
  the slightest scrap of difference.
Does that shock you?
It did us when we finally realised it.
But what shocked us more was that we'd no idea it was the case,
  no inkling whatsoever
  that we were simply going through the motions.
We thought we trusted completely,
  and, believe me, had you heard us praying

you'd have thought so too,
    but when our maid Rhoda burst in upon us,
    eyes wide with wonder,
    tripping over her words in her haste to get them out,
    that's when our lack of trust was laid bare.
'It's Peter!' she told us.
    'Here!
    Outside!
    Knocking at the door!'
And, do you know what? –
    we just sat there and looked at her, as though she were mad.
'Pull yourself together,' we told her.
    'Get a grip!
    You know where Peter is.
    We all do.'
Poor girl, she tried to argue,
    beside herself with frustration,
    but we just wouldn't listen,
    wouldn't even countenance the possibility
    that we might be mistaken.
So much for faith!
In the end she did what she should have done sooner –
    opened the door! –
    and there he was, just as she'd said,
    wondering what on earth had taken us so long.
He told us the whole story –
    his initial despair,
    the sudden burst of light,
    the mysterious deliverer,
    the joy of freedom –
    and then, before he left, he added one last thing:
    'Tell this to James and to the believers.'
Was it a gentle dig at our lack of faith?
I don't think so,
    yet it might as well have been,
    for it brought home again how little we'd trusted.
We'd believed him doomed,
    lost to us for ever this side of eternity,
    but God showed us otherwise –
    a glorious reminder that, though the well of faith runs dry,
    his faithfulness continues to flow
    in a never-failing stream!

Prayer

Gracious God,
  we do not find prayer easy,
  for there are many times when you do not seem to answer
  or when the answer you give is not quite what we hoped for.
Faith tells us one thing, experience another,
  and eventually it is experience, often all too painful,
  which wins the day.
There was a time, perhaps,
  when we would have asked for something
  fully confident you would grant it,
  but, as the years pass and that fails to happen,
  it becomes hard to keep on believing,
  and slowly our prayers become mechanical,
  offered more out of duty than expectation.
Yet you *do* hear, and you *do* respond;
  and, did we but know it, our failure to recognise your answer
  is often due to our failure to listen,
  or to the strait-jacket we subconsciously set upon you.
Teach us to recognise that you may say no, you may say yes,
  but you will always say something,
  and so may we pray with renewed confidence,
  trusting in your eternal purpose;
  through Jesus Christ our Lord.
Amen.

Silence

Slides and music

Etude in E Chopin, during which 2 Corinthians 12:7b-10 is read

Meditation of Paul

I could think about nothing else at the time
  but that affliction of mine,
  that thorn in the flesh, as I finally came to call it.
It dominated my whole life, and very nearly destroyed me,
  sapping my strength,
  destroying my confidence,
  eating into the very fabric of my faith.
Try as I might, I just couldn't get it out of my head –
  it was always there,

preying on my mind,
   lurking in the shadows,
   waiting to devour me.
When I woke up in the morning it was waiting to meet me,
   a constant reminder of my weakness.
When I walked in the street it pursued me,
   striking me down when I least expected.
When I talked with friends it was there too,
   breaking into our conversation.
When I turned to God in prayer, even there it turned up,
   insinuating itself between us.
And I was getting desperate,
   sucked ever deeper into a dark pit of despair,
   the laughter, the love, the life being drained from me.
Why? I asked.
Why me?
What sin had I committed?
What penance did I have to do
   before God would have pity and set me free?
I'd make it worth it, I told him,
   not just for me but for both our sakes.
I could do so much more,
   serve him so much better,
   if only he'd hear my prayer.
But there was no answer,
   no release,
   nothing.
I begged him again,
   angry,
   disappointed,
   resentful.
But it made no difference –
   still nothing.
So I left off for a while,
   until my patience could take it no longer,
   the frustration too much to bear.
And then once more I asked,
   grovelling this time,
   begging,
   pleading.
But yet again, nothing,
   just a blank, empty silence.

Or so I thought,
   until suddenly this picture of Jesus came to me,
   his eyes filled with pain, his body broken,
   and on his head a crown of thorns;
   the blood trickling down his tortured face,
   the hands outstretched in agony –
   and all at once I knew I was wrong.
He'd heard me all right,
   and answered,
   only I hadn't been ready to listen.
For it was there,
   in the sorrow and suffering of the Cross,
   that God fulfilled his eternal purpose;
   there,
   in what the world counts weakness,
   that God showed us true greatness!
So have I finally come to terms with this problem of mine,
   exorcised the demon that's haunted me for so long?
No, I can't claim that,
   for I still have my moments,
   still sometimes ask why,
   and still hope some day it might be different.
But when I catch myself feeling like that
   I stop and think of Jesus,
   and I realise again
   that in my weakness is God's strength.

Prayer

Loving God,
   we do not like living with weakness.
We want to feel strong, in control of our destiny,
   able to stand up against whatever life might throw at us,
   and we resent anything which threatens that sense of security.
Yet time and again across the years
   you have turned this world's expectations upside-down,
   your values totally different from our own.
You humble the proud, you bring down the mighty,
   you reduce the powerful to nothing,
   choosing instead to work through those
   who seem insignificant and vulnerable.
Teach us, then, when we find our weaknesses hard to accept,
   to recognise that you are able to use them

in ways beyond our imagining,
and to understand that in those very weaknesses
your strength is most perfectly seen;
through Jesus Christ our Lord.
Amen.

Silence

Slides and music
Pilgrims' Chorus (Tannhäuser) Wagner
during which Hebrews 11:32-12:2 is read

Meditation of the writer of the Hebrews
I was ready to give up, if I'm honest,
tired, scared, disillusioned.
We all were, every last one of us,
just about ready to call it a day.
You ask why?
Well, you wouldn't have if you'd been there with us,
if you'd heard the screams as we did,
the cries for mercy,
the gasps of agony,
the sobs of desolation as yet more martyrs went to their death.
It was hard, I can tell you,
and, worse still, we knew that at any moment
our turn might come –
the axe,
the sword,
the stones,
the lions,
all waiting for another victim to satisfy their hunger.
We'd lost hundreds,
good honest men and women,
honest,
devout,
dedicated,
led like lambs to the slaughter,
nothing and no one able to save them,
not even our prayers.
What could I say to bring hope in such times?
What possible message of reassurance could I give
when I was troubled and confused myself?

It was a crisis for me as well as them,
    every one of us struggling to make sense
    of such dreadful carnage,
    such appalling suffering,
    but there seemed nothing to say,
    no words which offered any hope or comfort.
Until suddenly I thought of Jesus,
    the pain he endured for us –
    gasping as the lash tore into his flesh,
    as the thorns pierced his head,
    as the nails smashed through his hands and feet;
    groaning as the cramps convulsed his body
    and the lifeblood seeped away.
He need not have faced it,
    but he'd done so willingly,
    faithful to the last for our sake.
And I knew then that, whatever might be asked of us,
    whatever we might suffer,
    it could never be worse than the agony he endured,
    the terrible total desolation he was asked to bear.
It wasn't an answer, of course, I can't claim that –
    it simply rephrased the question –
    but it was enough,
    for I knew then, and I could say then with confidence,
    that God is with us in our suffering,
    by our sides, whatever we might face.

Prayer

Living Lord,
    as well as the good times, life brings the bad –
    moments of pain, fear, sorrow and suffering.
Most of the time we are able to get by,
    tested but not pushed to the limit,
    but occasionally we question our ability to continue,
    so great are the problems we face.
We feel crushed, overwhelmed,
    our strength sapped and our spirits exhausted,
    even our faith hanging by a thread.
Be with us in such moments
    and give us courage to persevere despite everything.
Though the present seems bleak and the future looks hopeless,
    though our burdens seem many and our resources few,

help us still to walk the way of Christ,
   knowing that he has gone before us
   and is waiting to meet us at our journey's end.
Take our hand and lead us forward,
   for his name's sake.
Amen.

Silence

Slides and music

Moderato (Serenade for strings in E minor) Dvořák
during which Galatians 1:13-24 is read

Meditation of Paul

It looked impossible at the beginning,
   utterly beyond me.
And I don't mind confessing there were many times
   when I felt like giving up,
   throwing in the towel and cutting my losses.
Surprised?
You shouldn't be.
After all, just look what I was up against –
   me, Paul, called to take the gospel beyond Jerusalem,
   beyond Judea,
   out to the ends of the earth!
It was a tall order by anyone's reckoning,
   and when you remember how the Jews felt about the Gentiles,
   and how the Gentiles felt in return,
   well, you can begin to understand the scale of the problem, can't you!
I was up against it from the very start,
   doing my best to keep a foot in both camps to avoid causing offence,
   trying to share the good news,
   but forever keeping one eye over my shoulder,
   knowing the snipers wouldn't be far away.
It didn't help I suppose, with my own people anyway,
   me being a Jew myself,
   schooled as a Pharisee and expert in the law to boot!
They thought I was betraying my roots,
   reneging on my convictions,
   denying the faith of our fathers.
And as for the Gentiles, many simply wondered what I was doing,
   pushing my nose into their affairs.

So, yes, I had my doubts, to put it mildly!
Wouldn't you have felt the same?
Who was I to overcome that sort of prejudice,
    to break down the barriers between us,
    to bring people of such contrasting backgrounds together
    into one family of humankind?
Who was I to talk of a new way of thinking,
    of building a different sort of kingdom,
    of sharing a different sort of love?
Someone else perhaps – but me?
No way!
And yet the mystery is, I did!
Somehow, in a way I'll never understand,
    I found the strength and the words I needed
    when I needed them most.
I found energy to begin new tasks,
    courage to meet new people,
    faith to dream new dreams.
I unearthed reserves I never knew existed,
    and achieved results I never imagined possible –
    all kinds of people
    in all kinds of ways,
    discovering the joy of sharing and working together,
    discovering a faith that answered their deepest needs –
    a faith to live by.
It looked impossible, you can't argue with that –
    wonderful yet altogether ridiculous.
But it wasn't,
    for I've discovered since then,
    much to my amazement,
    much to my relief,
    that I can do all things
    through him who strengthens me.
Thanks be to God!

Silent meditation.

Prayer

Sovereign God,
    the challenges you set before us may be very modest
    compared with those faced by others over the years,
    but they can seem daunting nonetheless.
We feel inadequate to meet the task,
    acutely conscious of our lack of faith,

the limitations of our gifts
and our inability to serve you as we would wish.
Yet time and again throughout history
you have taken the most unpromising of material
and used it in ways defying all expectations.
You have turned doubt into faith,
weakness into strength, ~ *Sickness into health*
timid service into fearless discipleship, ~ *Fear into Courage*
and you go on doing that today
through the power of your Holy Spirit.
Give us, then, the faith to respond to your call,
trusting that, whatever you ask of us,
you will be by our side to help us see it through,
to the glory of your name.
Amen.

Silence _____ *Mothers M. Prayer, Gifts & Poems,*

Blessing — *Grace.*

Music   *Credo in unum Deum (Mass in C minor)* Mozart

APPENDIX
Visual Resources

The following collections of slides have all been used in conjunction with the meditations, readings and music offered in this book. Most powerful of all has been the pack of 144 slides in six sets based on the television series *Jesus of Nazareth* directed by Franco Zeffirelli, produced by the Bible Society.

Sadly, this and many of the other collections referred to here are no longer available from the producers, but the details given may be of help in tracing them, either through your local Diocesan Religious Studies Resource Centre if you have one or, perhaps, through a local library, school, college or university. Failing that, you might try:

Rickett Educational Media Ltd (formerly The Slide Centre Ltd)
Great Western House, Langport, Somerset TA10 9YU. Tel 01458 253636

As well as the collections mentioned, I have occasionally used slides of the Holy Land, particularly, for example, scenes of the wilderness to accompany meditations on Jesus' temptation or John the Baptist preaching in the desert.

(Note: An asterisk indicates that the resource is no longer commercially available)

Jesus of Nazareth 1: Jesus – Birth and childhood*
Jesus of Nazareth 2: Jesus – Begins his ministry*
Jesus of Nazareth 3: Jesus – Heals*
Jesus of Nazareth 4: Jesus – Cares*
Jesus of Nazareth 5: Jesus – In the last week*
Jesus of Nazareth 6: Jesus – Trial to Resurrection*

Colour transparencies from the TV series directed by Franco Zeffirelli. Was produced by The Bible Society.

In the Beginning*
A cartoon slide set produced in conjunction with a Ladybird Bible Book primarily aimed at children. Was produced by Scripture Union.

The Life of Christ – I-IV
Slides focusing on the annunciation, nativity, and childhood of Jesus, as 'seen through the eyes of the artist', produced by:
Visual Publications
The Green, Northleach, Cheltenham, Gloucestershire GL54 3EX
Tel 01451 860519

Jesus, the Child*
A cartoon slide set produced in conjunction with a Ladybird Bible Book primarily aimed at children. Was produced by Scripture Union.

Come, let us adore*
A series of 27 slides on the nativity. Was produced by Audio Visual Productions UK.

Oberammergau 1990
A sequence of 36 slides from the Oberammergau Passion Plays, produced by:
Huber
Drosselstraße 7, D-8100 Garmisch-Partenkirchen, Germany

Man of the Cross
A slide-sound presentation (code: 70P326), also available as a set of 15 posters (code 73P262), using a variety of artistic media, including photography, vividly portraying the Way of the Cross. Produced by:
St Paul MultiMedia Productions
199 Kensington High Street, London W8 6BA. Tel 020 7937 9591

He Carries Our Cross*
An audiovisual programme for liturgy, prayer and reflection, including slides of line-sketches, focusing on the events of the Passion under two subsections: (a) Journey to Jerusalem, and (b) Journey to the Cross. Was produced by St Paul MultiMedia Productions.

Bread and Wine*
Pictures of the elements of the Eucharist, particularly suitable for meditations on the Last Supper. Was produced for the Church Pastoral Aid Society by Falcon Audio Visual Aids.

St Paul*
A radiovision slide set consisting of 45 picture slides. Was produced by the BBC.

The Story of St Paul*
A picture slide set produced in conjunction with a Ladybird Bible Book primarily aimed at children. Was produced by Ladybird Books.

The Gospel: Life of Jesus*
A cartoon slide set. Was produced by St Paul MultiMedia Productions.